About the editors

Ineke Buskens works internationally as an independent research, facilitation and gender consultant and has published on qualitative and emancipatory research methodology; women's health and HIV/AIDS; gender and information communication technology; and open development. Ineke was head of the Centre for Research Methodology at the Human Sciences Research Council, Pretoria, from 1991 to 1996, where she designed and facilitated South Africa's first experientially based, qualitative research education modules and provided some of the first opportunities for social science researchers of different ethnic backgrounds to learn together. Ineke has been the GRACE Network's research director and project leader since its inception in 2004 and this has been the highlight of her career so far.

Anne Webb focuses on the design and coordination of qualitative research and learning processes to address and reduce gender inequality in Canada and internationally. To this end she has been working with communities and research teams for over twenty years, involving people from many walks of life and locations in Canada, Europe, the Middle East and Africa. Anne's approach to feminist qualitative research brings together elements of participatory action research, socio-economic analysis and critical self-awareness. She is currently designing and coordinating a two-year multi-country research and learning process. From 2005 to 2013 she was the research coordinator of GRACE.

More praise for *Women and ICT in Africa and the Middle East*

'In this welcome addition to the growing literature in the field of women, development and ICT, a range of case studies elucidate both the emancipatory nature of ICT and the formidable structural and cultural obstacles that remain.'

(Valentine M. Moghadam, Northeastern University)

'This is a rich, challenging and rewarding read for anyone interested in better understanding the role of ICT in women's empowerment. This book offers reasons to be optimistic about the transformative potential of ICT without losing sight of the power structures in which they are embedded.'

(Martin Scott, author of Media and Development)

WOMEN AND ICT IN AFRICA AND THE MIDDLE EAST

changing selves, changing societies

edited by Ineke Buskens
and Anne Webb

Zed Books

LONDON

Women and ICT in Africa and the Middle East was first published in 2014 by Zed Books Ltd, 7 Cynthia Street, London N1 9JF, UK

www.zedbooks.co.uk

The research presented in this publication was carried out with the financial assistance of Canada's International Development Research Centre.

Typeset in Arnhem by Newgen Knowledge Works

Cover designed by www.roguefour.co.uk

A catalogue record for this book is available from the British Library

Library of Congress Cataloging in Publication Data available

ISBN 978-1-78360-043-4 hb
ISBN 978-1-78360-042-7 pb
ISBN 978-1-78360-044-1 pdf
ISBN 978-1-78360-045-8 epub
ISBN 978-1-78360-046-5 mobi

Printed and bound by CPI Group (UK) Ltd, Croydon, CR0 4YY

Contents

Foreword

The significant problems we face cannot be solved at the same level of thinking we were at when we created them. (Einstein)

We've all had that 'ah-ha' moment when suddenly things become a whole lot clearer. It is as if a veil has been lifted and we are seeing the world with new eyes. Sometimes it is as if the world itself, and our position in it, are forever changed.

Such insights come only when we are ready for them. This is a natural part of the process of human growth. Only when we are mature enough do we begin to see our parents as humans with their strengths and weaknesses. And, as Steven Covey explains in his book *The 7 Habits of Highly Effective People*, only after we have become truly independent beings can we begin to accept and take advantage of the reality of our interdependence.

This book is the end product of a long journey that has intertwined research and personal growth. The research and methodologies in this book were made possible by the experiences from the first GRACE Network, which cumulated in the path-breaking book *African Women and ICTs: Investigating Technology, Gender and Empowerment*. Each step along the way since then not only saw a deepening of the substantive knowledge of the interaction between gender and information and communication technologies (ICTs) (first in Africa, later to be expanded to the Middle East) but was equally a process of deepening self-awareness for all involved.

In a world where the subjugation of women isn't always disturbingly blatant, but rather exceedingly subtle and hidden from our day-to-day consciousness, buried under layers of deep-seated, calcified assumptions and identities, researchers have to be able to bring these subtleties into consciousness. Only then is it possible for those researchers to do justice to the lived realities of research respondents and researcher-selves, both from an empirical and from an engagement-for-change perspective. As this book clearly reveals, research then becomes as much an empirical examination of the external world as an internal process of self-reflection.

But the unique methodological approach applied by the researchers in this book is not just a contribution to ICT for development (ICT4D) or ICTs and gender research; rather it is applicable to research for development writ large. It is a means and process that provides researchers with the tools to counteract deeply ingrained biases, and helps keep them aligned with their ultimate purpose of making the world a better place. This coherence is critical – otherwise we increase our risk of being unwitting participants in or even contributors to the social injustices that we seek to overcome.

Humanity is pressed with deep and systemic challenges: poverty, climate change, pervasive inequality. To address these challenges, Einstein's proverb is more relevant than ever. Changing our level of thinking, however, is not easy – but it is possible. What the experiences within this book teach us is that, if we want to change our level of thinking in order to solve a problem, perhaps we should first seek to change our level of being.

Matthew L. Smith
International Development Research Centre
4 October 2013

Acknowledgements

In the first place, we want to thank our main donor, the International Development Research Centre (IDRC) for their ongoing financial support. We particularly want to thank Heloise Emdon, Matthew Smith, Ramata Thioune and Adel El Zaim without whom this book would not have become a reality: thank you for believing in us and accepting the challenges that we presented to you.

We also want to thank our partners, families and friends who kept the home fires burning (sometimes even financially) when we were elsewhere writing or travelling, bringing home sometimes disturbing thoughts and experiences, and drawing our inner circles into our cauldron of change. Thank you for standing by us, for being the sounding boards we needed, for staying with us and changing with us.

Working with the women and men who shared thoughts, emotions, experiences and perspectives with us has been an absolute privilege and honour. Thank you for sharing and collaborating with us. We hope that we have been able to do justice to you and to your sharings, and that the changes our projects have already set in motion and may further effect in the future, will bring benefit to all of you.

As a network of twenty-two teams (twenty-one research teams and the coordinating team) spread over fifteen countries, so many individuals, organizations and institutions have helped us along the way that it would be impossible to mention them all. We appreciate you and your support deeply. We hope that the bonds of collaboration that were forged and strengthened in and through this work will make other good work possible in the future.

We also want to thank ourselves and each other for our focus, patience and tenacity as researchers and for staying with our knowledge quests until we reached satisfactory levels of insight. Even though this research discipline at times took all that we had and all that we were, this book stands as evidence that surrender to a knowledge quest yields rewards commensurate with commitment. Lastly, whilst this book represents a temporary closure in our work, we are satisfied with this outcome and will gladly welcome any feedback that will contribute to our ongoing journeys of learning and becoming.

Introduction

INEKE BUSKENS

The time and space we live in

With this book on women, gender and information communication technology (ICT) in Africa and the Middle East we, as the Gender Research in Africa and the Middle East into ICTs for Empowerment (GRACE) Network, are, for the time being, concluding our work as a research network, which has focused on the nexus between women's empowerment and ICT since 2004. The twenty-one research projects conducted in fourteen countries that are the ground from which this book has emerged were conducted in the period 2008–12, a period that presented both great opportunities and great challenges, not only for ourselves and our research associates and respondents but also for people across the globe.

Our time is the era of the networked society, of the information or knowledge society. GRACE, as a network, would not even have existed without the technology that allowed us to connect when we wanted to and share what we needed to. ICT is enabling effortless and almost instantaneous sharing and is making scientific collaboration and therefore the scientific enterprise as a whole exponentially more exciting and effective.

Furthermore, many resources (books, articles) have become available for free download from the Internet, making it possible for scholars and activists from the Global South, such as ourselves, situated in areas or countries sometimes without access to well-stocked libraries and bookstores, to become acquainted with and hence participate in recent thinking and debates.

And yet this time is also one of rising inequality, of crises, wars and disasters (Ryan-Collins et al. 2009; Cohen 2012). In our particular regions we experienced revolutions, sectarian violence and civil war and ongoing occupation.[1] Globally the scramble for the natural resources that are needed to sustain our 'modern' way of life has created unprecedented destruction of social and natural habitats. How unsustainable our 'developed' and now increasingly global way of life actually is has become painfully clear over the past few years. As Naomi Klein (2011) put it: 'The new normal is serial disasters: ecological and economic.'

As the place where many of the resources coveted by the 'developed' North are located, the global South has had more than its fair share of the fall-out of this scramble. Minerals, oil, agricultural produce, currencies (Jabbar 2013) and human talent continue to be extracted from southern lands, facilitated by civil war and unrest, by slave labour prices and practices and by the crippling debts that participation in the global financial system has created for many countries in the South.

Increased liberalization and expansion of international trade, which occurred in the aftermath of the Cold War, has exacerbated the level and intensity of conflicts in resource-rich African countries to such a degree that there is indeed reason to speak of 'the resource curse'. The minerals that are essential for the production of ICT electronics, such as mobile phones, laptops and MP3 players, are, to a large degree, extracted from the Congo. Called 'conflict minerals', coltan,[2] cassiterite, wolframite and gold have thus prompted renewed debate around the tension between African national sovereignty and property rights reform on the one hand and the transnational governance of minerals on the other (see Gorilla Organization 2008).

While e-resources travel from the South to the North, e-waste has started to travel more and more from the North to the South (see Greenpeace 2009). One of the new hotspots for this dumping is Accra, Ghana, where the way in which the waste is processed presents grave health risks for the people handling it.[3] The irony is, of course, that the people who mine the minerals and process the waste, while probably happy with the fact that this provides them with a livelihood, are not in the position to really make full and empowered use of the technology that is created and disposed of by their work.

Although the above just touches the surface of the way power (economic and financial) and ICT can intersect in our globalized world, it may help to sketch the contours of the complex dilemmas facing scholars in development studies in general and ICT for development (ICT4D) in particular (Gurumurthy et al. 2009), especially when they are from the global South, as we are. Acknowledging how the current neoliberal global economic and financial systems are causing pervasive damage to our ecosystems and endangering the well-being of so many people especially in the South, we had to carefully examine how to think about the way we worked. While focusing on development as freedom (Sen 1999) and realizing the powerful and empowering experience and manifestation of individual choice (Kleine 2013), we had to acknowledge both the constraints and enablers that were our respondents' realities in a profoundly sexist and deeply unjust globalizing world (O'Hearn 2009). The following questions presented themselves to us:

- Will it be possible to turn ICT into a force for the go
  ing world, or will ICT, despite its tremendous capac
  sharing, mobilization, communication and educa
  the already growing inequalities between rich and p
  izations and individuals? *(techno determinir* ?)
- Since ICT has become an inseparable part of our
  economic life, how might ICT as space, as way of
  and as science be influenced and formed by notions of social justice
  and sustainability? *(social - determinist)*

Summing it up for us was the question: 'What value systems should guide us and how should we be guided by those values?' In the broadest sense, the GRACE research vision is aligned with a world where all people are free, a world that is grounded in social justice and sustainability. The question of how this almost trans-personal and transcendental vision should guide the research had to be answered and realized by each researcher individually. The researchers did not align their projects to this purpose in the sense of action steps that would lead to this goal in a linear progression. The overall vision functioned rather as a 'true north', a magnet that would influence decisions on all matters of research choice.

Research for the purpose of social transformation

Since it was imperative to bring what we were envisioning, planning, designing and conducting in line with a loving, just and sustainable world, we needed to develop our capacity for ethical agency and learn how to bring this to bear on both research purposes and processes (Van der Velden 2008). In the first GRACE phase (2005–08), researchers' agency was also important, but more as a methodological asset in the sense that being in touch with one's own agency sensitizes one to understanding respondents' capacities, opportunities and hindrances for agency better; this was the overall purpose of this phase (Buskens 2009, 2010).

Within this second phase, which started in 2008, after the completion of the first book, *African Women and ICTs: Investigating Technology, Gender and Empowerment*, the research projects were grounded in intentional purpose-aligned thinking on various levels (Buskens 2011b, 2013). Researchers would formulate not only a research question but also three social change purposes that they would love to see their project contribute to: one that was specific for their project, one for their region and one for the project as a whole. This purpose-aligned thinking strengthened their conative, intentional mental capacity (Huitt and Cain 2005; Huitt

d helped them to become cognizant of their own agency in rela-
to their own aspirations and environmental conditions and learn
w to develop it.

The researchers chose their individual project purposes for strategic
reasons in relation to the most prevalent forms of gender inequality in
their country, and on the basis of personal research interests and/or
methodological or theoretical strengths. The overall GRACE Network purpose was 'women's empowerment through ICT'; the regional purpose for
the Africa group was 'the transformation of Africa in the sense of Africa
taking its dignity back' and the regional purpose for the Middle Eastern
group was 'to see women thrive and flourish'. The vision of a better world
for all bound these purposes together.

While this purpose-aligned research approach was innovative in its
ontological and epistemological aspects and normative in its alignment
with the various levels of values the researchers embraced, methodo-
logically the projects followed traditional protocols and quality criteria
that were appropriate for the respective methods and techniques. The
studies included quantitative approaches, mixtures of quantitative and
qualitative methods, qualitative descriptive research (sometimes with
participant observation), collaborative inquiry, participatory action
research and normative action research processes. In terms of research
participants, some researchers worked with academic groups, some with
professionals, some with unskilled/semi-skilled women and some with
mixed groups. The research methodology and research-capacity-building
methodology that formed and informed the knowledge-construction processes that ground this book are further explored in Chapter 22.

Gender and ICT4D research: conforming, reforming and transforming

The approach we have chosen to work with in the field of gender and
ICT4D is by no means the only one. Taking as a point of departure the
view-points of researcher perspectives, both on gender relations and on
the socioeconomic-political-religious structures that support them, combined with researcher intentionalities regarding the social change they
want their research efforts to contribute to, presents us with the distinction between conformist, reformist and transformist gender research
approaches (Buskens 2014). Although all three stances will result in projects that bring about personal and social change, they do so in very different ways and the ultimate effects will also be very different.

In assisting women to conform to existing gender relations and society as it is, researchers will inevitably contribute to maintaining and

4

strengthening the status quo. Reformers want to see measures taken to address gender inequality through education and various policies but without directly challenging the existing societal and economic context. In a sense, reformers will also contribute to maintaining the status quo, although reformed gender relations can lead to profound changes in society, as can be witnessed in advanced economies in the Global North. Transformers, on the other hand, want to see society transformed in all its aspects since they see systemic gender biases not only as problems in themselves but also as symptoms of a deeper problem plaguing human societies (Jain and Elson 2010, 2011). Transformers will thus want to address in and through their research the underlying reasons that society has always and almost everywhere been a non-level playing field for women (Buskens 2015).

Transformation has been the leading thought in efforts towards gender-mainstreaming of policies and regulations. Indications are, however, that gender-mainstreaming has failed as a strategy towards effective and sustainable change towards gender equality and women's empowerment in development interventions (Brouwers 2013). Transformation in the form of gender-mainstreaming could theoretically also inform research processes, but, given the fact that the most important research instrument remains the researcher's own mindset and that all environments and cultures are still sexist to various degrees (Eichler 1991), gender–mainstreaming efforts that would focus on conceptual and procedural research design and process decisions while excluding the persons of the researchers would probably have limited success. The most successful approach towards transformation as a strategy for gender equality in development research in general and ICT4D research in particular would be one where researchers engage transformation of their own gendered selves in and through their research processes.

The process of transformation in and through development research thus differs qualitatively from the processes of conformation and reformation for all stakeholders. In processes of transformation, personal and social change are on the agenda for everyone: in critiquing received values and identities crafted in response to environments that are grounded in and constitute such values and identities, personal change will bring about social change and social change will affect the sphere of the personal. Since research with the purpose of transformation will inevitably affect researcher selves (to the degree and depth that they allow this), a 'methodology of the personal' will thus have to be integrated into research design, research processes and capacity-development. These dynamics are further explored in Chapter 22.

Researching for or researching with?

In her study 'Designing for trauma: the roles of ICTD in combating violence against women', Sarah Revi Sterling brings to the fore the dilemma of design for women's empowerment in a sexist world: 'we are designing for criminal events that should not happen to anyone, but do' (Sterling 2013: 160). Questioning the feasibility of participatory design (how to design with rapists and rape victims?), Sterling problematizes design that presupposes that there is such a thing as a typical rape or attack: 'What does prototyping entail when there is no archetypal attacker – but there are cultural patterns of movement and behaviour in each community, as well as regional and local discourses of sexuality and violence?' (2013: 160).

In raising the question whether it would be possible to design in an iterative, participatory way for a rape-prevention technology, Sterling distinguishes between intended design impact and preferred design methodology. This is a crucial distinction that can be made in the field of ICT4D research in general. Although there is a definite resonance between knowledge interests and research approaches,[4] they cannot be equated. However, since participatory design processes are (when conducted well) often experienced as intrinsically empowering, it is possible that designing with is perceived as more transformatory than designing for. In the efforts towards gender equality and women's empowerment, however, this is not necessarily the case (Buskens 2015).

Women's adaptive preferences (Nussbaum 2000) – the ways they have learnt to live with and think in terms of a discriminatory reality – and the ways gender relations and technology socially co-construct each other (Wacjman 2009), could even make women co-researchers agents of their own disempowerment. Especially in participatory approaches, it will thus be important for women to develop next to their capacity for critical agency (Sen 2001) and critical voice (Buskens 2011a) their capacity to aspire (Appadurai 2004). When normative action research design is infused with researchers' perspectives and intentionalities, aligned with gender equality and women's empowerment, and grounded in the possibility for dialogue (Smaling 1995, 2008), it can be more transformatory in process and impact than participatory action research, where the knowledge quest is led and defined by women respondents and researchers adapting to such without questioning or dialogue.

This book

In our first book, *African Women and ICTs: Investigating Technology, Gender and Empowerment*, the authors described how they had witnessed women use ICT and function in ICT space supported by their internal and external resources and endeavouring to overcome both internal and external barriers (Buskens and Webb 2009). Unaided by policies, programmes or projects and often acting as leaders and innovators, women have taken part in the information society on their own initiatives (Odame 2005; Buskens and Webb 2009).

ICTs can benefit women greatly and contribute to women's empowerment and gender-equality endeavours (Hafkin and Taggart 2001; Arun et al. 2004; Gurumurthy 2004; Huyer et al. 2005; United Nations 2005; Melhem et al. 2009; Bonder 2011; Hafkin 2012; APC-WNSP 2014). Hence, the field of ICT4D holds great promise for women, when the realities of gender inequality and the way these become inextricably intertwined with the way women participate in the knowledge society are taken into account (Webb 2012), and potential adverse local effects of globalisation processes can be mitigated.

While the first book's projects were grounded in research that was mostly descriptive and, although aligned with personal and social transformation in terms of women's empowerment, not designed to accomplish such in and through the research projects themselves, this book is more explicitly about the processes of personal and social change that (need to) take place when women in the South set out to explicitly empower themselves in and through the use of ICT, by participating in ICT space and by enhancing their being, doing, becoming and relating through ICT. Furthermore, while the first book only comprised studies about African women, this book has expanded to include studies about women in the Middle East. However, the formula of researchers studying their own contexts and sometimes their direct environments, in their own languages, and including themselves where appropriate in these processes, for purposes directly related to gender equality and women's empowerment as they see these, has remained the same.

The purpose-aligned conceptual framework that grounded the GRACE approach in this second phase and informed the knowledge-construction processes that form the basis of this book can be framed as normative action research. While some projects took this transformatory methodological perspective as their main research design, others implemented more conformist and reformist research designs and project purposes. Yet all projects retained a critical-constructive, future-oriented perspective, with the researchers making their paradigmatic and pragmatic decisions in response to the interplay between their particular research focus and the reality of sexism and social and gender in-equality in their environments.

Thinking aligned with purposes of social change inevitably challenges disciplinary, theoretical and methodological boundaries, procedures and habits because of its intrinsically transdisciplinary nature, but it enables researchers to construct knowledge that speaks directly to the development needs, experiences and discourses of all stakeholders and especially to those of women seeking gender equality and empowerment.

The chapters

Because of the academic, professional, cultural and methodological differences between the research teams, the research projects yielded a complex kaleidoscope of data, knowledge, information, experiences, stories, analyses and perspectives. Yet a certain order has emerged that seems to highlight certain stages or clustered experiences women typically encounter on their journey towards empowerment with ICT, through ICT and in ICT: women's agentic use (as opposed to unaware, unintentional, automatic use) of ICT, their participation in ICT space and their ICT-enhanced being, doing, relating and becoming.

Part one – Agentic ICT use: the aspiration for emancipation versus the power of gender traditions

As has been argued convincingly by ourselves and by others, ICT provides women with the spaces and means to make their lives better in various ways (Hafkin 2000; Hafkin and Huyer 2007; Buskens and Webb 2009; Buskens 2010; Webb 2012). Chapters 1 to 7 show that the use of ICT can indeed contribute to women enhancing their personal and professional lives and that ICT as a professional arena can offer women rewarding career opportunities.

However, the deeply held societal beliefs and structures that emphasize male dominance and superiority and foreground women's main (albeit unrewarded) role of supporting husbands and families are brought by both women and men to the practices and discourses around the use of ICT. Attractive as the aspiration towards emancipation may be to many women, gender traditions in the form of gender roles and gender norms may be a greater power. Since social harmony is grounded in gender inequality in so many contexts, the disruption to the social order that the equal potential of women and the equalizing potential of ICT could bring about may be unacceptable to many.

The chapters in this section therefore speak of conflict and disappointment on various levels: Hibatulla Ali et al. argue that, for resource-constrained Yemeni women to be able to use ICT in their health-seeking

8

behaviour, the gendered socialization of women as passive and unable to take care of themselves for their own sake needs to change fundamentally. Mubarak points towards the fact that, while gendered relations are external, gendered images of women as inferior have been internalized by female students to the degree that they influence their relationships with computers. Mbambo-Thata and Moyo involved both computer-science students and teachers in their study of classroom sexism and revealed how this sexism influenced the majority of female students to drop the prestigious study subject of programming, which resulted in limited career options. Sexism in society pervades the workplace, as Omamo and Aluoch show through their study of ICT career women in Kenya: even women who are passionate about this interesting and competitive field have to deal with sexism and face a workplace that is not organized to accommodate workers who are also women and mothers with responsibilities outside the workplace. Sané describes how, in the highest echelons of power, ICT can offer women political leaders in Senegal an opportunity to participate in political meetings 'at a distance' when they cannot physically be present, either because of domestic responsibilities or because of morals (a decent woman is not seen outside at night). However, while ICT can be a blessing in this regard, it can also hold women back: this gendered use of ICT is clearly two-sided. Ben Hassine's conclusion resonates with this finding: Tunisian university women's use of ICT does not mean that their burdens of work get lighter and it might even make their lives harder, driven as they are by a need to fulfil both traditional and modern expectations. The final chapter in this section, by Ismail and Shamsher Ali, touches on the freedom that the use of ICT can bring to women suffering from domestic violence and yet also points to the limitations of the technology in a sexist environment.

Part two – Developing critical voice in and through safe ICT-created space
In Chapters 8 to 14, the authors describe how women develop their capacity for critical voice in safe ICT-created spaces. The studies by Foda and Webb, by Al-Saqqaf, by Oweis and by Baboun show how the researchers instigated such spaces for female students and worked with the students both online and offline. Using various forms of collaborative inquiry processes, these researchers together with their students explored ways in which ICT could contribute to young women learning how to integrate gender awareness into their understanding of their immediate environment and the world at large, exploring ways of being, relating and knowing that were more authentic, self-caring and self-empowering of their 'woman-selves' than the modes they were socialized in.

Comfort and Dada, Muller and Quawas acted as observers and participant observers in groups that used ICT space as a safe haven from sometimes violent (Comfort and Dada), blatantly sexist (Quawas) and girl-child-unfriendly (Muller) social realities.

When women are expected to be silent, a woman's voice itself is an act of resistance. Women speaking up about what is meaningful to them as women is furthermore intrinsically problematic in a male-dominated world. Women's authentic voice is thus a powerful form of female agency. ICT allows women to convey their social discontent in a relatively safe and very effective way. Whatever ICTs they had at their disposal, whether community radio, television, film or mobile phones and whether through social networking, blogging or mailing, the women actors in this section, both researchers and research respondents, conveyed very effectively both their critique of society and their hope for social change.

This power of speaking out and being heard is emphasized by all authors in this part: speaking about what troubles them in a space that is safe and secluded from normal social life leads women to instigate change because this kind of talking leads to action. Women develop agency through speaking up and speaking out.

Having empowered themselves through exercising their newly found critical voices, these women are either on the verge of taking their new selves into the world or have started to do so already. Both Al-Saqqaf's and Baboun's students developed leadership capacities in and through the safe space of engaging with the gendered world and situating themselves in that world. And Comfort and Dada describe how, in the sanctuary of the Fantsuam Foundation and the safety of their mobile phone connections, women explore their own rationality and common sense and extend their new expanded beingness into a torn world to repair what was damaged.

These projects raise the exciting prospect that ICT-created spaces can become, as Oweis demonstrates, a safe womb where women can, instead of withdrawing from society, find temporary refuge in which to gather the strength and perspective needed to contribute to society from a more authentic and autonomous place.

Part three – ICT-enhanced relating and becoming: personal and social transformation

The chapters in this part, 15 to 21, show how the processes of personal and social change are interwoven and how ICT can accelerate and augment these dynamics by enhancing women's being, doing, becoming and relating. Women can create a space of dignity and freedom in which to own their sexuality on social networking sites in Zambia, and, as Abraham reveals, the very act of engaging in self-development for their own sake makes women agents of social change in various ways. This is not only because women are in virtual space breaking the gender norms that are prevalent in physical space but also because seeking group affiliation on the basis of shared interests instead of traditional alignments is bound to change the structure of society.

As shown by Ahmed Mahdi and Buskens and by Nour Ibrahim in their chapters about female genital mutilation/cutting and premarital sex in Sudan, the use of ICT makes communication about issues that are actually unspeakable in traditional social space easier. In societies that place great value on an individual's respect for and responsibility towards their community, individuals change with and within changed social space that they have helped to change. Since individual actors are as much subjects and creators of their realities as they are created by them, social realities change together with the individual agents who change with them, within them and through them. Meguid shows how web accessibility and special assistive software in combination with mobile phones help mothers of disabled children to overcome their isolation and social exclusion. From this study and the supportive and cohesive group it created, a centre for children with special needs has emerged, along with a powerful political leadership advocating for the plight of these children and their mothers, changing society from within.

Community radio has the potential to produce fora for community dialogue that can create new connections for caring and sharing and bring communities back to traditional values of responsibility and respect. The personalities of the radio presenters are important in this regard, as the Bakesha and Yitamben studies show: in order for community radio to instigate such important social and individual changes, programme presenters have to be both independent and community minded. When they are prepared to use their personality as an instrument for social change, they will also, however, benefit personally.

The chapters in this section emphasize the importance of connection for processes of personal and social transformation: connections were needed for processes of transformation to unfold and such processes in turn changed the various connections. Chapter 21 makes this visible in a particularly personal way: in describing two parallel and interrelated empowerment processes, that of herself and that of the female landowners she was working with, El-Neshawy shows how, with all their personal and social differences in terms of orientation and ambition, all these women, the researcher included, were striving towards strengthening their relationships: with their land, with their male relatives and in and through these connections with themselves.

Even where the women who take centre stage in this section did not set out to change their world, as they were changing themselves within their world, their personal changes set in motion social changes in their direct environments. In the dialogues that researchers and/or facilitators started with their communities, they changed their immediate environments, influenced the wider social and political structures and organizations in their countries and also changed profoundly on a personal level themselves.

The seeds of transformation in connection

Because of the emphasis in the GRACE Network on transformation and on the crucial role of respondent and researcher agency, a very specific picture has emerged of what a successful gender and ICT4D project would look like. Reading the chapters more closely will reveal that the three conceptual categories ordering the various chapters are relevant to most respondents and researchers in their journey towards empowerment in all the projects: in the agentic use of ICT, most women will encounter the power of gendered traditions; on their journey of self-expansion, they will need the nurturing that a safe ICT-created space can provide (indeed, the GRACE Network itself is such a space); when women set out to bring empowerment to their communities they themselves become receivers of the gift that change entails; and when they set out to empower themselves the ripple effects on their environments are inevitable.

Emphasizing researcher agency implies respect for individuals and thus unique processes of creating meaning. The theoretical frameworks that the researchers used or constructed in and through their research processes vary widely and speak not only to the difference in research topics and research respondents but also to a difference in mindset: to how different people approach a given situation, as the unique beings that they are. Honouring this researcher uniqueness made the diversity in research processes, results and representations possible and hence also created the wealth of perspectives, experiences and understandings from which the beginning of a more theorical understanding about women, gender and ICT could emerge.

In hindsight, it seems logical and almost inevitable that in acknowledging and working with individual uniqueness the crucial role of connection would become so visible: the connection between researchers and respondents, the connection between respondents, the connection between researchers and last but not least the almost trans-personal relationship that the connection with a just, loving and sustainable world provides. The space that is created by such a trans-personal connection influences all other relationships in a profound way. As the chapters in this book show, the various forms of connection enrich and strengthen each other and are all very pertinent to the success of the gender and ICT4D projects that are discussed here.

This collection of texts presents a perspective on gender research in ICT4D in particular and on development in general that is different from the more directive top-to-bottom approach of constructing a conceptual framework to make sense of a variety of local research inputs instead of letting a general understanding emerge from the bottom up. Our approach will not easily lead to the provision of tools and services on a large scale or to a standardization of so-called best practices that are applicable in a wide variety of contexts. But the knowledge the researchers have constructed can be transferred to other contexts when it is properly decontextualized and the processes the researchers have designed will be widely applicable when the principles underlying the process decisions are understood. The processes of change that have unfolded in and through these projects speak to the validity and effectiveness of the approaches the researchers have taken.

Calling for a more modest approach to development grounded in a more truthful relationship to the world, Majid Rahnema (1997: 392) spoke of 'that genuine and extraordinary power that enables a tiny seed, in all its difference and uniqueness, to start its journey into the unknown'. As both researchers and respondents have sown their tiny seeds, the effects of their extraordinary efforts will, no doubt, continue to make themselves known.

Notes

1 I am referring here to the recent revolutions in Tunisia, Egypt and Yemen, the sectarian violence in Nigeria and Kenya, the political upheavals in Sudan, the civil unrest in Zambia and the ongoing occupation in Palestine.

2 The full name for coltan is columbite–tantalite.

3 See http://en.wikipedia.org/wiki/Agbogbloshie.

4 Habermas distinguishes knowledge interests between the drive to control and predict, the drive to communicate and the drive to emancipate and links these with the empirical-analytical paradigm, the interpretive-hermeneutic paradigm and the critical-emancipatory paradigm (Habermas 1972). These paradigms can be loosely linked to quantitative research, qualitative research and (participatory) action research, although, as Smaling establishes, paradigms are

underdetermined by methods and methods are underdetermined by paradigms (Smaling 1994).

References

Appadurai, A. (2004) 'The capacity to aspire: culture and the terms of recognition', in V. Rao and M. Walton (eds), *Culture and Public Action*, Palo Alto, CA: Stanford University Press, pp. 59–85.

Arun S., R. Heeks and S. Morgan (2004) 'ICT initiatives, women and work in developing countries: reinforcing or changing gender inequalities in south India', Development Informatics Working Paper Series, Manchester: Institute for Development Policy and Management.

Association for Progressive Communications Women's Networking Support Program (APC-WNSP) (2014) 'Gender and information and communication technology: towards an analytical framework', www.apcwomen. org/work/research/analytical-framework.html, accessed 12 January 2014.

Bonder, G. (2011) *Why is it Important that Women Fully Participate in the Construction of the Information/ Knowledge Society?* Buenos Aires: FLASCO, www.catunescomujer. org/catunesco_mujer/ documents/2011_mujeres_SI_ bonder_ENGLISH.pdf, accessed 5 June 2014.

Brouwers, R. (2013) 'Revisiting gender mainstreaming in international development: goodbye to an illusionary strategy', International Institute of Social Studies Working Paper 556, http://repub.eur.nl/res/ pub/39504/wp556.pdf, accessed 20 May 2014.

Buskens, I. (2009) 'Doing research with women for the purpose of transformation', in I. Buskens and A. Webb (eds), *African Women and ICTs: Investigating Technology, Gender and Empowerment*, London: Zed Books/IDRC, pp. 9–21.

— (2010) 'Agency and reflexivity in ICT4D: research – questioning women's options, poverty and human development', *Information Technologies & International Development*, 6: 19–24.

— (2011a) '"Observation as freedom", a response to: "Women and the Internet: objectification and human capabilities" by Martha Nussbaum', Human Development Capabilities Approach Conference, The Hague, 6–8 September.

— (2011b) 'The importance of intent: reflecting on open development for women's empowerment', *Information Technologies & International Development*, 7(1): 71–6.

— (2013) 'Open development is a freedom song: revealing intent and freeing power', in M. L. Smith and K. M. A. Reilly (eds), *Open Development: Networked Innovations in International Development*, Cambridge, MA: MIT Press, pp. 327–52.

—(2014), 'ICT and Gender', in R. Mansell and P. H. Ang (eds), *The International Encyclopedia of Digital Communication and Society*, Oxford, Wiley Blackwell.

— (2015) 'Infusing a gender perspective in indigenous knowledge technology design: some reflections and suggestions', in N. J. Bidwell and H. Winschiers-Theophilius (eds), *At the Intersection of Indigenous* and *Traditional Knowledge and Technology Design*.

Buskens, I. and A. Webb (eds) (2009), *African Women and ICTs: Investigation Technology, Gender and Empowerment*, London and New York: Zed Books.

Cohen, T. (ed.) (2012) *Telemorphosis: Theory in the Era of Climate Change*, vol. 1, Ann Arbor, MI: Open Humanities Press, http://hdl.handle.net/2027/spo.10539563.0001.001, accessed 10 September 2013.

Eichler, M. (1991) *Non-Sexist Research Methods: A Practical Guide*, New York: Routledge.

Gorilla Organization (2008) 'Conflict coltan and cassiterite', http://gorilla.wildlifedirect.org/2008/10/02/conflict-coltan-and-cassiterite, accessed 5 June 2014.

Greenpeace (2009) 'Where does e-waste end up?', 24 February, www.greenpeace.org/international/en/campaigns/toxics/electronics/the-e-waste-problem/where-does-e-waste-end-up, accessed 24 May 2014.

Gurumurthy, A. (2004) 'Gender and ICTs: overview report', Brighton: BRIDGE, Institute for Development Studies, University of Sussex.

Gurumurthy, A. with P. J. Singh and A. Kovacs (2009) 'IT for change: recasting the Bejing Platform for Action through the information society lens – a conceptual and action framework', input into the UNESCAP High-Level Intergovernmental Meeting on the Review of Implementation of the Bejing Platform for Action, Bangkok, Thailand, 13–15 May.

Habermas, J. (1972) *Knowledge and Human Interests*, London: Heinemann.

Hafkin N. J. (2000) 'Convergence of concepts: gender and ICTs in Africa', in E. M. Rathgeber and E. O. Adera (eds), *Gender and the Information Revolution in Africa*, Ottawa: International Development Research Centre, pp. 1–16.

— (2012) 'Gender', in G. Sadowsky (ed.) *Accelerating Development Using the Web: Empowering Poor and Marginalized Populations*, http://public.webfoundation.org/publications/accelerating-development, accessed 20 May 2014.

Hafkin, N. J. and S. Huyer (2007) 'Women and gender in ICT statistics and indicators for development', *Information Technologies & International Development*, 4(2): 25–41.

Hafkin, N. J. and N. Taggart (2001) *Gender, Information Technology and Developing Countries*, Washington, DC: Academy for Educational Development.

Huitt, W. (2007) 'Success in the conceptual age: another paradigm shift', paper presented at the 32nd Annual Meeting of the Georgia Educational Research Association, Savannah, GA, 26 October.

Huitt, W. and S. Cain (2005) 'An overview of the conative domain', *Educational Psychology Interactive*, Valdosta, GA: Valdosta State University, www.edpsycinteractive.org/papers/conative.pdf, accessed 20 May 2014.

Huyer, S., N. Hafkin, H. Ertl and H. Dryburgh (2005) 'Women in the information society', in G. Sciadas (ed.), *From the Digital Divide to Digital Opportunities: Measuring Infostates for Development*, Québec: Claude-Yves Charron, pp. 135–96.

Jabbar, S. (2013) 'How France loots its former colonies', *This Is Africa*, 24 January, http://thisisafrica. me/france-loots-former-colonies, accessed 5 June 2014.

Jain, D. and D. Elson (eds) (2011) *Harvesting Feminist Knowledge for Public Policy: Rebuilding Progress*, New Delhi: SAGE/IDRC.

— in collaboration with the Casablanca Dreamers (2010) 'Vision for a better world: from economic crisis to equality', www. inclusivecities.org/wp-content/ uploads/2012/07/Jain_Elson_ UNDP_Crisis_to_equality.pdf, accessed 20 May 2014.

Klein, N. (2011) 'The fight against climate change is down to us – the 99%', *Guardian*, 7 October, www.theguardian.com/ commentisfree/2011/oct/07/fight-climate-change-99, accessed 20 May 2014.

Kleine, D. (2013) *Technologies of Choice? ICTs, Development and the Capabilities Approach*, Cambridge, MA: MIT Press.

Melhem, S., C. Morrell and N. Tandon (2009) 'Information and communication technology for women's socio-economic empowerment', World Bank Working Paper 176, Washington, DC: World Bank.

Nussbaum, M. C. (2000) *Women and Human Development: The Capabilities Approach*, Cambridge: Cambridge University Press.

Odame, H. H. (2005) 'Introduction', in *Gender and ICTs for Development: Setting the Context in Gender and ICTs for Development*, Amsterdam and London: KIT and Oxfam, pp. 13–25.

O'Hearn, D. (2009) 'Amartya Sen's *Development as Freedom*: ten years later', *Policy & Practice: A Development Education Review*, 8: 9–15.

Rahnema, M. (1997) 'Towards post-development: searching for signposts, a new language and new paradigms', in M. Rahnema and V. Bawtree (eds), *The Post-development Reader*, London: Zed Books, pp. 377–405.

Ryan-Collins, J., A. Simms, S. Spratt and E. Neitzert (2009) 'The great transition – a tale of how it turned out right', New Economics Foundation, www.neweconomics. org/publications/entry/the-great-transition, accessed 13 October 2013.

Sen, A. K. (1999) *Development as Freedom*, Oxford: Oxford University Press.

— (2001) 'Many faces of gender inequality', *Frontline*, 18(22), www.frontline.in/navigation/?ty pe=static&page=flonnet&rdurl=f l1822/18220040.htm, accessed 14 October 2013.

Smaling, A. (1994) 'The pragmatic dimension: paradigmatic and pragmatic aspects of choosing a qualitative or quantitative method', *Quality & Quantity*, 28(30): 233–49.

— (1995) 'Open mindedness, open heartedness and dialogical openness: the dialectics of openings and closures', in I. Maso, P. A. Atkinson, S. Delmont and J. C. Verhoeven (eds), *Openness in Research*, Assen: Van Gorcum, pp. 21–32.

— (2008) *Dialoog en Empathie in the Methodologie* [Dialogue and Empathy in Research Methodology], Amsterdam: SWP Publishers.

Sterling, S. R. (2013) 'Designing for trauma: the roles of ICTD in combating violence against women', in *Proceedings of the Sixth International Conference on Information and Communications Technologies and Development: Notes – Volume 2*, New York: Association for Computing Machinery, pp. 159–62.

United Nations (2005) 'Gender equality and empowerment of women through ICT', www.un.org/womenwatch/daw/public/w2000-09.05-ict-e.pdf, accessed 12 January 2014.

Van der Velden, M. (2008) 'What's love got to do with IT? On ethics and accountability in telling technology stories', in F. Sudweeks, H. Hrachovec and C. Ess (eds), *Proceedings of Cultural Attitudes towards Technology and Communication 2008*, Perth: Murdoch University, Perth, Australia, pp. 26–39.

Wacjman, J. (2009) 'Feminist theories of technology', *Cambridge Journal of Economics*, 34(1): 143–52.

Webb, A. (2012) 'ICT in a gender inequality context', *ICT Update: A Current Awareness Bulletin for ACP Agriculture*, http://ictupdate.cta.int/en/Regulars/Q-R/Une-inegalite-hommes-femmes-seculaire, accessed 14 October 2013.

ONE | **Agentic ICT use: the aspiration for emancipation versus the power of gender traditions**

[handwritten annotations:]

techno-utopia re fountain?

- ICT diffusion & use → Africa + ME
- Emancipatory (women + dev)
- Practitioner / activist
- "Women" ≠ feminist

↪ what are the factual assumptions why women? fact or presumption?

ye.g. Lack of access?

→ Technological determinism?
→ Overly optimistic? → tech can X, Y, Z

✳ Risks? Not RCT

1 | Healthy women, healthy society: ICT and the need for women's empowerment in Yemen

AHLAM HIBATULLA ALI, HUDA BA SALEEM, NADA AL-SYED HASSAN AHMED, NAGAT ALI MUQBIL AND ABEER SHAEF ABDO SAEED

> When health is absent, wisdom cannot reveal itself, art cannot manifest, strength cannot fight, wealth becomes useless, and intelligence cannot be applied. (Herophilus)

Introduction

The state of women's health in Yemen is deeply worrying. Reproductive health studies have shown that Yemen's maternal mortality ratio is among the highest in the Middle East and North Africa region (World Bank 2012). According to the Yemeni National Strategy for Reproductive Health (Republic of Yemen 2011), 'Yemen has a high maternal mortality rate of 365 deaths per 100,000 live births so that amounts to approximately seven to eight women dying each day from childbirth complications'. Ranking as the country with the highest overall gender gap among 136 countries, Yemen also has the highest gender gap in the Middle East and the highest in the lower-middle income category (Haussman et al. 2013: 12, 13, 17, 20). With an adult male literacy rate of 81.18 per cent and an adult female literacy rate of 46.79 per cent, the gender inequality in terms of education is striking (Index Mundi n.d.).[1]

As professional Yemeni women working in the fields of science and medicine, we, the Yemen GRACE Health Research team, all firmly believed that women's reproductive health problems could be resolved by raising awareness among Yemeni women about more effective forms of health care. We were aware of studies that suggested that information and communication technologies (ICTs) could contribute to improving women's health, and we saw in these a ray of hope. We assumed that ICTs, such as radio, television, mobile phones, computers, e-mail and the Internet, could be used to disseminate valuable health information to Yemeni women and improve their health-seeking behaviour.

Inspired by both personal success with ICTs and international research about the potential of ICTs in disseminating evidence-based knowledge, empowering people and significantly improving the health of vulnerable groups (see e.g. Mechael 2005; Maitra 2007; Buskens 2010), through our research project we intended to explore and investigate possibilities of empowering Yemeni women with information through ICTs (old and new) related to their reproductive health and well-being. We focused on women's reproductive health because of risks involved with pregnancy and the high rate of mortality during childbirth, which, if appropriate measures are taken, in many instances can be prevented. We chose Aden, Yemen's economic and commercial capital, as our area of research, and did our fieldwork in the districts of Salah-al-Deen, Fuqum, Al-Buraiqa and Madinat Al-Shaab. These areas are all characterized by a culture of strict conservative beliefs as well as under-use of health services.

We hope that our findings will be useful to efforts to improve women's reproductive health care in Yemen and beyond, particularly those involving the use of ICTs for dissemination of health-care information.

Study rationale

Studies have shown that use of ICT can have a positive health impact in developing countries, especially in remote areas where long distances and poor infrastructure hinder the movement of physicians and patients (Geissuhler et al. 2003). ICTs, especially mobile phones, are emerging as powerful tools in the facilitation of health-care message delivery, knowledge-sharing and health-care service delivery (Mechael 2005). ICTs are also believed to 'play a decisive role in behavioural change communication and safe motherhood. ICTs will help in improving connectivity for individuals and communities, which in turn may provide access to critical transformational information' (Maitra 2007: 1).

Given this potential of ICTs, we felt that if adopted correctly they could also play a significant role in Yemen: raising awareness about the importance of maintaining a healthy lifestyle, clarifying misconceptions about reproductive health care and equipping women with information relevant to good reproductive health.

Research approach

In our research we posed the following questions:

• To what extent do women in these areas of Aden use ICTs as sources of reproductive health information?

- Who is/are the decision-maker(s) in the family pertaining to women's reproductive health care?

Our research respondents were women aged between fifteen and forty-nine years who attended reproductive health clinics in public polyclinics and lived in the Salah-al-Deen, Fuqum, Al-Buraiqa and Madinat Al-Shaab districts.

The research process had the following phases:

- pre-intervention, where we administered a baseline questionnaire to 201 women;
- intervention (six months), with delivery of health messages through television and radio: these messages focused on issues of reproductive health such as family planning and contraception, negative consequences of early marriages, advantages of regular visits to health centres, etc.;
- post-intervention, where we reintroduced the same questionnaire to four hundred women;
- interviews, where thirteen women were interviewed to obtain a better insight into issues;
- closure, with a final follow-up with health professionals who had administered the questionnaire at the health clinics.

Health professionals at the targeted clinics, who were trained by the research team for that purpose, administered both the pre-intervention and post-intervention questionnaires. From among the women visiting the targeted health clinics, 201 women selected through convenience sampling participated in the pre-intervention phase.

During the following six-month intervention period, we sent out health messages through the local radio station and Aden television channel. Our messages had a special design so that they could be easily identified from others sent out by the Ministry of Health and Population. However, our plan to send health messages via mobile phone did not work out because the mobile phone companies (we approached Yemen Mobile and Saba Phone) were not interested in collaborating with us on this issue.

After the intervention phase, the post-intervention questionnaire was administered to four hundred women visiting health clinics in the targeted areas. However, this questionnaire had a methodological flaw: the question pertaining to the mobile phone intervention that we had planned but that did not happen was not removed from the questionnaire, so when health professionals administered it this question remained.

TABLE 1.1 Receiving our project
health messages through ICT tools
(n = 400).

Medium	No.	%
Television	16	4.0
Radio	14	3.5
Mobile phone	13	3.2
None	357	89.3

The post-intervention questionnaire was followed by thirteen in-depth interviews, from which we hoped to gain a better insight into women's health information sources and health-seeking behaviour. Regarding the interviews it needs to be noted that we approached many women over a period of three weeks but most declined, saying that sharing personal information with a stranger would be inappropriate. We therefore included all those women who agreed to be interviewed.

To check data reliability the team leader interviewed all of the health professionals involved in the research process, both in person and over the phone, after data collection had been finalized.

Findings from the pre- and post-intervention questionnaires

Processing health information

In the pre-intervention questionnaire we asked participants which ICTs they used as information sources. In the post-intervention questionnaire we asked participants the same question as well as whether they had seen *our* health messages on television or listened to them on the radio. We made sure that respondents knew what we were talking about by explaining the characteristics pertinent to our messages.

Most of the women said they had not noticed our health messages. Interestingly, though, a small percentage (3.2 per cent or thirteen women) said they had received messages via mobile phone, which was puzzling because we did not have a mobile phone intervention (Table 1.1). We could not find any other source that would have sent health messages via mobile phone in that period.

What are women's sources for obtaining reproductive health information? While trends in terms of health-information-source use remained more or less the same in the six-month intervention period, women professed that they used television more than listening to health staff, relatives or friends or listening to the radio; they also used mobiles minimally. The results from the pre-intervention questionnaire

TABLE 1.2 Main source of reproductive health information.

Medium	Pre-intervention (n = 201)		Post-intervention (n = 400)		χ^2
	No.	%	No.	%	
Television	80	39.8	219	54.5	18.9 p<0.0005*
Health staff/ relatives/friends	68	33.8	87	21.8	
Radio	47	23.4	69	17.3	
Mobile phone	6	3.0	25	6.4	

* Highly significant.

TABLE 1.3 Decision-makers in reproductive health issues.

Decision-maker in reproductive health issues	Pre-intervention (n = 201)		Post-intervention (n = 400)		χ^2
	No.	%	No.	%	
Husband	114	56.7	176	44.0	38.56 p<0.0005*
Both husband and wife	58	28.9	132	33.0	
Self-decision	11	5.5	83	20.8	
Mother-in-law	18	8.9	9	2.2	

* Highly significant.

differed considerably from those from the post-intervention question-naire (Table 1.2).

Making health decisions

Who was/were the decision-maker(s) in the family pertaining to women's reproductive health care? In terms of decision-making, the trends shifted in the intervention period. In the pre-intervention stage, mothers-in-law featured more prominently as decision-makers (8.9 per cent or eighteen cases) than self-decision (5.5 per cent or eleven women); in the post-intervention phase, self-decision accounted for a much higher per-centage than the mothers-in-law (20.8 per cent (83) versus 2.2 per cent (9)) (Table 1.3).

What did not change, however, was that the husband appeared to be the major decision-maker in both the pre-intervention and post-intervention stages (56.7 per cent (114 cases) and 44 per cent (176 cases) respectively), followed by the group that favoured a joint decision by both husband and wife in both the pre- and post-intervention stages (28.9 per cent (58 cases) and 33 per cent (132 cases) respectively).

Reflection on the quantitative results

As the respondents reported that they had not received our health messages, we could not explain the difference between the pre- and post-intervention results. Before drawing any conclusions we decided to contact the health professionals who had administered the questionnaire. The team leader set out to interview these health professionals both in person and over the phone to gain further insight into the process behind the data collection.

These follow-up interviews revealed some interesting information. In three of the targeted areas – Al-Buraiqa, Fuqum and Salah-al-Deen – the health professionals who administered the questionnaire stated that most of the women participants came thinking they would receive something in return for filling out the questionnaire.

Furthermore, referring to the illiterate women participants, health professionals in Al-Buraiqa, Fuqum and Madinat Al-Shaab stated that it had taken a long time to explain the questions to them. Some of these women had answered the questions positively – giving the feeling that they just wanted to be done and leave – and others had asked the health professional to fill in what they thought appropriate.

Health professionals in Salah-al-Deen and Al-Buraiqa pointed out that they had mentioned to the participants that health messages would be sent through radio, television and mobile phones.

Findings from the interviews

When talking about our thirteen women participants we use pseudonyms in all cases.

Roles of ICTs in women's lives

The results from the interviews showed that some women, such as Husun, lacked access to the devices themselves: 'I don't listen to radio programmes. TV is [on] all the time with my teenage kids.' Others, such as Gala, could not comprehend the television language: 'Awareness? Radio? No. TV? The programmes are difficult to be understood and nobody watches the Yemeni channels.' Some, such as Latifa, remained engrossed in household chores: 'No one listens to the radio, and I am too busy with housework to watch TV.'

A role for ICTs in obtaining health information?

Husun considered medical counselling and neighbourhood women's gatherings as good sources of health information. Gala indicated her health-information sources as (in order, from top to bottom): husband, neighbours, teenage children and finally doctors, and believed these were adequate, explaining: 'No one reads journals or watches TV as people are struggling for their needs; they need food and medicine.' Tawadodd had a similar view of ICTs:

> I don't like radio. Sometimes I watch TV but I do not understand everything they say. I'm sad that I didn't go to school because if I'm educated, I will understand better and become well informed. I think it is better to ask doctors or midwives. I can ask them everything in privacy.

The other women who were interviewed did not rely on ICTs (television and radio) for information either, except Aysha, who had a university degree.

Health decision-making

Women's health-seeking decisions varied from self-made decisions to joint decisions to having no voice in the matter. Hasna'a confirmed: 'I made the decision and I cleared it to my husband! My in-laws don't have any word in it. As a family, we are taking our own decisions.' Hasna'a said: 'I made it, I told you, I don't care if he gets a new wife', indicating that making her own health decisions is not without controversy in her family. Husun mentioned that, as long her house, kids and husband's needs are taken care of, she is free to meet the neighbours or go to the doctor.

Warda explained that her mother-in-law is the decision-maker on household issues as well as family planning. Tawadodd and Mariam said they had family members make decisions for them. Asma, Fathiya, Wahida and Latifa said they made joint decisions (related to family planning).

Poverty

Poverty affected the lives of the women we interviewed in various ways. Tawadodd, a poor woman suffering from infertility, visited private clinics but money became an issue so she then came to the public clinic. For Tawadodd, both health and good food cost money – money that she did not have. She lived under the fear that, if she did not conceive, her husband would remarry and divorce her, as he could not financially support two wives.

Latifa, whose husband's income was 17,000YR ($81) per month, was pregnant with her third child and felt distressed, saying that the child was a mistake as they could hardly afford good food (meaning meat, chicken, fish, salad, fruit). Driven by poverty, some of the women we interviewed sought family planning to avoid the financial burden of having more children to take care of, and we noticed a joint decision in such cases.

Health care, self-care?

The women we interviewed realized the need for a healthy lifestyle, but their health consciousness did not seem to stem from a sense of self-love but rather as a means to an end: to take care of their family. As Warda expressed it: 'I have to put myself first sometimes or no one will take care of my children and husband.' Asma placed herself last when she told us that taking care of herself was essential for her kids and husband, and lastly for herself. Husun took care of herself because 'we need to be healthy … Otherwise, our husbands will get new wives and our children will be taken away. Finally, we will only suffer.'

Latifa did not believe in regular check-ups, and said: 'Even when I am sick I take some medicine that my husband gives me. I go to the clinic when the kids are sick' (before this visit, her husband had seen that she was very sick so he had insisted she visit the clinic). Similarly, Fathiya ate well and took care of herself but went to see a doctor only when she felt unwell. Hasna'a, however, said: 'First my health, then my children's sake. We have to put our priorities – we are not stupid, most people are careless.'

Discussion

Our endeavour to investigate the possibility of using ICTs as a means of empowering Yemeni women living in conservative and under-resourced areas with limited reproductive health information led us to discover a complex reality that challenges the very implementation of ICTs, particularly the new ones, for this purpose.

Poverty was the major impediment to the use of new ICTs in our research environment. In poverty-stricken households such as those of Tawadodd and Latifa, computers, mobile phones and the Internet were unheard of. Poor families that are trying to meet their basic needs cannot afford a mobile phone or Internet service. The monthly bills would place an insurmountable extra burden on an already inadequate income. Almost half of the women in our study were illiterate,[2] and this emerged as another major factor impeding the use of ICTs, since both text messaging and the Internet require reading skills. It has been established that factors such as poverty, illiteracy (which includes computer illiteracy) and language barriers constrict women's use of ICT (United Nations Development Programme 2005: 7).

The third factor impeding women's use of ICT for health-care purposes is linked to their understanding of what they think they are entitled to in terms of health care and the capacity to take actions towards such health care. Women's health-seeking behaviour is grounded in their early gender socialization. Unlike the boy child, the girl child's education is grounded in obedience and care for others. Raised to be a good, obedient wife and mother, she receives early training in domestic activities and agricultural work, including transportation of water in rural areas (Hommad and Al-Basha 1992; see also Al-Rabee 2003: 3). In a climate so charged with gender inequality, it is therefore not surprising that women such as Latifa and Asma prioritize family needs and household chores over their self-health and self-care; nor is it surprising that decisions made by husbands for their wives' well-being are accepted as a matter of course. As Mosedale (2005: 244) explains, 'definitions of empowerment usually include a sense of people making decisions on matters which are important in their lives and being able to carry them out'. Our findings, however, testify to the fact that, in relation to health matters, Yemeni women's main orientation is about deferring to others' authority and not about independent thinking and making decisions on their own behalves. These findings confirm research elsewhere (Oxaal and Baden 1996) and are consistent with earlier research findings in Yemen (Hommad and Al-Basha 1992; see also Al-Rabee 2003). Hommad and Al-Basha (1992: 3) have found that 'Over one-third (36%) of women have their health care decisions made by their husband alone. Another 58% of women make these decisions jointly with their husbands. And 2.3% make such decisions themselves.' These percentages approximate ours very closely.

We therefore have to conclude on the basis of our findings that, in conservative and/or under-resourced areas in Yemen, where ICTs would be most needed, their implementation and success remain debatable.

In the course of our study we also discovered certain factors that form an impediment to the viability and validity of research with women who live in conservative and under-resourced areas.

In the first place, the fact that the mobile phone companies refused to collaborate with us in sending out female reproductive health messages, while these companies would regularly send out all kinds of other messages, alerted us to the fact that women's well-being and reproductive health are not matters of public concern in Yemen. Since, to our knowledge, no reproductive health messages have been sent via mobile phones in Yemen as yet, or any other health messages to women for that matter, we were struck by the fact that these companies did not respond enthusiastically towards this innovative use of mobile telephony.

In the second place, Yemeni women's gender socialization makes research a challenging endeavour. As became apparent in our qualitative research phase, many women did not feel free to interact with a stranger. Furthermore, many of the women who did participate misconstrued the purpose and the meaning of the research: quite a few women had expected to receive gifts because of their participation and 3.2 per cent of the respondents indicated that they had received mobile phone messages while such were not sent. It is highly likely that illiteracy was a factor in these misunderstandings since illiterate women would be dependent on others for understanding and would probably not have a frame of reference to understand a research process.[3]

In the third place, since the qualitative interview sample was self-selected, comprising those women who felt free enough to participate in the interviews, the qualitative research findings are biased towards a specifc type of woman. On the basis of our research findings and our intimate knowledge of the context, we postulate that the women who did not want to be interviewed might be more disempowered, which in this context would mean having even less decision-making power than the women who participated. Our qualitative interviews were therefore biased in a helpful way: they enabled us to hear what it would take to 'break the norm' for a Yemeni woman from an under-resourced environment, by hearing it in her own words.

In order to safeguard the validity of our research results, we only analyzed the qualitative interview data and the quantitative data that pertained to the questions focusing on women's decision-making processes.

Conclusions and recommendations

Our recommendations are twofold since they pertain to two sets of findings: methodological insights regarding health research with women in Yemen and the research insights pertaining to women's health-seeking behaviour and the possibility of increasing their health awareness through ICT.

Researchers focusing on women's health in Yemen should take into account that Yemeni women's disempowerment will interfere with processes of data collection: women may not always be reliable conversation partners when they lack the voice and the confidence to speak for themselves, and women may not always have the frame of reference to interpret research processes, purposes and contexts appropriately. Researchers thus have to keep verifying what women actually 'hear', how they understand what has been asked and what they think this means. Furthermore, working with a self-selected sample comprising women who would feel free enough to participate in research biases the research results. Researchers have to understand what such bias means in relation to the research question and purpose.

Regarding health outcomes, in order to save Yemeni women from untimely deaths, we need to see profound changes in women's perceptions about their self-worth and in their capacity to make their own decisions to seek the health care they need. Based on our results we make the following recommendations:

- Urgent investment is needed into the type of female education that will give girls a sense of their rights and the opportunity to grow their self-esteem and self-confidence. Education can equip women with negotiating capabilities, allowing them to discuss issues related to their reproductive health with husbands and other relatives in positions of authority over them.
- Parents should be educated about the importance of raising and dealing with their daughters and sons equally. They should realize that both females and males have a right to education.
- Husbands should be involved in health-care awareness campaigns to help them understand their wives' health-care needs and the rights they have to make decisions about such needs.
- In designing health messages for women using ICTs, both old (radio and television) and new (mobile phone, Internet), policy-makers need to take into account that women seem to process health information together with friends and relatives and not so much on their own.

Finally, for Yemeni women to become more healthy and for the shocking female mortality rate in Yemen to become a thing of the past, the social, cultural and religious beliefs that inform Yemeni women's gendered sense of identity and as a consequence their health-seeking behaviour have to change. Only when the culture of gender discrimination and sexism, so prevalent in Yemeni society, is transformed towards mutual care and respect between women and men will it no longer be strange for women to take care of their health for reasons of self-respect and self-care. A healthy Yemeni society means healthy women – and healthy Yemeni women mean a healthy Yemeni society.

Notes

1 Adult literacy rate is the percentage of people aged fifteen and above who can, with understanding, read and write a short, simple statement on their everyday life. Illiteracy is falling in Yemen, with the gender gap becoming slightly less pronounced. The Index Mundi 2010 youth literacy rates are 96 per cent for men between fifteen and twenty-four and 74.08 per cent for women of the same ages (Index Mundi n.d.).

2 This is a slightly better average than the national 2010 rate, with 81.18 per cent literacy for men and 46.79 per cent for women (Index Mundi n.d.).

3 Women might have 'heard' that they would be helped (because they were interviewed in a health-care clinic) or that they would receive something (possibly a radio, a TV mobile phone, because this is what the interviewers mentioned), and so they may have answered the question focusing on whether they had received a message via an ICT as whether they would want such an ICT.

References

Al-Rabee, A. (2003) 'Adolescence and youth reproductive health in Yemen: status, policies, programs, and issues', www.policyproject. com/pubs/countryreports/ARH_ Yemen.pdf, accessed 20 May 2014.

Buskens, I. (2010) 'Agency and reflexivity in ICT4D research: questioning women's options, poverty, and human development', *Information*

Technologies & International Development, 6, 19–24.

Geissuhler, A., O. Ly, C. Lovis and J. L. Haire (2003) 'Telemedicine in Western Africa: lessons learned from a pilot project in Mali, perspectives and recommendations', *AMIA Annual Symposium Proceedings*, Washington, DC: AMIA, pp. 249–53.

Haussman, R., L. D. Tyson and S. Zahidi (eds) (2013) *The Global Gender Gap Report 2013*, World Economic Forum, www3.weforum.org/docs/ WEF_GenderGap_Report_2013.pdf, accessed 27 May 2014.

Hommad, N. A. and A. Y. Al-Basha (1992) *Legal Aspects and Its Reflection on Yemeni Women's Status and Their Roles in the Political, Economical, and Social Fields*, Sana'a: Yemeni Association of Family Planning.

Index Mundi (n.d.) 'Yemen – literacy rate', www.indexmundi.com/facts/ yemen/literacy-rate, accessed 6 April 2014.

Maitra, A. (2007) 'Safe motherhood and ICT tools in BCC', http:// unpan1.un.org/intradoc/ groups/public/documents/un/ unpan036503.pdf, accessed 20 May 2014.

McCarthy, J. and D. Maine (1992) 'A framework for analyzing the determinants of maternal mortality', *Studies in Family Planning*, 23(1): 23–33.

Mechael, P. N. (2005) 'Case study from Egypt: Mobile phones for mother and child care', *Information for Development*, 3: 15–17.

Mosedale, S. (2005) 'Policy arena – assessing women's empowerment: towards a conceptual framework', *Journal of International Development*, 17(2): 243–57.

Oxaal, Z. and S. Baden (1996) 'Challenges to women's reproductive health: maternal mortality', BRIDGE Report 38, www.bridge.ids.ac.uk/reports/re38c.pdf, accessed 21 May 2013.

Republic of Yemen (2011) *Yemeni National Reproductive Health Strategy 2011–2015*, http://yemen. unfpa.org/demo/uploaded/Yemen%20NRHS%202011-2015%20Final%20English%20version%20_1.pdf, accessed 27 May 2014.

United Nations Development Programme (2005) 'Gender equality and empowerment of women through ICT', www.un.org/womenwatch/daw/public/w2000-09.05-ict-e.pdf, accessed 21 May 2014.

World Bank (2012) *World Development Indicators*, http://data.worldbank.org/sites/default/files/wdi-2012-ebook.pdf, accessed 27 May 2014.

2 | Computer proficiency and women's empowerment: gendered experiences of ICT at the University of Khartoum

AMEL MUSTAFA MUBARAK

Introduction

This chapter focuses on female and male students' experiences of the policies, practices and environments of integrating and using technology at the University of Khartoum. The University of Khartoum adopted a policy of equal access to computers for all students by allowing one hour of use a day for students at BSc level and two hours or more for post-graduate students, irrespective of gender, in order to distribute access to the limited ICT resources equitably to a maximum number of students. The university also provided a compulsory computer course for all students during their first year.

It was assumed that such policies would provide equal benefits to both male and female students. Little emphasis is placed, however, on gender analysis or building the capacity to redress gender inequalities in the education sector in Sudan. The introduction of ICT into the educational sector in Sudan has thus created new forms of social and gender inequalities. As a study conducted at the University of Harare in Zimbabwe has shown, so-called gender-neutral access policies at universities tend to favour men (Mbambo-Thata et al. 2009).

ICT-related activities have a long history of being viewed as a male domain (Brosnan and Davidson 1996; Liff and Shepherd 2004; Huyer et al. 2005). New technologies introduced into the global marketplace as gender neutral, having equal potential to be used by either men or women (Rathgeber 2000), are affecting women's and men's lives, activities and sense of self differently. The common belief that women are less interested in technology than men – and that this explains their slower rates of adopting technology, thus making the issue 'natural' and not worthy of investigation or policy concern – is exacerbating this trend of gender-inequitable use and benefit. This divide is having generally unrecognized implications for women's sense of their capacities and their self-development.

Through investigating the gendered nature of the relationship female students have with computers and the Internet, we seek to identify the gender-related factors that work against their uptake of ICTs. We recognize that an individual's low level of ICT functioning can be mistakenly understood to reflect inequalities in competence if the factors contributing to low functioning are not well understood.

According to Sen's capability approach, an individual's achieved well-being is evaluated by considering the level of valued functionings, or the 'beings' and 'doings' that can be attained (Sen 1999). This chapter explores female students' functionings in terms of their computer and Internet use and the implications this has for their sense of well-being and hence for their agency and self-development. For women's own sake and to enhance the contribution they can make to their community and to influence their country's development, it is important for policy-makers and institutions of higher learning in Sudan to understand the matrix of issues involved in female students' ICT proficiency, and how best to reduce gender-related barriers and create opportunities for enhancing female students' capabilities.

Methodology

This research took place at the Shambat campus of the University of Khartoum, where relevant and significant progress has been recorded in the development and use of ICTs (relative to other institutions in Sudan). The Shambat campus consists of the faculties of Agriculture, Forestry, Veterinary Science and Animal Production. My focus was female students (undergraduates and post-graduates) using computer labs at the campus. Male students were also included in the statistical data and focus groups in order to enrich and complement the data and information generated and to facilitate a gender analysis.

The data sources for the study were: (1) statistical data on the female and male students' use of the computer labs collected daily by the lab supervisors for a period of six months; (2) observations made by myself during several visits to the computer centres both within and outside the university, and observation of classrooms, offices and homes in order to learn about gender differences in use of ICTs; and (3) interviews with female students and four focus groups of eight to ten students held separately with female and male students at Shambat campus.

Results

The number of female students using computer labs was fewer than the number of male students in all faculties at the university and at all education levels (undergraduate and post-graduate). This was despite the

TABLE 2.1 Number of male and female students using computer labs at Shambat Campus (December 2009 to May 2010).

Faculty	Male	%	Female	%	Total
Agriculture	2010	58.4	1430	41.6	3440
Forestry	512	67.5	246	32.5	758
Veterinary	774	52.5	700	47.5	1474
Animal production	927	52.5	839	47.5	1766
Other	87	61.3	55	38.7	142

Females represent 43.1 per cent of the total users, while males represent 56.9 per cent. Female users per month represent only 21.5 per cent of the total female students at Shambat campus, while males using the computers each month account for 79.7 per cent of the total male student population.

fact that the number of female students at the university campus (71.2 per cent) was much higher than that of male students (28.8 per cent).

Table 2.1 shows the number of male and female students using computer labs at Shambat campus between December 2009 and May 2010.

ICT access and skill: gender differences

Results from interviews showed that most of the female students in this study shared similar socioeconomic characteristics and social situations: they had no or one common personal computer (PC) shared by all family members; no or a low level of computer and Internet skills acquired from a single computer course offered by the university or by a male family member; and no time at home for computer use due to household responsibilities, with males being given first access to the computer. These factors contributed to less computer use in the home by female than male students.

A female student, Abeer, remarked: 'Although there is a computer at home I have no incentive to use it since I have many duties after returning home or it may be occupied by somebody else in the house.' Ayat sadly described her computer use at home as follows: 'It is not important for me to use the computer since I must leave the device once my brother wants to use it, my dad says to me leave it for him and you can use it another time to avoid a quarrel.'

A major barrier that most female students seem to face is lack of training in the use of computers. Most female students' first experiences with use of ICT are at university, where they are offered a preliminary computer course during their first year. The majority of male students began using computers and the Internet before enrolment at university.

Female students only have access to computers at the university and at home, since there are more social restrictions on females they have many duties and obligations within the family. Females are not allowed, for example, to go to an Internet café, to stay at the university after class or to go with friends to their home, while males enjoy all these options. Family approval is crucial in women's choices. Using these access options, the male students improve their skills and it becomes very easy for them to use computers efficiently at the university.

Perceptions and inferiority

During a focus group discussion (FGD), when asked for opinions about male skill in computer use, a male student said: 'Men must know everything such as how to use computers, how to drive a car ... so as not to be described or named by certain local names, known between us, like the word *fara* [in Arabic]'; *fara* means 'female mouse' and is a derogatory description for males as it refers to inferiority. Men apparently do their best to acquire competence and need to feel that they are in a superior position, so as not be seen to be like women. This need to feel superior motivated them when among others to look for any new technology, learn quickly from each other and show their knowledge and be proud of it. 'I use the computer and Internet every day, not necessarily for academic purposes but for chatting, playing games and sending emails,' reported one student from the Faculty of Animal Production during an FGD. Another asserted: 'Using the computer makes you open to the world – you can easily receive and send information and quickly communicate knowledge.'

Female students, however, often doubted their capacities and saw themselves as less competent than men in using ICTs. 'Males are open-minded, they learn everything quickly' and 'they have the chance to learn from each other, to be outside the home for long periods, to come home late, to go to public Internet cafés and all these chances are not available for females', reported two female students during FGDs. Comparing themselves with male students and realizing that they were not like males deepened their feelings of inferiority. Because of this self-perception of limited competence, female students preferred to use a PC together, in little groups, while male students would rarely sit in groups. 'I have no skill in using computers, so I used to go to the lab with my friend Sara who has good skills in computer use and can help me,' admitted a female student from the Faculty of Forestry. Realizing that some of their friends had good computer skills created awareness among female students that it was possible for women to develop this level of skill.

A 'gender-neutral' policy in a gendered context

Male students made maximum use of the available resources to their benefit, while female students showed less interest in using the available access to computers and the Internet. Female students reported that one hour is not enough for them to accomplish any task due to their poor skills, while male students can benefit fully from the time. 'I am not interested to go to the computer lab because one hour is not enough for me to complete any task, so I just copy the assignment done by my colleagues,' stated one female student from the Faculty of Agriculture.

Female students also did not find the computer course that was offered by the university useful, since it was an introductory course and mostly theoretical and because there were not enough PCs to train the large number of students in the class. Some female students intended to take a computer course at a computer centre to improve their competence in ICT use. 'It is better for me to register in a formal course in order to be organized and not miss any information. By self-learning I will not learn everything,' stated one of the female students during an FGD.

Although the male students also did not find the university course useful, it did not represent a problem for them. They had acquired a high level of competence in computer use by individual trial and self-learning and felt confident: 'Learning computer use is an easy task – I can train myself and I will not behave like a woman by making it a big problem and learn at a computer centre,' reported one of the male students.

Female student computer proficiency

Constraints on their time and activities were experienced by all female students, but some were further ahead in terms of their capacities with computers because of the greater opportunities afforded to them by better access to ICT resources, better training and more family help and support. Female student Nada had had experience with ICT since primary school in the United Arab Emirates, where she took all her studies prior to entering university. She had a laptop and Internet access at home, and enjoyed family encouragement. She felt very confident in her skills and herself. When I asked her about male skill in using computers, she was confident that she could do better with computer tasks than most male students: 'I cannot afford not using the Internet during a day – I have to check my mail, chat with my group on Facebook many times during the day, and use search engines for many topics,' she reported.

Nada was not constrained by a sense of inferiority like other female students, and instead felt confident; her supportive environment provided space, equipment and know-how for her to become proficient with the technology and confident in her abilities.

Discussion

Social norms and their effect on capability

The gendered social norms in Sudan and at the university are maintained in men's and women's relationships with computers. The social space males enjoy and the peer pressure on male students to be better than females give them incentives and the feeling of being more competent takes the form of more self-confidence and more computer use than female students. Being raised in a culture that associates power and control with males, the environment in which they learnt computer skills and knowledge was supportive of their skill development. It is possible that the fear the male students articulated of being identified as inferior, like women, had driven them hard to succeed and that this success brought them the self-confidence they displayed. It is also possible that their self-confidence was partly a mask to hide their fear of being (seen as) inferior.

While the female students were aware that there were multiple access points but at the same time unequal opportunities, having limited computer access heightened their sense of having less computer competence and subsequently made their sense of inferiority more acute. These feelings, along with the accompanying recognition of having less power to shape their own lives, confirmed the females' assumptions and perceptions of being less competent compared to males and their tendency to posit men as more competent with technology. These feelings of being less than men, and that they cannot help themselves in the way men can, manifest in them having less interest in taking up technology and its benefits. So the sociocultural norms that restrict women's being also restrict women's exploration and the expansion of their abilities and capabilities, reducing their avenues for expressing and applying themselves.

Although there is recognition by some female students that greater computer skill is possible for young women should they be given the chance (as shown by Sara and Nada), female students still hold themselves back from using their full potential and act in ways that reinforce their acceptance of their lesser competence, and subsequently their sense of being inferior. The sense of and experience of inferiority becomes 'normal' when the social condition of being considered less competent and less than equal is internalized: 'As social perception of stigma shows, there is almost no link between the real situation of the individual and the reasons for (her) stigmatization' (Klimowicz 2007: 5).

Students' sense of well-being in relation to their agency

The female students know how important accessing knowledge is and thus they are acutely aware of the importance of ICT. While they are aware of the potential benefits of ICT, they are also just as aware of their own restrictions; they realize that males will be in a better situation compared to them because they have better knowledge and information, stemming from the fact they use computers and the Internet more than women do. These various thoughts and emotions strengthen each other and become a Gordian knot that becomes too difficult to disentangle and that deepens women's sense of lower competence and inferiority. Some young women intended to join a computer centre so as to acquire the necessary competence for using computers, unlike the males, who were mostly self-taught. It was obvious that there were different attitudes towards acquiring competence in using technologies, as reflected in male students expressing the need to be competent and self-confident and tending towards independent learning to gain the competence and skill they felt they needed in computer use. Most female students felt an increased sense of inferiority and less self-confidence in the context of the males' apparent capacity to learn quickly and to benefit from their greater access options.

In both the female and male students it can be seen that their response to the issue of gaining computer competency is aligned with accepted behaviours favoured by their society. However, a significant difference is the scope of accepted behaviours one has: 'In social relationships in which the individual is in a subordinate position, the ability of the individual to choose is typically favour-dependent … Choices within the household and elsewhere may be … restricted, with varying penalties for making unapproved choices' (Hill 2003: 120–1).

Female students' choice of pursuing formal learning is favour-dependent, since this activity has to be approved by their families, unlike the options available for males. Male students have many choices approved by society, giving them a wide scope for making the favour-dependent choices that suit them, such as undertaking self-learning. The males stayed within what was socially accepted and expected of their gender – the demonstration of mastery.

Unlike the males, the female students' expectation is that they will not be able to use computers by themselves and will have to go to a computer centre in order to be able to do that: 'Most likely, perceived ease or difficulty of performing a behaviour reflects beliefs about the presence of internal as well as external factors that may further or impede performance of a behavior' (Ajzen 2002: 676). Female students adapt their preferences (affected by their internalized acceptance of marginalization in relation to computer learning) to being less competent than men, and in doing so keep the sociocultural practices and concepts alive. In this way they maintain their subordinate position through their decision to seek help from others and not try self-learning like males do.

Implications of women's perceptions of their capabilities and functionings

The perception of women students of being less competent than men made them less confident in themselves, particularly regarding using ICT in the context of this study, thus adding another barrier to benefitting from ICT. On the other hand, the more confidence and power that males enjoy, the more they use ICTs. The inequitable distribution of rights, resources and power – as elements of repressive cultural rules and norms – constrains many women's capacity to develop their abilities and benefit fully from computers and the Internet.

It is apparent that simply providing apparently equal resources (in this case ICT infrastructure and training) does not result in the same level of functioning or outcome for everyone. Individuals have different abilities to convert resources into actual functioning – that is, improved access to information through the use of ICTs, as Sen (1999) and Nussbaum (2003) stress in their capability approach. These different abilities to convert resources to maximum benefit are a result of self-perception, which is highly influenced by one's contextual factors (including the experience of marginalization).

Women taking the opportunity: greater self-confidence and technological engagement

Nada's story demonstrates how women students who are less encumbered by inequitable, gendered social norms and (self-) perceptions of low ability can be as competent with computers as males. Nada lived in an environment that was different from that of the other female students; for her, gendered social relations were less constraining for girls. A supportive environment and options, combined with better skill, Internet facilities and social encouragement from the family, increased Nada's self-confidence, enhanced her use of ICTs and made her more technologically engaged. According to Bandura (1991: 257; see also Bandura 1993: 128, 1997: 700; Bussey and Bandura 1999), 'efficacy beliefs play a pivotal role in the exercise of personal agency because they not only operate on behavior in their own right but also through their impact on other classes of motivators such as outcome expectancies and goals'.

Even when Nada moved to a different environment with social and cultural norms that were more inequitable for women and enforced by all around her, her belief in personal efficacy still informed her goals, outcome expectations and perceived environmental opportunities and impediments to her motivation. This made her see herself differently from how the majority of females around her perceived themselves and their capacities; in fact, Nada saw herself as doing better than males in computer and Internet use.

Another aspect is that female students who are proficient in ICT don't have the peer pressure that male students have, or the fear of appearing inferior (as this is already assumed) to cope with, and thus can freely express confidence and that they can do a better job on computers than males, as Nada expressed. In a context where developing computer expertise is seen as normal for females and males, it is demonstrable that female students will develop a relationship with computers and a sense of their capacities similar to those of male students – although perhaps less encumbered by the need to demonstrate mastery; this is a change that we would love to see women achieve.

Conclusions and recommendations

This research shows how different social freedoms, expectations, norms and senses of self produce different results in relation to computer proficiency and the user's sense of her/his capacities and self-empowerment. The repressive cultural rules and norms constrain many women's ability to benefit from ICTs, whereas the perception of women students being less competent than men (increasing their sense of inferiority) made them less confident in themselves. In this study this was particularly the case regarding use of ICTs, and this led to women suppressing their contribution to their own development as well as that of their communities and countries.

In contrast, the higher social power that males enjoy, together with fear of inferiority, peer pressure and expectations of mastery and confidence, results in a very different relationship with ICTs and with themselves, where they feel more confident in themselves and enjoy ICT use. The results also show how female students take the full benefits of computers and the Internet when situated in an environment that is usually associated with male students in the context studied – where there are no barriers to access or to learning and working with computers, where there is support and encouragement and where developing computer expertise is seen as normal. Consider the story of Nada, who had a long relationship with computers and had a confident sense of her capacities. Her story will give hope to many women, because it shows how the limitations that female students experience are not innate.

This research recommends that, in order for women to have empowering relations with computer-related ICTs and to experience benefits equal to those of men, it is not enough just to provide equipment or resources. Equality of opportunity may not be enough to redress the historical oppression and disadvantages of women. Because of their different positions in society, women and men may not be able to take advantage of equal opportunities to the same extent (UNDP 2001).

Gender analysis offers information through which to understand women's and men's access to and control over resources that can be used to address disparities, challenge systemic inequalities (most often faced by women) and build efficient and equitable solutions. Institutions of higher learning and others involved in women's development and empowerment have to realize that women live and learn in gendered environments, and that they bring these environments with them as internalized perceptions of who and what they are and what they think they are capable of. The need for confidence in one's self and one's capacities (to learn, to help oneself and to teach oneself) is a prerequisite to benefitting equally from the technologies that are available.

It is therefore recommended that great efforts be made in the interest of skill acquisition and training for women to recognize both their capacities and the socioeconomic and cultural issues that marginalize their capabilities. Furthermore, women have to be encouraged to appreciate themselves for what they can do, so that they can overcome their internalized feelings of inferiority. In order to ensure that ICTs benefit women in the same way and to the same extent as men, inclusion of a gender analysis in the design, policy and methodology of educational and training opportunities and environments is therefore crucial.

References

Ajzen, I. (2002) 'Perceived behavioral control, self-efficacy, locus of control, and the theory of planned behavior', *Journal of Applied Social Psychology*, 32(4): 665–83.

Bandura, A. (1991) 'Social cognitive theory of self-regulation', *Organizational Behavior and Human Decision Processes*, 50: 248–87.

— (1993) 'Perceived self-efficacy in cognitive development and functioning', *Educational Psychology*, 28(2): 117–48.

— (1997) *Self-Efficacy: The Exercise of Control*, New York: Freeman.

Brosnan, M. and M. Davidson (1996) 'Psychological gender issues in computing', *Journal of Gender, Work and Organisation*, 3(1): 13–25.

Bussey, K. and A. Bandura (1999) 'Social cognitive theory of gender development and differentiation', *Psychological Review*, 106(4): 676–713.

Hill, M. T. (2003) 'Development as empowerment', *Feminist Economics*, 9(2–3): 117–35.

Huyer, S., N. Hafkin, H. Ertl and H. Dryburgh (2005) 'Women in the information society', in G. Sciadis (ed.), *From the Digital Divide to Digital Opportunity: Measuring Infostates for Development*, Montreal: Orbicom, pp. 134–94.

Klimowicz, T. (2007) 'Stigma and disdain – a negative setting of identity', paper presented at the Inter-Disciplinary.net 6th Global Conference, Budapest, 2–5 May.

Liff, S. and A. Shepherd (2004) *An Evolving Gender Digital Divide*, Oxford: Oxford Internet Institute.

Mbambo-Thata, B., E. Mlambo and P. Mwastsiya (2009) 'When a gender-blind access policy results in discrimination: realities and perceptions of female students at the University of Zimbabwe', in I. Buskens and A. Webb (eds), *African Women and ICTs: Investigation Technology, Gender and Empowerment*, London and New York: Zed Books, pp. 67–76.

Nussbaum, M. (2003) 'Capabilities as fundamental entitlements: Sen and social justice', *Feminist Economics*, 9(2–3): 33–59.

Rathgeber, E. M. (2000) *Gender and the Information Revolution in Africa: Women, Men, and ICTs in Africa: Why Gender Is an Issue*, Ottawa: International Development Research Centre.

Sen, A. (1999) *Development as Freedom*, New York: Knopf.

United Nations Development Programme (UNDP) – Gender in Development Programme (2001) 'Learning and information pack – gender analysis', www.undp.org/content/dam/undp/library/gender/Institutional%20Development/TLGEN1.6%20UNDP%20GenderAnalysis%20toolkit.pdf, accessed 5 June 2014.

3 | Towards non-gendered ICT education: the hidden curriculum at the National University of Science and Technology in Zimbabwe

BUHLE MBAMBO-THATA AND SIBONILE MOYO

Introduction

In 2004 the government of Zimbabwe introduced the National Gender Policy (NGP). The policy states that 'to promote and encourage girls to take on science, mathematics and technology at all levels of education' universities will lower entrance requirements for females in order to attract more female students into higher levels of education (Government of Zimbabwe 2004: 16).

The National University of Science and Technology (NUST) executed this policy as follows: minimum entry level for all students into university is a pass in any two advanced-level (A-level) subjects relevant for the course to be taken. The maximum number of points one can have in three subjects is 15. This means anyone with two points can qualify for entry into university. Competition for places means an additional criterion had to be used, that of the number of points for A level. Depending on the pass rate of applicants, a cut-off point is set for entry into a particular programme. Students with the highest points are taken first. In executing the NGP affirmative action policy, female students were allowed into NUST with lower points than male students.

Implementation of this policy has led to an increase in the female student population to approximately 40 per cent over the five years up to 2010. For the Computer Science department, however, during the same period the percentage of females hovered at around 20 per cent. Of the 20 per cent of females graduating with a degree in Computer Science, 22 per cent chose a career in software development while the rest were in the soft side of computing, which is mainly oriented towards support and application. Such careers include jobs in systems support, systems administration and information systems management.

We discuss the relationship between careers that NUST's female Computer Science graduates choose and how this relates to the teaching and learning processes they participate in. We suggest ways in which the unexamined sexism that forms and informs the Computer Science department's hidden curriculum and classroom atmosphere can be transformed into a supportive learning environment for female Computer Science students.

The intended impact of the NGP will not be realized while women graduates are unable to break gender barriers preventing them from choosing traditionally male career options such as computing design and programming. In order to ensure the NGP's success it is critical that female learners do not limit themselves in their career choices.

Research methods

A combination of research methods was used in this research. We did a gender analysis of the career selections of NUST former graduate students. Graduates from the years 2006, 2007 and 2008 were located to identify their areas of employment. From a list of 188 graduates (of whom 43 were females), 117 were located through the Internet and e-mail. Those who responded were invited to participate in Focus Group Discussions (FGDs) and interviews.

Four FGDs were held: the first two with former female students, one with current female students (twelve final-year and nine second-year students) and the last with two male and two female NUST staff (Computer Science lecturers) and six female gender activists. For all these discussions an open invitation was sent to the target populations, and the researchers dealt with those who were available. The groups were, in a sense, self-selected. Respondents made themselves available to participate.

The intent behind the FGDs with current female undergraduate students was to validate data gathered from past students. The last FGD, with NUST staff, focused on the discussion of findings that emanated from the FGDs with current female students and former students. This study did not include male students and their realities and perspectives.

After the FGDs some former student participants who were available and those who had unique stories were invited for in-depth interviews. As a conversation technique we used the free attitude interview, a qualitative in-depth interview method that enabled us to understand how our respondents perceived their realities in their own terms (Buskens 2005).

We also did classroom observations during teaching sessions and afterwards interviewed individual programming lecturers and students. The observations were meant to verify the issue of lack of participation in class by female students, as well as the issue of neglect raised by former students during FGDs. The interviews with individual lecturers were meant to obtain the lecturers' views on the performance of female learners in programming courses and what they could recommend as remedies

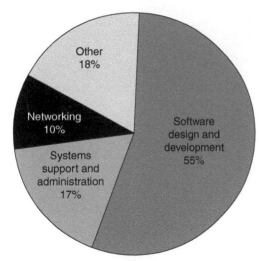

FIGURE 3.1 Career distribution of male NUST Computer Science graduates.

to address issues raised by students. With the students we discussed our observations of their behaviour in class.

Results: what did we learn?

Gendered career distribution

The results in the pie charts in Figures 3.1 and 3.2 show a gendered distribution of careers of NUST graduates in the computer industry. Most female Computer Science graduates (61 per cent) held posts as systems support personnel or administrators, while 22 per cent were in software design and development, 17 per cent were in other fields and none were in networking.

The distribution of careers among males is quite different, with a higher percentage (55 per cent) as software developers (compared to 22 per cent of females), 17 per cent as systems administrators, 18 per cent as other and 10 per cent in networking. In the absence of a national study there were no data to compare the gender distributions of Computer Science graduates of other universities in Zimbabwe.

The stereotype that female students are incapable of learning programming

It emerged from the current and past female student respondents that some lecturers perceived female learners as weak in programming courses. Some female students were told, 'Go and get married if you cannot do programming.' One former student indicated, 'At that point I would

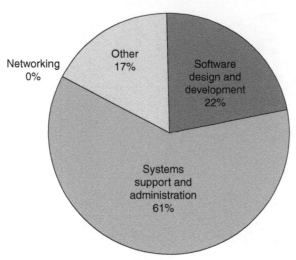

FIGURE 3.2 Career distribution of female NUST Computer Science graduates.

stop listening to him, instead I would go and work with classmates after the lesson.' This particular student resorted to seeking an alternative and informal learning arrangement due to these remarks: group discussion with her peers. However, there were also female students who could not find alternative learning spaces, and failed programming or resorted to copying from others. This has career implications since programming is the core and backbone for a software-development career.

Lecturers' gendered performance expectations and student support

One former student indicated that some male lecturers tended to support male learners as opposed to female learners, particularly in programming courses. This student further indicated that these lecturers showed concern when they saw that men did not understand programming concepts:

> At the return of class tests, lecturer X would have this to say if a male student performed badly, 'John [not his real name], what happened? You did not do well this time.' Yet when females performed badly in programming assignments, the lecturer would say, 'Ah well, it is Jane ...'

This created the impression with the students that the lecturers accepted failure by women in programming courses as normal, but when men failed the lecturers would be sympathetic and supportive.

A female tutor in the department, a graduate of NUST herself, felt that female students divorced themselves from learning programming when they thought the subject matter was difficult. Having gone through the course and having perceived programming as difficult, she recalled how she would sit back in class and concentrate on other subjects, depending on male students to grasp the concepts. During study group meetings they would tutor her in programming, and in return she would share what she had understood from the subjects she had concentrated on. The students bartered their knowledge. According to her, this assisted her to learn programming as she found it easy to ask her male classmates and study-mates if she did not understand a concept. Instead of asking the lecturer, the students created an alternative learning environment that worked for them.

Female students do not participate in class

We observed that most female students did not participate in class. On probing during an FGD with final-year female students, one student said she felt shy about giving wrong answers. The students indicated that lecturers teased and ridiculed them if they got the answers wrong. The students further confessed that as students they did not realize that participation in the classroom would help them learn. They said, if this research and the FGD had been held when they were in their first year, they would have realized the value of participation and been more participative in class. They urged the researchers to hold similar discussion groups with first-year students in order to raise awareness that participating would help them learn.

Female students who excelled in programming

There were, however, exceptions to the norm, and 22 per cent of the female graduates (Figure 3.2) have successful careers in software development. Input from these respondents is reported below.

Support from lecturers

According to some former students, there were lecturers who had shown skill and passion for the programming course, resulting in students developing an interest for that particular course. According to one respondent, the lecturers had a passion for programming, which created an engaging environment for her to participate in effectively: 'For me lecturer X and Y were my inspiration. I liked the way they taught the programming courses.' The respondent, a successful female programmer, indicated that in her case the style of teaching by the lecturer inspired her to take up a career as a programmer. The programming lecturer was said to be 'engaging' with both male and female students, built up the enthusiasm of students and developed their liking of the subject.

Industrial attachments (internships)
It also emerged from these students that in most cases what they did during their year of industrial attachment influenced what they went on to do after completing their degree. In particular, those students who were attached to software-development houses had higher chances of continuing in the field after graduation. These students came back to college with sharpened development skills after having been in the software-development field for one year; they excelled in their programming courses when finishing their degrees.

Availability of resources
Related to the issue of industrial attachment was the availability of computing resources for practising programming. Students mentioned that, since programming was a practical course, it needed a lot of practice for learners to succeed. One participant cited that in her case the desktop computer her brother had bought her enabled her to practise programming at home after hours, and thus she was able to master the concepts.

Rising to the challenge
Some students indicated that it had actually been the denigrating attitude of teachers that stimulated them to excel. One highlighted how she had been subjected to discouraging remarks from one lecturer, who often advised her 'to go and get married' if she could not cope with the demands of programming. She said, 'I worked hard to prove him wrong!'

Computing lecturers gain awareness of their sexist attitude and its effects
During a group discussion with NUST staff it emerged that most lecturers who were present were gender-blind. They indicated that they did not realize their teaching methods had a negative impact on female students. One of the male participants in an FGD said: 'When I tell women learners to go and get married if they fail their programming assignment, I am trying to encourage them to work hard.' He said he was not aware that female students took his remarks negatively.

The lecturers affirmed that the FGD opened their eyes to biases in their teaching. They professed that findings discussed in the FGD came as a surprise and were an eye-opener as far as gender issues were concerned.

For the first time they realized that their own teaching style could have contributed to reducing the number of females succeeding in programming, diminishing women's chances of careers in software design and development.

Discussion: impact on the female students' career choices

As researchers we observed a correlation between the gendered distribution of careers and gendered performance of students in Computer Science at NUST. We observed that women students were less engaged in the classroom. This impacted negatively on their learning and acquisition of programming skills. On graduation these students thus lacked the necessary foundation for careers in software development. This most probably contributed to the skewed distribution in careers, with fewer women taking up careers in software development.

This phenomenon has to be understood more deeply. We have turned to the concept of the 'hidden curriculum' to help us get a deeper understanding of what students in the NUST Computer Science programming classes were facing. The hidden curriculum is, according to Johnson (2000),

> a concept used to describe the often unarticulated and unacknowledged things that students are taught in school. This is distinct from the publicized curriculum that defines what students are supposed to study and learn – subjects such as mathematics and literature. The hidden curriculum is an important issue in the sociological study of how schools generate social inequality. Students who are female, for example, or who come from lower-class families, or who belong to subordinate racial or ethnic categories, are often treated in ways that create and reinforce inferior self-images as well as low aspirations and expectations for themselves.

In a very general sense, women in a male-dominated society get the message that they are less than men: less important, less capable, less gifted, in short less in all the aspects and fields that really matter. In the context of the NUST classroom environment, the 'hidden curriculum' was not even that hidden: next to the open curriculum of teaching Computer Science, the hidden curriculum was the belief that women cannot do programming. Two aspects of this hidden curriculum seem relevant:

- stereotyping – as evidenced by support being given only to male students in a classroom environment and ignoring female learning, the consequence being that the majority of female students were not participating in the classroom and deferred to males;

- the perspective that talent or ability is acquired and that learning and hard work do not play as important a role: 'ability as a gift' (Dweck 2007: 48).

The impacts of these two aspects strengthen each other: stereotyping increases the impact of the conceptualization of 'ability as a gift' as it discourages learners who are perceived not to have this gift and affirms those deemed to possess it. It was obvious that this dynamic was at play at NUST, as these utterances by Computer Science lecturers testified: 'if girls cannot do programming they should go and get married', and 'girls came in with lower points and therefore are incapable'. However, research by Dweck (2007) indicates that ability in a subject can be learnt.

The teacher–student relationship and classroom environment reflect the social and cultural environment in which students and lecturers relate to each other and is gendered. Learning processes are influenced by gender relations and perspectives and as a result female students find themselves stereotyped and tied into the 'science as gift' myth that permeates society in general and institutions of higher learning specifically.

A combination of these two factors completely undermines the policy intentions of including women. If NUST is to succeed in including women and enabling them to select careers in science fields of their choice, then the issues discussed above need to be addressed to eliminate gender stereotyping and the view of programming ability as a gift.

However, while a classroom environment communicating the assumption of male superiority in computer skills discouraged most women from learning computer programming, there were some women who had a different response. Instead of giving in to the negative remarks, these women put in extra effort to prove their abilities. This could be due to the aspect pointed out by Mwansa and Winschiers (2004: 199) when they say, 'As a result, they feel under constant pressure to prove themselves.' It would seem that successful students made a decision to oppose the negative remarks, which propelled them to work harder.

Unfortunately it seems that the majority of students were not able to take their teachers' gender-stereotyped attitude as a challenge to perform and transform a potentially harmful 'curriculum' into motivation to excel. Most female graduates indicated that they had longed to be supported in the same way as male students were. If similar attention and assistance were given to them, it would create an environment more conducive to learning for more female students. This is corroborated by Green (1989, cited in Sellers et al. 2007: 34): 'Students who sense that more is expected of them tend to outperform students who believe that less is expected of them – regardless of the students' actual abilities.' It could be inferred that the majority of female students who sensed that not much was expected of them in programming performed badly.

The teacher or lecturer wields the stronger power in relations with learners, and thus determines classroom interaction. As a measure to demystify difficulty in Computer Science, Shaikh (2007: 94) recommends encouragement of classroom interaction between students through discussions and group tasks, clarification of theory and concepts in the context of their practical uses and applications, and assessing students with a more formative and collaborative approach in which they share and discuss their solutions in class.

Some lecturers have expressed the view that at NUST the lack of confidence and poor performance of female students in the classroom could be a result of them being enrolled at university with lower A-level points, as allowed by the NGP. This suggests that they would not be as capable as their male counterparts. However, the university admissions policy stipulates that a student with two A-level points may be admitted to the university. The women students admitted into the programme meet the minimum qualifications for university admission. Furthermore, there is no existing evidence to link male and female students' performance to their measure of A-level points.

There ought to be congruence between policy interventions and classroom practices. It cannot be assumed that the existence of an inclusive policy such as the NGP will result in practices that support policy. As many of the female students indicated, derogatory remarks by lecturers had a negative impact on their learning. Such remarks not only undermine the students but also undermine the policy that seeks to be inclusive of women. As such, this practice stands in contradiction to the university management's implementation of the NGP, and therefore needs urgent attention.

Conclusions and recommendations

According to the findings 22 per cent of female NUST Computer Science graduates were employed as software designers. The research also showed that the classroom atmosphere discourages participation of female students, and that the success of female students in programming remains minimal. We make recommendations of ways to improve the classroom environment.

As researchers we want to promote a learning platform where women are able to learn optimally, leading them to make their own choices as to what career they prefer, without having to contend with man-made obstacles. We trust that, when the classroom environment responds to policy imperatives, is sensitive to the needs of women students and is supportive of women students and not hostile to them, access to success will be ensured for students pursuing careers in programming.

We believe that a changed learning environment will eventually lead to an increase in the selection of careers in design and development. We look forward to the day when the percentage of women entering the field of software development is increased.

We thus recommend:

- Mandatory training in gender sensitivity and awareness in teaching and learning for all lecturers. Such training sensitizes the lecturer to value the female learner in male-dominated courses such as programming.
- Peer learning to be instituted among students. Students could be paired or put in small groups at the beginning of a semester so that they learn together, do assignments together and thus deal with the neglect of lecturers if this were to persist. In these peer learning environments female learners should not be overshadowed by males in numbers or activities.
- Female students to be trained to actively engage in the classroom. Through seminars students should discuss the importance of student involvement in the learning process.
- Female students to be encouraged to seek industrial attachment in a programming environment if they intend venturing into the software-development field. This gives them the opportunity to practise programming, besides beefing up their curriculum vitae for consideration by programming companies when they complete their studies.

While the NUST Computer Science curriculum itself remains substantial in producing software developers, it would appear that it is not the curriculum that is inadequate but that it is the hidden curriculum that determines the eventual success of female students, and this needs to be addressed.

The continued belief by some lecturers and members of society that because women are not men they cannot do Computer Science (and, if they happen to do it, they are relegated to less creative aspects) perpetuates the cycle of women's under-representation in software design and development.

Our research showed that only 22 per cent, or less than a quarter, of former female Computer Science graduates are working in design and development. The research also demonstrated how the classroom environment contributes to limited success of women students in programming. It is evident from the research that, if women are given the platform to learn and practise programming, they can succeed in it.

It remains for the institution to learn from these research findings and determine a transformation agenda that seeks to create an environment for learning that will push the figure beyond 22 per cent. It is hoped that, if our recommendations are put into practice, the number of female graduates taking up careers in software development should increase, and the software-development industry in Zimbabwe will benefit as a result.

References

Buskens, I. (2005) *Free Attitude Interview Manual*, http://issuu. com/gracenetwork/docs/fai__ final, accessed 20 May 2014.

Dweck, C. S. (2007) 'Is math a gift? Beliefs that put females at risk', in S. J. Ceci and W. M. Williams (eds), *Why Aren't More Women in Science? Top Researchers Debate the Evidence*, Washington, DC: American Psychological Association, pp. 47–56.

Government of Zimbabwe (2004) *National Gender Policy*, Harare: Gender Department, Ministry of Youth Development, Gender and Employment Creation.

Johnson, A. L. (2000) *The Blackwell Dictionary of Sociology*, Oxford: Blackwell.

Mwansa, M. and H. Winschiers (2004) 'Women, a critical factor in information technology – not just a quota issue', International Conference on Cybernetics and Informatics Technologies, Systems and Applications, Orlando, FL, 21–25 July.

Sellers, S. L., J. Roberts, L. Giovanetto, K. A. Friedrich and C. Hammargren (2007) *Reaching All Students: A Resource for Teaching in Science, Technology, Engineering and Mathematics*, www.cirtl.net/ ReachingAllStudents, accessed 7 November 2010.

Shaikh S. A. (2007) 'Participation of female students in computer science education', *Learning and Teaching in Higher Education*, 3: 93–6.

4 | Equal opportunities on an unequal playing field: the potential for social change in the ICT workplace

SALOME OMAMO AND EDNA R. ALUOCH

Introduction

This topic represents and captures in a nutshell the assumptions and lack of awareness of inequalities experienced in ICT work environments that emerged from our study. It also represents hope for change in a traditionally gendered career.

Information and communication technology (ICT) professions[1] constitute a unique research area for investigating relationships between gender and work organization. ICT companies often identify themselves as being at the leading edge of organizational changes: flat hierarchies, project work, multi-skilled teams, continuous skills update, flexible and extended working-time patterns, responsiveness to customer pressure and so forth. Yet, despite the flexibility expected and unconventional workplace, the employment conditions in ICT companies are often unfriendly to women, particularly to those with children or other caring responsibilities. Women consequently drop out of ICT employment in particularly large numbers after maternity. They also leave in significant numbers in their forties and fifties, apparently in order to regain control over their working hours and to work more flexibly, away from the pressures of the ICT work environment (Department of Trade and Industry 2005).

A study in Kenya indicates that women are highly optimistic, embracing ICT as a practical mechanism for achieving entry into the labour market. There is continued high demand from the public in many sectors to acquire relevant skills to access ICT, given the close link between such skills and employment and/or career progression inside and outside the country in both the public and private sectors (Amadi et al. 2007).

There is a substantial gender gap in ICT professions. The issue of equal opportunities is an ongoing challenge for women pursuing and maintaining careers in ICT, and work organization is one of the explicative hypotheses for the gender gap in ICT professions. Some specific organizational features of ICT jobs, such as unpredictable working rhythms, customer-driven location and continuous time pressure, raise barriers to women's access and careers (Valenduc and Vendramin 2005), as similar features in their domestic responsibilities compete for their time and attention. These workplace features are best suited to and based upon workers with few competing demands on their time and energy.

Research methodology

Our study was conducted between 2010 and 2012 and examined the professional work environments of ICT companies in Nairobi, Kenya. The purpose was to work with companies that were interested in making the work environment better for women by promoting gender equity and job satisfaction in the workplace. In order to do this, an in-depth understanding of the ICT work environment had to be developed. In-depth interviews and key-informant interviews were carried out with twelve human resources (HR) managers. Out of the twelve companies, focus group discussions (FGDs) were held in a total of six companies (one FGD per company) with professional women in ICT.

In order to conduct research for empowerment appropriately we, the researchers, had to be able to make women participants' agency visible, and where appropriate engage it effectively. This approach was adopted to help with self-reflection for both the researchers and the respondents, and to create an open space in which both researchers and respondents could explore and speak their truth as they see it in their current world, enabling them to further seek deeper and alternative truths/insights for the possibility of a better and changed world. We identified with the reasoning that, for researchers to be able to recognize and engage respondents' agency, they must be able to recognize and enhance their own (Buskens and Webb 2008). Capacity-building was provided for the researchers on the importance and use of this research approach.

ICT work demands

Central to traditional industrial definitions of 'the job' and 'the worker' is the expectation of a continuous and uninterrupted performance of duties and tasks (Acker 1990, 1992). This is also the model in Kenyan-based multi-national and national ICT companies. Within this ideal worker norm, the fulfilment of job requirements necessitates an employee's willingness to put the organization before all other considerations (Williams 2000; Rapoport et al. 2002). This commitment is reflected by an individual's investment of time in paid work (Rapoport et al. 2002), and it has been suggested in businesses and work environments that the value and worth of an individual worker are predicated upon his/her ability to display dedication to the corporation (Kanter 1977; Acker 1990; Rao et al. 1999; Williams 2000; Rapoport et al. 2002).

According to Rao et al. (1999), there is a culture of heroic individualism within work institutions that is perpetuated by a culture of winning and success. The organizational 'hero' is one who works day and night 'to meet deadlines against insurmountable odds' (Rao et al. 1999: 4). This ideal worker is historically most closely emulated by men (Pateman 1988; Acker 1990, 1992). The male worker, traditionally the 'breadwinner', has conventionally been expected to show a greater commitment to his career over active involvement in childcare, extended family, household and societal activities. As hierarchies within organizations are built on this ideal, value is placed on employees with few or no commitments outside the productivity and success of the corporation (Acker 1990).

Our FGDs with women in ICT professions revealed the gendered implications of this corporate work culture. The sector is characterized by long working days and attending courses after hours to constantly keep pace with quickly changing technology and new knowledge. This keeps many women who are trying to balance a family life with work away from the ICT sector. Women have to cope with tight project deadlines and the need to put in extra hours to meet those deadlines, with little or no relief from traditional gender roles and responsibilities in the domestic and social spheres. FGDs with women who have children and other domestic responsibilities found these workplace practices and expectations to be stressful, particularly as they sometimes had to work individually or in teams with male counterparts in an extremely competitive way. There is a high expectation of availability by companies, by colleagues and also by company clients. Career advancement appears to depend on working long hours and having the time to demonstrate commitment to the work and the organization in this way.

One female information technology department manager (IT support) had this to say:

> We are also required to be ahead of everybody so as to offer solutions
> to customers. This requires doing a lot of research. It's quite
> challenging because one has to be up to date with new ideas, new
> solutions, etc. and keep pace with changes while at the same time
> maintain a work–life balance.

Being up to date has to happen on one's own time, and one has to do personal research in order to stay relevant and updated in the highly volatile ICT field. Other than major training organized for all staff, the research aspect is seldom integrated into the work day.

Our discussions revealed how women in this field are passionate about this career path, although they expressed their need for extra support both from home and at work. Some mentioned that, despite discouragement and a lack of support from others, including their spouses, they have chosen to do what they are passionate about.

Interviews and FGDs with managers in ICT revealed that women in this field, especially in the technical arena, still face challenges brought about by stereotypes and discrimination. An example is women who work with men who see them as incapable, just because they are female. Some HR managers also discriminate in terms of hiring, working on the assumption that women cannot do certain jobs. When women go to offer services and support to clients, they are sometimes regarded as incapable and continuously have to prove their capability.

Said one female IT manager:

> I had a problem joining this company in IT because my husband was not very encouraging. He saw this as a male domain where only men could handle the pressure that came with the job. That's how men see it. Even if you ask men if they'll marry a woman in the IT field, they will not be enthusiastic. My husband told me that I was better off working with the government, my previous employer, since although the pay was less and I was at a lower position, it was less demanding than the private sector. By the way, some men will tell you, 'If it is stressing you, just come home and look after the children, I'll pay the bills.'

Our findings also indicate that women have had to contend with or come up with their own solutions to the challenges that they experience. Most of the women we spoke with in ICT careers have accepted the workplace challenges as part of what they have to cope with, and therefore do not see them as gender-based discrimination. However, during the interview process, when discussing the nature of the challenges, they recognized and acknowledged that these challenges do not have to be accepted as normal, and that they have to speak out. In-depth interviews with some of the HR managers also revealed that they were ready to listen to the women employees and find solutions or a way forward:

> Maybe we have never ever sat down to talk about our challenges, because we're working in an environment where it is work, work until it's done. So we have just been doing that. I think we've never sat down to look intensively at what is not right. But we realize that there are many things to be raised. What I think we can do is perhaps sit as professional ladies in IT and list our issues, discuss and agree then

follow up with the department leaders or HR. Because there are things we are holding on to, there are too many things. We've just accepted that we are professionals and so we have to deliver. (IT support officer)

This [interview] has been an eye-opener. We can keep talking about our issues instead of just keeping quiet. I think from the discussion it's evident that we shouldn't settle for something just because that's the way it has been. We should always strive to make it better, to make it bigger. We must not just say we are ladies, we started out being managed by men and that's just the way it is. We should engage our human resource managers and even our heads of department. I mean, how do we do it differently? I think discussing our challenges as women in ICT is something that we should pick up on. (IT department team leader during an FGD)

Gender awareness among HR managers

Findings from the in-depth interviews with HR managers in ICT companies revealed that more than half of those who participated lack awareness of gender issues; very few HR managers were trained to think from a gender-equality perspective. Of all the HR managers interviewed, only one male was interviewed. This was by default, since it happened that most of the companies contacted had women as HR managers. Three-quarters of the managers mentioned that they practised equality and that there was no bias for any gender. When asked about their awareness of the challenges women in ICT professions face that may interfere with their work, most of them mentioned that they didn't have any idea since they perceived all careers to be equal:

In fact you are the ones enlightening me on these things. There are some things I've never really sat down to think about, such as these challenges that you are talking about. The only challenge I think about is that of sexual harassment. Men tending to harass women and maybe also threatening them position-wise, you know some ... when your boss is a man he tells you, oh you have to give me, if you don't, the position is at risk. There are other challenges like men or people having this mentality that some jobs cannot be done by women. I've never really thought about other challenges. (HR manager)

It was evident from the discussions that companies that acknowledge the various challenges that women face – such as sex-role conditioning and stereotyping, sexual harassment, the perception of computing and ICT professions as a male domain, the lack of a critical mass of women in ICT and the rate of change in the industry, which makes it difficult for women to re-enter after a break for childbearing and rearing – offer some support (however limited) to women recommencing their careers.

Despite the fact that some managers are aware of the challenges that women in ICT face, they do not do much about it, as they see ICT as a career like any other and perceive that women have to accept or cope with the challenges once they choose to become ICT professionals. They do not take into account that the challenges women face in traditionally male careers and work environments have evolved on the basis of male norms and terms, in the context of gender inequality, and that professional demands are not the same in all careers.

These companies do not see the workplace norms and standards as based on individuals who can dedicate their time to their careers. They therefore have left it up to the women to counter male-defined work models and to challenge stereotypes, and have not ventured into finding out whether there is any form of inherent workplace inequality that should be dealt with:

> You know when it comes to performance, we treat everyone at par. So yes the ladies need to do that much more given their other responsibilities, but again it's an issue of do they know where their career needs to go? Yes it's a challenge, but it's a challenge because that's the career path that they have chosen. When they chose that career path they knew it was not going to be an easy path. It is the same for doctors. Just the same way a male doctor's going to be on shift, the female doctor has to be on shift. So it's up to an individual to say, if this is the way it's going to be, how do I rise up to that challenge? And not sit back and say it's a challenge. It's a challenge from the day one gets in. (HR manager in an IT company)

HR managers advocate for equity without fully understanding what gender equality means with regard to work–life balance or gendered workplace norms and expectations. For these managers fair treatment means giving equal opportunities to both male and female employees, not taking into account the fact that the playing field is not equal for men and women. There is a general absence of understanding that what seems 'normal' is based on traditional notions of male and female roles, and inequality between women and men in the determination of these.

ICT companies' HR managers take the approach that a 'level playing field' should be created within the company for every staff member, and that every individual should be able to execute their chosen career path. Unfortunately, the understanding of what comprises a level playing field does not include recognition of socially and economically normalized asymmetrical and exploitative gender relations:

> Everything we do is actually square and just. You see when it comes to the work environment, basically what we've done is to try to ensure that people are comfortable, because again if we try to favour a particular gender over the other, it may not just be for women alone, but even for men, you'll find that there will be issues. So again, as HR practitioners it is our mandate as part of our professional ethics that we observe equality and justice and through that we try to cut down on any discriminatory practices. (HR manager)

Almost all the companies admitted that they did not have gender-equality policies, apart from a blanket policy on discrimination where each employee should be treated equally or in which recruitment is based on merit and there is no gender bias. However, others mentioned that they have company practices that are not necessarily on paper but are created to support women. The only written gender policy practised by the companies was that of three months' maternity leave, as required by the government. Some HR managers argued that gender-equality policies should be in place right from childhood; it becomes a challenge to introduce them when people have moved into their careers.

Our findings also revealed that there is a missing link in HR–employee relations. Although the managers mentioned that there was an open-door policy, the FGDs revealed that women in ICT professions didn't approach HR with their problems. Contributing factors that were identified include that the women have accepted the situation as it is, and that the managers are generally not aware of or do not fully understand the challenges women in ICT face. These two parties failed to recognize that there was a gap between the apparent intent and potential of HR policies and systems and the workplace experience of the women ICT professionals.

There is also a disconnection between apparent advocacy of equality and notions that with special support the workplace can become more responsive to women employees' needs. The competitive dedication to the company work culture was accepted and unquestioned. There was no mention of pursuing more substantive change to how the work is perceived, organized and practised.

Reflections on support and profitability

Individuals who are dependent upon work as their primary means of subsistence are often forced to participate in systems whose values run counter to their own: 'Workers' dependency on paid employment affords a privileging to employers that enables the desire for productivity and profit to exceed the needs of men, women and their families' (Acker 1998: 199). By viewing workers as disembodied, asexual beings, the corporation is free to pursue competitive market goals with little consideration given to the human individuals and families that they are affecting (Acker 1998).

Several HR managers brought up the argument that there are very few women compared to men in the technical and engineering departments of ICT companies. It would therefore be a costly affair to bring in support systems for the few women in these departments, and the companies constantly work on minimizing costs. However, some managers mentioned that they took the issue of employee welfare seriously and offered support to ensure job satisfaction and productivity.

Some HR managers recognized the dynamism of the ICT field and that the work culture was bound to change in the future. It was therefore important, they believed, for them to put systems in place (such as being able to work from home) that would ensure that IT managers stayed relevant and cost-effective. However, such ideas were yet to be implemented by almost all of the companies, but were being considered:

> Well in ICT and the way it's going, I can't give you a time frame, but it's getting too expensive to have everybody working in the office. Office space is expensive, parking is expensive and power is expensive. So I can give you a laptop and access to the network. Then I tell you what I expect and I am able to measure output. We can get to that level of trust whereby I would support people working from home. This can be very beneficial for the women. (HR manager)

What is the motivation towards changing the system and what are the assumptions involved in such an idea? This HR manager makes it clear that the focus is on the bottom line, and the assumption is that women will continue to carry three jobs (at work, in the family and in the community) in a gender-exploitative social and economic context.

The various support systems offered by some of the ICT companies included training and retraining, team-building exercises to build cohesion and support between male and female employees, gym facilities, a crèche, counselling, motivation and flexible work hours. All were aimed at helping women cope with the way things are in ICT work while also maintaining their other demanding social and domestic roles. These forms of support, however few, are appreciated by professional women in ICT as they facilitate their management of their multiple, traditionally female roles:

We're in the ICT world, we have our own special needs that probably the men do not have, so can you listen for those needs and try and equip ... it could be something as simple as having a room where I can be able to attend to my child, I am just from maternity leave, so there's somewhere that I need to be able to express milk or breastfeed. So just understanding that there are some things I need to be able to do and it's those little things. (IT systems support manager)

Going beyond obscurity: understanding choices and the concept of gender equality

In Dorothea Kleine's 'choice framework', an individual's resource-based agency (based on specific procedures) can operate within a given structure to achieve degrees of empowerment, such as recognition of the existence of choice, sense of choice, use of choice and achievement of choice (Kleine 2010).

Women in ICT make the choice to go into ICT careers despite the fact that there are many challenges. Their awareness of the existence of this choice coupled with the sense of choice makes them study ICT courses and get into ICT careers. However, having the sense to choose this career doesn't assure them of complete achievement of purpose. Again, this is due to social and environmental factors not recognized by employers or their representatives – the HR managers in the case of our study. There is, furthermore, also a level of non-recognition on the part of the women ICT professionals. When freedom of choice and the achievement of that choice are consciously valued by women, those women are better equipped to recognize and accept that there are forms of discrimination that they need to speak out on and not accept or contend with as fate.

HR managers fail to distinguish between what people choose/settle for, given the way things are and what people would prefer, all other things being equal. Arguably, even if by accepting situations as they are women are doing the best they can for themselves in the circumstances, many would prefer to make their choices in different circumstances.

In short, there is strong empirical evidence that suggests that, at least in the labour market, a good deal of the difference between the choices that men and women make can be accounted for by the differences in their circumstances and opportunities, which are often locked in by the impacts and implications of their choices. Failure to recognize how choice is circumscribed permits the assumption that women have the same options as their male counterparts do.

A study reported points out that professional women there are 'forced to slide down the career ladder to find jobs that allow them to spend time with their family', with nearly a third of female corporate managers being forced to take a more junior position after having a child. In contrast, men feel no such effect. Given the experience and skills wasted when highly trained women are forced out of jobs they are well qualified for, the authors of the report correctly argue that this constitutes a 'hidden brain drain' to society (Peacock 2006).

A similar argument is seen in a study in Kenya, which reveals that in ICT professional women's career progression is slower than that of men, since women have to take breaks and are overtaken by their male counterparts. Most women with families also avoid jobs that require travel to clients, despite the fact that this has a negative impact on their pay and career progression (Abagi et al. 2009).

The market appears to treat women as individuals in their own right. However, so long as women carry the double burden of unpaid work in the reproduction and maintenance of human resources, and a societal role and paid work producing goods and services, they are unable to compete with men in the labour market on 'equal' terms, where what is equal is based on an 'uncritical adoption of an unmarked male template ... as a universal standard' (Jackson 2012: 1001).

It became apparent from our study that, however much HR managers mentioned that they operated on the basis of equity and merit and that there was no gender bias, this did not help to counter gender inequalities within the companies. HR managers speak of a level/equal playing field where no individual is favoured – yet the mere fact that they are not aware of or do not understand the challenges that career women in ICTs face indicates that they do not recognize that women, with their three-tier responsibilities, are expected to deliver equally in a male-dominated dynamic industry, without provision of any kind of balancing of unequal aggregate workloads or change.

For these HR managers, careers in ICT are like any others where people face challenges, and therefore women have to compete on the same level as their male counterparts. They are expected to do this without any recognition of how these careers are biased towards traditional male gender norms, where social and domestic functioning is excluded from men's core responsibilities and attended to by women. Both HR managers and women in ICT professions fail to recognize that this work environment, developed on the basis of a gendered division of labour and traditionally gendered careers, is in need of change.

Conclusions and recommendations

For the ICT sector to continue to grow and provide the innovative solutions that will drive productivity and economic prosperity, we must create an environment and working conditions that encourage women to enter and stay in this industry, or return to it after having a family. After considering ICT businesses as sites dependent on the gendered division of labour, it is evident that the attainment of true gender equity 'requires changes on many levels: changes in policies and practices (at work, in the family, and in [the] community) [and] broad cultural change' (Rapoport et al. 2002: 167). Therefore, policy-making in technological fields should not ignore the needs, requirements and aspirations of women.

It is only when ICT companies, including professional women in ICT, recognize that a level playing field should include recognition of socially and economically normalized asymmetrical and exploitative gender relations that progress will be made towards making the work environment a better place. The current work culture, developed on the basis of a gendered division of labour and traditionally gendered careers, is in need of change. Assumptions and lack of awareness of inequalities experienced in ICT work environments need be dealt with, as highlighted in this chapter.

New ways of addressing issues of inequality need to be grounded in the deconstruction and reconstruction of the underlying assumptions on which the institution of paid work is created: 'Moving away from the principles of traditional management ideology where resources are devoted to changing and adjusting individuals' (Ressner 1987: 66). Women should be empowered in the context of knowledge societies to build up their abilities and skills to gain insight into the issues affecting them and also build up their capacity to voice their concerns. This requires a concerted effort between the company management, employees and other development actors.

Sensitizing the management and staff of ICT companies, the women's organizations and civil society in general to the gender impact of ICT policy issues may pay great dividends, in terms of raising the awareness of a large segment of society to the social implications of technology policy. But one should also think of:

- organizing more formal schemes of continuing training and skills update, including specific schemes for particular women's situations (after maternity leave, or when re-entering after a career break);
- promoting informal women's networks for skills upgrade and professional development;

- improving the work–family balance through targeted measures such as better training of project managers in terms of time management, family-friendly initiatives in companies and women-friendly time scheduling.

The hope for change in this traditionally gendered career will only become a reality if these issues are addressed by exploring and pursuing solutions and alternatives such as those mentioned above. This will increase employee satisfaction and ensure retention of workers. Given the commitment, experience and skills wasted when highly trained women are forced out of jobs they are well qualified for and passionate about, companies stand to gain much when they are able to retain the best brains and committed IT professionals. Women who enter or are already in the ICT profession should look forward to career progression, an enjoyable workplace free of discrimination and harassment, and encouragement to remain in their profession while having other interests and responsibilities.

This chapter aims to contribute to the hope and possibility of pursuing that necessary change.

Notes

1 ICT professions include ICT manufacturing (computers, telecommunication equipment and cables, consumer electronics, automation and measuring equipment); telecommunications construction and maintenance of telecom networks and network services; ICT services systems, software, software products, consultation and expert services and data-processing services; and digital media and digital entertainment or educational content production. The delivery method is 'cross-media'.

References

Abagi, O., N. Sifuna and S. Omamo (2009) 'Professional women empowered to succeed in Kenya's ICT sector', in I. Buskens and A. Webb (eds), *African Women and ICTs: Investigating Technology,* *Gender and Empowerment,* Ottawa: Zed/International Development Research Centre, pp. 169–82.

Acker, J. (1990) 'Hierarchies, jobs and bodies: a theory of gendered organizations', *Gender and Society*, 4(2): 139–58.

— (1992) 'Gendering organizational theory', in A. J. Mills and P. Tancred (eds), *Gendering Organizational Analysis*, Newbury Park, CA: Sage, pp. 248–60.

— (1998) 'The future of "gender and organizations": connections and boundaries', *Gender, Work and Organization*, 5(4): 195–206.

Amadi, A., V. W. A. Mbarika, L. Kvasny and F. C. Payton (2007) 'IT education and workforce participation: a new era for women in Kenya', *Information Society*, 23: 1–18.

Buskens, I. and A. Webb (2008) 'GRACE 2 proposal',

www.grace-network.net/ publications/GRACE2_Proposal_ Final.pdf, accessed 5 June 2014.

Department of Trade and Industry (2005) 'Statistical press release', http://stats.berr.gov.uk/ed/sme/ smestats2005-ukspr.pdf, accessed 26 November 2010.

Jackson, C. (2012) 'Speech, gender and power: beyond testimony', *Development and Change*, 43(5): 999–1023.

Kanter, R. M. (1977) *Men and Women of the Corporation*, New York: Basic Books.

Kleine, D. (2010) 'Policy arena: ICT4WHAT? – using the choice framework to operationalise the capability approach to development', *Journal of International Development*, 22: 674–92.

Pateman, C. (1988) *The Sexual Contract*, Cambridge: Polity Press.

Peacock, D. (2006) 'Strategies for increasing men's involvement in the care economy', www.genderjustice. org.za/199-strategies-for- increasing-men-s-involvement- in-the-care-economy-2/file.html, accessed 6 June 2014.

Rao, A., S. Rieky and D. Kellehar (1999) *Gender at Work: Organizational Change for Equality*, West Hartford, CT: Kumarian Press.

Rapoport, R., L. Bailyn, J. K. Fletcher and B. H. Pruitt (2002) *Beyond Work–Family Balance: Advancing Gender Equity and Workplace Performance*, San Francisco, CA: Jossey-Bass.

Ressner, U. (1987) *The Hidden Hierarchy: Democracy and Equal Opportunities*, Brookfield, VT: Avebury.

Valenduc, G. and P. Vendramin (2005) 'Work organization and skills in ICT professions: the gender dimension (workshop 1: ICT and skill change: opening the black box?)', ICT, the Knowledge Society and Changes in Work, The Hague, June 9–10.

Williams, J. (2000) *Unbending Gender: Why Family and Work Conflict and What to Do About It*, Toronto: Oxford University Press.

5 | Can new practice change old habits? ICT and female politicians' decision-making in Senegal

IBOU SANÉ

Introduction

My research focuses on the use of information and communication technology (ICT) by women political leaders in Senegal. As in many African countries, the political space is characterized more by the 'outward show' of female political participation than by actual integration of women as political partners on equal terms. Politics in Senegal remains a space of male domination in the way roles and authority are distributed and in the way the party political hierarchy favours, to varying degrees, political participation in activities that take place within the structures of its domain.

Given the numerical importance of women (52 per cent of the population and 51 per cent of the electorate) and the 'dramatic show' of female support for political leaders, many observers of political practices have commented on the 'paradox' between the massive involvement of women in politics and their limited presence in places of power (Diaw 2004: 232). Women's demographic weight and passionate, even militant political participation stand in contrast to their political under-representation; their great political engagement is not balanced with a commensurate representation in political institutions.

This imbalance is significant: the means women have available to participate in decision-making bodies will determine the socioeconomic changes and political mutations they can effect. Equal participation of women and men in decision-making processes will establish the potential for a gender-power balance and will of course also be more coherent with the conceptualization of a society that is committed to strengthening democracy. Furthermore, equality in decision-making will give women the weight that is needed to integrate a perspective of gender equality into the political arena and the way politics is done.

As ICT use in Senegal has become widespread, I wanted to investigate whether the use of ICT enhances or hinders political participation of women political leaders in Senegal. This chapter comprises three parts: the first is devoted to the theoretical framework and the research methodology, the second interrogates the notions of equality and parity and the third reflects the results of my investigation.

Theoretical framework and methodological approach

I chose to locate my research in the conceptualization of Pierre Bourdieu's 'habitus' (Bourdieu 1980), which facilitates an understanding of the representation practices of individuals and groups. The habitus is a system of socially produced internalized patterns that structure the behaviours and actions of individuals as well as their social positions in social space, in society. The conditionings that go with particular social positions and conditions of existence produce systems of durable and transposable dispositions and so feed and recreate a structure that is arranged to function as a *restructuring* structure – that is to say, as a normative generator and organizer of practices and representations. I can say with the German sociologist Max Weber (1978: 546, 554, 571, passim) that the habitus is located in behaviour, in ways of doing things, in gestures and postures. Using the notions of habitus, social structure and social domination I was able to get more insight into the intricacies of the male–female relationships in this research.

It was not easy to obtain information from women leaders who use ICT as part of their modes of political outreach and learn from them what approach they preferred. I realized that these women were very busy with their duties and obligations of personal (family), professional, social and political natures. Therefore it was necessary to define at the outset an investigation strategy and a work plan that would enable us to obtain an understanding of the political universe in Senegal. I embarked on an exploratory inquiry process using both qualitative and quantitative methods, identified the political parties that legally constituted the political space and organized meetings with key informants, who in this case were the leaders of political parties and influential women leaders. Several meetings were held with such leaders or 'resource persons' in order to explain the purpose of the research and the decision to focus on women political leaders. It was necessary to keep all stakeholders informed about the research process and results as the study unfolded. The results referred to here are those achieved at the end of the meetings with political leaders and resource persons.

About equality and parity: towards reducing gender inequality

Women's exclusion from political decision-making bodies is an issue engendering much debate in Senegal and is linked to human rights. The concept of equal opportunities is an important principle for Senegalese women's organizations. However, the political arena is still an exclusively male world and is characterized by much de facto discrimination against women. Equal participation of women in decision-making bodies is one of the major challenges for gender equality and democracy, and is also crucial to sustainable development.

Although Senegal claims to be a democratic country, it nonetheless remains a fact that discrimination against the female sex in decision-making bodies continues to exist. It seems that we often forget that equality is part and parcel of democracy, and that human beings aspire to egalitarian social relations. The Senegalese political field functions as and within a male democracy that prevents female leadership from having real influence. The question therefore arises whether the equality that women desire is realistic – or at least not utopian – in the Senegalese context.

In order to understand the prevalence and widespread acceptance of male domination, we have to go back to tradition. Traditional society is organized in such a way that men gain more access to power than women. The resistance to gender equality and democracy therefore has to be understood culturally, as male domination is legitimized within traditional society. In his book *La Domination masculine* (Masculine Domination), Bourdieu (1998: 174) discusses the power of the male order and how it is embedded in cultural customs and actualized through the internalization of beliefs and norms. Bourdieu's exposition facilitates appreciation of the extent to which male domination and female exclusion are grounded in and form the basis of cultural norms in Senegal.

However, at this moment the effects of male domination are not as systematically pervasive in Senegal as one might think; the critical work of women's organizations, particularly the feminist movement, has managed to influence this trend in the social space to a considerable degree. There is also quite a strong tradition of Senegalese women remonstrating against their exclusion with the purpose of improving their political chances and capacities. It was in 1957 that they began to denounce the fact that they were not integrated into the political decision-making processes within their parties and that they were not invited to important meetings. This prompted them to engage actively and militantly in politics, and in 1963 Caroline Faye Diop became the first female member of parliament in Senegal – one of eighty parliamentarians of the second term (1963–68). Diop was at the vanguard of the struggle for awareness-raising, advancement and emancipation of women. In 1978 President L. S. Senghor appointed her as Secretary of State for the Status of Women.

However, it was not until the political turnaround that occurred in 2000, when Mame Madior Boye was appointed prime minister, that women's political leadership received a powerful impetus.

As women continued to fight for gender equality, parity became a strategic rallying point. Parity reflects equal representation in the political arena with the purpose of reducing gender inequalities and, while it is not an end in itself, it is an important step towards gender equality. Important supporters of parity were the Senegalese Women's Council (COSEF), the Caucus of Women Leaders for Parity and the Association of Senegalese Women Lawyers. The slogan '50/50', from a campaign launched by the Women's Environment and Development Organization, was used. These groups organized campaigns together with the political parties, trade unions and others for a more balanced representation of women on candidate lists.

In 2002 President Abdoulaye Wade engaged with the organization Femmes Africa Solidarité, which was then under the leadership of Binetou Diop,[1] to support the project of parity before the African Commission on Human and Peoples' Rights. Since that time the issue of parity has engaged the minds of people in Senegal. In 2005 the demand for institutional gender parity grew into a movement of national proportions. On 14 May 2010, Law No. 10 of 2010 on parity was finally passed in the National Assembly and the Senate, conclusively establishing parity in elective office. By adopting the law on parity, Senegal made a historic shift that is allowing it to rebuild its societal and political values.[2]

Parliament is indeed the place where strategic parity must be established; this is where the use of national resources is determined and where laws that decide the future of Senegal are voted upon. In cases where the number of votes becomes a critical factor, it is important that women and men are adequately represented so that both can put their specific concerns across.[3]

Research findings

Politics, gender and the sociocultural order

Generally Senegalese men do not give much respect or credibility to women who appear to function without guardianship (whether from husbands or parents), and women are almost never independent or autonomous. In keeping with this traditional perspective, among my study group, there were women who viewed political activity as men's terrain: 'Women are motivated to support men and derive their satisfaction from helping them in their accession to power', said F. Niang, a forty-eight-year-old female teacher with two children.

TABLE 5.1 Percentage of women in the Senegalese Parliament, 1959–2012.

Legislatures	Total delegates	Total women	% women
22 March 1959 to 1 December 1963	80	0	0
9 December 1963 to 25 February 1968	80	1	1.25
7 March 1968 to 28 January 1973	80	2	2.5
9 March 1973 to 31 March 1978	100	4	4
1 April 1978 to 31 March 1983	100	0	0
2 April 1983 to 31 March 1988	100	13	13
6 April 1988 to 30 June 1993	120	18	15
9 June 1993 to 3 June 1998	120	14	11.66
1998 to 28 April 2001	120	19	15.83
29 April 2001 to 3 June 2007	140	23	16.4
From 3 June 2007	150	27	18
1 July 2012	150	64	42.7

Source: Archives of the National Assembly.

From the responses of women with political ambitions, a picture emerged of conflict and tension in the relationships between men and women, because of the mechanisms developed by men to maintain their privileges and the attempts of women to redistribute political power.

Most female respondents said that, despite the impact of modernity, they were not always free to do what they wanted. Their situation very often forced them to remain defined by and confined within the domestic sphere for fear of violating social gender norms. They feared bringing pressure upon their social relations and evoking a crisis that might result in, among other things, divorce and/or disputes with their husbands and in-laws. (In Senegal the husband's family plays a major role in the couple's married life, and married women must negotiate with their in-laws to make their marriage a success.) Thus, women were often not able to create a space in which they could participate in political affairs.

When women did manage to pursue a political career they were not supported in their political ambitions either by their husbands or (to a large extent) their families, as quotes from the following two respondents show. K. M. S., a fifty-nine-year-old community organizer with six children, said: 'My husband does often not agree, although he sometimes tolerates the situation. When I go to meetings, he does not give me his agreement, he does not feel concerned and he takes little interest in what I do.' S. G., a forty-eight-year-old woman with four children, said: 'After many arguments with my husband, he created a lot of problems for me and we ended up divorced. He did not succeed in making me change my mind.'[4]

In case upon case my findings revealed how psychological pressure was exerted on women when they became successful. Some men left their wives, while others intimidated or blackmailed them. Others simply offered their wives a divorce. Sometimes a husband would be amenable at first, but, when the woman's stature and position increased dramatically, their relationship would crumble. As a consequence the women would find themselves in situations of open conflict with their partners. It was common to see women faced with the dilemma of hesitating between continuing their political struggle or confining themselves to their role as wife and mother.

Women still have far to go in politics, and in order to understand what is at stake economic, religious and cultural factors have to be taken into account. This is an account of a fifty-seven-year-old respondent with three children of her political career and her relationship with her husband:

> I must say that I have had quite a rich political career and very early on I took on certain responsibilities, which subsequently created problems for me, with my husband, my surroundings, the *marabouts* [Muslim holy men], in-laws and men in general. I come from a family where all our forebears were involved in politics because we thought it was the only way to get rich and become respected in life. Very young, I followed my parents who were leaders in their political parties. They were great activists. And being born into such an environment, I walked all the paths that facilitated my entry into a very complex and masculine universe, which required sacrifices and political compromises. I thus had to choose when I started to assume responsibilities because I had a macho husband, for whom the rule applied: 'Kill me' or 'I'll kill you'.
>
> One day I attended a meeting of the political bureau of my party from 5 p.m. until 5 a.m. the next morning because the agenda was very important for me and required on my part a decision that would impact the life and the future of militants such as we were. When I got home between 6 and 7 a.m., I found to my surprise a woman lying on a couch; she had just been married to my husband. He had got exasperated by my frequent meetings and my working at night. He came up to me, rosary in his hand, and said in a firm voice: 'Well then, will politics marry you? Will politics give you more children?' But as luck would have it, the next day he heard on South FM radio that I had been named as Minister ... He rushed to congratulate me and asked if I

could come back home because, as he said, I had children who needed my education and human warmth. I replied that politics had lifted me up to an elevated height and he had remained small because of his petty opinions.

The husband is gone, but I have succeeded in my political career through sheer determination, conviction and tenacity. Today I am a personality and my husband is still pursuing me. When his brother saw me recently in a shiny car, he could not help himself, he could not contain himself and screamed it out, both his hands in the air. He never thought that I would be able to get to where I am now.

There were, however, men who felt that the rights, duties and challenges that accompany political life were the same for women as for men. 'You cannot have your cake and eat it', claimed a sixty-five-year-old male politician, an engineer, adding:

Our women want to have it too easy. We too have our problems. Who says that my wife is happy with me when I come very late? Who says that my children are pleased with me when I do not see them when they go to bed at night? If women want to do politics, they have to make sacrifices; they have to talk to their family, firstly to their husbands. Everything is negotiable. This also applies to men.

Political women leaders not only had difficulties with husbands and in-laws but also often experienced conflicts with other women in the party or in the immediate environment in which they operated. It appeared that solidarity among women was lacking. Jealousy, *maraboutage* (witchcraft), quarrels and petty fights characterized their interpersonal relationships. As T. S., a fifty-six-year-old, concurred:

There are many altercations between us women, especially when it comes to occupying a particular station in the party. There is hypocrisy, because when it seems that you are winning, they'll shower you with flowers, laurels, but it only takes you losing the position to a man, and they will turn away from you.

It is obvious that this lack of female solidarity made it even more difficult for female politicians to shape a life, defined and confined by the limiting gender norms that consolidated male domination and female exclusion, in a more empowering way. Applying Bourdieu's thinking to this situation suggests that these women limited themselves in two interrelated ways: by the actual physical limitations their culture imposed on their practices, and which they learnt to accept; and by their thinking, which conditioned them to accept these limitations. So male domination was concealed and the gender power imbalance was maintained and strengthened in an insidious way, without it becoming obvious that the women were doing much of the 'work of domination' themselves.

Scope and limits of the use of ICT

Since 1997 Senegal has implemented a strategy to strengthen and facilitate access to ICT. Some political parties are open to the use of ICT in their communication and outreach activities; others have not yet institutionalized its use. Where women leaders use ICT in such cases, it is in the same sense as the general public and the men in their parties would do.

However, a gender-specific use of ICT is emerging where women feel 'forced' to use ICT. As women are often not able to attend political meetings that are held in the evenings – not only for security reasons but also because it is not deemed proper for Senegalese women to go out at night on their own – using (mobile) telephony and the Internet (the two most popular forms of ICT in Senegal) enables them to participate in political meetings while they are physically absent. In this way they can give their opinions and defend their points of view on the issues under discussion without having to leave their houses.

As F. Ndiaye, a forty-five-year-old married businesswoman with two children, informed us:

> For important political issues, I used ICT to influence the decisions. To do this, I would have to negotiate with politburo members one by one. This is not easy. Sometimes some of them would ask me to come and be physically present, knowing full well what would happen at home if I did that. We must raise awareness and sensitize people about these issues ... I use ICT (mobile and Internet) for our meetings, our discussions and general meetings. But it is especially the SMSs [text messages] we send to men and women of the politburo in order to influence their decisions, especially when we need to counter their decisions.

Women who used ICT appreciated using SMSs because the messages they sent had more 'substance' than an ephemeral telephone conversation. The man chairing the particular political session would have the option of showing other members the content of the SMSs the women had sent them, and in this way each member could see those messages for themselves. Of course the chairman could respond in two ways: he could agree to reveal the content of the messages when he deemed the situation favourable and conceal the content when he deemed it unfavourable. In the first case he could involve a few people in the decision process and devote the necessary energy to convincing his comrades to agree with him. In the second case he could exercise a 'blackout' policy and ignore the SMS, unless another party member who received the same message spoke about it to others. It sometimes happened that the woman who sent the SMS would be asked to come and physically defend her point of view.

It is obvious, however, that even though the use of SMSs gave women some form of political agency, everything still depended on the judgement and goodwill of the men in power. At least their responses reflected their openness towards gender concerns and their willingness to work with ICT. These men also often recognized the value of using video-conference tools or social networks (Twitter), and were found to be willing to install computers and communication equipment (Internet, wi-fi) in their party offices.

ICT control and training were issues to be considered, as not all women and all parties could carry the costs involved. Furthermore, using ICT from home or an office to participate in political meetings could also become a limiting factor in the physical and active participation of women. While attending meetings in person, women would have the opportunity to establish their point of view, refine their arguments and convince men in the dialogue of the moment. Staying at home and using ICT to vote, without men having to take their views seriously, could therefore definitely be to women's disadvantage.

There were, however, also male leaders who, while acknowledging the existence of what they ironically called 'the electronic vote', were not willing to accept these innovations in their ambit of power. This refusal of men to allow women to use ICT in this way would, of course, in the gendered political landscape of Senegal, limit women's political participation considerably if not totally.

Discussion

Use of ICT for the purposes of political reaching out, connecting and influencing does not have the same meaning for men as it has for women. While for men use of ICT can be an expansion of their capacity for political communication and influence, strengthening and diversifying their face-to-face capacity, women's use of ICT seems to have three dimensions: first, ICT is an expression and even a consolidation of their gendered and limited capacity for face-to-face political communication; second, women use ICT in an attempt to overcome this gendered and limited capacity for face-to-face political communication; and third, women's ICT use is an expansion of their capacity for political communication that strengthens and diversifies their face-to-face capacity in a similar fashion as it does for men.

The question that framed this research was whether the use of ICT by women political leaders would promote or hinder their participation in the decision-making bodies of their political parties. It has become clear that there is no simple answer to this question, as the use of ICT can be both advantageous and disadvantageous for women in their efforts to enhance their political participation. The general use of the technology definitely enhances the ease and effectiveness with which women can participate in the activities of their political parties. On the other hand, there is reason to doubt that ICT can make a substantial contribution to women's political participation, because the nature of the political process often requires interpersonal face-to-face communication for effective interventions.

If one considers women political leaders as actors in the development of their country because they use their expertise to establish the modes of organization and operation that their parties need, how can we refrain from considering the ways they have at their disposal to augment their power to act? Hence, the obstacles to such power – cultural systems of gender difference – as well as the guidelines for implementing such systems have to be reviewed through the prism of the maxim 'What you want to see done happens through the person who can do it'. ICT has, despite the caveats I have discussed here, a definite role to play in overcoming some of the obstacles women face in the political arena. Enabling women to use their right to speak and the opportunity to participate in elections and in party politics, on an equal basis with men, is a very valuable contribution.

Conclusions and recommendations

It is essential that women in Senegal continue to fight for political parity. The 2010 Gender Parity Law, which enabled Senegal to accomplish a 42.6 per cent female presence (64 women of a total of 150 delegates) in the National Assembly, is indeed an important step forward. But women must continue their fight against the religious and sociocultural determinants that define and consolidate their positions as second-class citizens. The ultimate focus for social change should not be on under-representation of women in political decision-making bodies but on that which generates and maintains this under-representation in its current form; that is, the representations and multiple exclusionary practices that form, inform and are caused by gender socialization that is grounded in power differentiation.

The fact that among the new female representatives in the National Assembly some are second or third wives seems to indicate that male hegemony is still firmly in place even in the highest political echelons of the country, echelons that are expected to uphold, promote and protect democracy, social justice (including gender justice) and development (Hirsch 2012). This leaves room to wonder whether gender parity in the political arena assisted by the use of ICT will actually be able to balance the power differentials between the sexes in Senegal.

Gender parity can, however, become a step towards the elimination of gender inequality and, to this end, the following actions are recommended:

- The parity law must be clarified and popularized, because women no longer consider the parity law to be a magic solution.
- Obstacles to the participation of women in decision-making processes need to be eliminated. The fact that women are capable of holding positions of political responsibility needs to be widely discussed with political and religious actors and women's organizations must take up that challenge.
- Because men continue to hold meetings in the night, which requires women to be away from home, programmes need to be developed to strengthen ICT capacity to support empowerment benefit without losing sight of the barriers that limit women's accessibility.
- Women across the Caucus of Women Leaders for Parity and the Association of Women Lawyers should mobilize for the application of absolute parity in all decision-making bodies, particularly on the level of local communities and the Economic, Social and Environmental Council, where women are not represented according to the country's gender ratio (which amounts to 52 per cent women).

Notes

1 Binetou Diop was named one of the one hundred most influential people in the world in 2011 by *Time* magazine (Les Afriques 2011).

2 On 28 June 2013 the Nationality Act was passed, allowing women to pass their nationality to their spouses and children. Finally, in July 2013 the Divisional Commissioner Anna Sémou Diouf was appointed Director General of the National Police Force.

3 In terms of gender parity, Senegal is third in Africa (42.66 per cent), behind Rwanda (56.3 per cent) and Seychelles (43.8 per cent). Worldwide, in 2013 it was in 6th place out of 189 countries (Inter-Parliamentary Union 2013).

4 We have taken care to specify the marital status of the respondents because of the arguments used by men to oppose the political

commitment of their wives. A married woman with children is not in the same situation as a single mother or a childless woman.

References

Bourdieu, P. (1980) *Le Sens pratique* [The Logic of Practice], Paris: Editions de Minuit.

— (1998) *La Domination masculine* [Masculine Domination], Paris: Editions du Seuil.

Diaw, A. (2004) 'Les femmes à l'épreuve du politique: permanences et changements' [Women in the test of politics: continuity and change], in M.-C. Diop (ed.), *Gouverner le Sénégal: entre ajustement structurel et développement durable* [Governing Senegal: Between Structural Adjustment and Sustainable Development], Paris: Karthala, p. 227–45.

Hirsch, A. (2012) 'Has Senegal's gender parity law for MPs helped women?', *Guardian*, 15 November, www.theguardian.com/global-development/2012/nov/15/senegal-gender-parity-law-mps-women, accessed 27 September 2013.

Inter-Parliamentary Union (2013) 'Women in National Parliament on 1 July 2013', www.ipu.org/wmn-f/classif.html, accessed 27 September 2013.

Les Afriques (2011) 'Bineta Diop parmi les 100 personnes les plus influentes du monde: pauvreté des femmes, féminisation du sida ... les combats continuent' [Bineta Diop among the 100 most influential people in the world: poverty among women, feminization of AIDS ... the struggle continues], www.lesafriques.com/actualite/bineta-diop-parmi-les-100-pauvrete-des-femmes-feminisation-du-sida-les-combats-conti.html?Itemid=89, accessed 27 September 2013.

Weber, M. (1978 [1921]) *Economy and Society*, Berkeley: University of California Press.

6 | Personal expansion versus traditional gender stereotypes: Tunisian university women and ICT

OUM KALTHOUM BEN HASSINE

Introduction

Public policy in Tunisia has both recognized the legal rights of Tunisian women in its Personal Status Code (PSC)[1] and supported the development of ICT since the 1980s (Kamoun et al. 2010). Especially notable were the launch of the 'family computer program' (Babnet 2005; OECD and Banque africaine 2009), the promotion of use of the Internet at reduced costs and the widespread teaching of Computer Science to students of all ages (Hamdy 2007). Furthermore, particular efforts have been made to promote the capacities of women in ICT (Ministère des Technologies de la Communication 2008).

These state-level commitments made very early in the development of this sector and its policies saw Tunisia being declared by the World Economic Forum in 2008–09 as first in Maghreb and Africa and third in the world in promoting ICTs. This situation warrants exploration of the degree of women's access to, use of and mastery of ICTs, and the implications of accomplishments in ICT for women's equality.

In Tunisia the legal rights of women were not recognized as a result of the women themselves fighting for equality, as was the case in the West, where women resisted their serfdom and ardently pushed for equality (Gilligan 1986). In Tunisia the genesis of the movement for the emancipation of women is the will of the political leaders of independent Tunisia, and is punctuated with male names (Rabaaoui-Essefi 2001), a peculiarity and singularity in this domain.

One of these men is Habib Bourguiba, the first president of the Tunisian state. He judged that Islam has the capacity to evolve to adapt itself to modern life, and therefore granted Tunisian women the status of full citizens with promulgation of the PSC. He believed that the lifeblood of the nation, including the women, must be mobilized to lead the battle against under-development (Slah-Eddine Baly, cited in Lakehal-Ayat, 1978: 5). Subsequently, women had access to education and employment, and contributed to the development and economic growth of independent Tunisia.

In this way, 'the state has been the chief agent of change, not only in introducing some enviably progressive legislation, but also in seeking to alter the productive and reproductive roles of women to an extent that justifies use of the term state feminism' (Murphy 2003: 169). However, this did not prevent the persistence of gender inequality and disregard of the legal rights of women in practice.

Similarly, the expansion of ICT is the result of a policy initiated by Tunisian leaders with the aim of developing the ICT sector and increasing economic growth (Kamoun et al. 2010). This too warrants reflection on its actual effects.

Instead of bringing well-being to all members of the population, the economic development of Tunisia, generated by an economy that adopted a process of reforms and liberalization from the mid-1990s (Wilmots 2003), has exacerbated inequalities between citizens and regions (Organisation Internationale du Travail 2011). In this situation of exclusion and marginalization, 'the voices defending Islam had grown louder and Islamic fundamentalism had changed from a cultural phenomenon into a political threat' (Charrad 1997: 300) by unambiguously coveting state power (Charrad 1997, 2001), and, while the 'regime offers women tolerance and secular empowerment, the Islamists offer the reassurance of cultural authenticity and traditionally defined gender roles' (Murphy 2003: 170).

These fundamentalists, who are 'organized into tight networks at the grassroots level', especially among poor sections of the population and those who are excluded from development, have called for a return to patriarchy and traditional models of gender (Charrad 1997: 304). Inequitable development and unjust sharing of economic growth in Tunisia therefore generated a regressive trend by pushing a large part of the population to take refuge in traditional values promoted by Islamists who preach male domination (Ruedy 1994).

Various studies indicate that Tunisian women have not achieved true equality of opportunity with men, particularly in employment and decision-making, key factors for changing the status of women (CREDIF, 2000a, 2000b, 2000c, 2001, 2002a, 2002b, 2003a, 2003b; Ben Hassine 2005; Sinha 2011). In the context of the present era of increasing Islamisation, there are further pressures towards upholding traditional inequitable gender norms. The legal protection of women's equality, which does not reflect a mass movement, is only respected by those who share the same values. Thus, while it is indisputable that the PSC, which is unique in Arab countries and has been in existence for more than fifty years, recognizes Tunisian women's equal status and rights, it is also clear that this legal

TABLE 6.1 Number of respondents who completed the questionnaire and who participated in focus groups and individual interviews, by category and gender.

		Administrative staff		Teachers		Students	
		Female	Male	Female	Male	Female	Male
Questionnaire		50	45	71	50	809	259
Focus groups	First	9	2	5	0	11	9
	Second	6	0	9	0	11	0
Individual interviews		4	2	6	0	5	0

provision has not eradicated the inequality entrenched in social and cultural gender norms and practices (Collectif 95 Maghreb – Egalité and AFTURD 2008).

Research methodology

To explore how this situation of women's legal rights, existing cultural and social norms and access to ICTs plays itself out in terms of equality and self-determination for women at the Faculty of Sciences at Tunis El Manar University, we undertook an exploratory investigation using quantitative and qualitative methods. Our questionnaire was distributed to all 539 teachers, including 252 women, spread over 6 departments (Biology, Geology, Mathematics, Computer Science, Chemistry and Physics); to all 262 administrative staff and workers, including 110 women; and to 10 per cent of the 10,481 students in several disciplines (of whom 6,227 are female) (Ben Hassine 2011). In total 930 women and 354 men completed the questionnaire, 62 individuals took part in focus groups and 17 people agreed to participate in individual 'free attitude' interviews (Buskens 2005), as shown in Table 6.1. The data collection and primary analysis took place over a period of one year, in 2009 and 2010.

Research findings

We investigated the degree to which female Tunisian academics, students and university staff have access to computers and the Internet, and whether how these tools are used is biased by gender. This was followed by an exploration of the impact of the Tunisian context and its contradictions (the PSC, maintenance of traditional standards, ICT expansion and economic growth, maintenance of social inequalities and the rise of Islamism) on the lives of women and their self-awareness, self-development and self-determination.

Gender-sensitive ICT policy does not ensure equality of use,
mastery or benefit

In our study, extensive quantitative data, confirmed by qualitative data, show that equity of ICT availability has been achieved at Tunis El Manar University (Ben Hassine 2011). Integration of ICT into Tunisian educational and professional domains has contributed to the achievement of the equal availability of these tools. However, women's limited self-determination of use of their time, which was pointed out by women during the focus groups and interviews, restricts their access to ICTs and their use and particularly acquisition of ICT skills.

Given this situation, what are the benefits to women of equal availability of ICTs if they do not have the same amount of use as men and 'cannot freely extend their work hours, or access these tools at home until the household tasks are done and until the children are in bed'? The majority of the female administrative staff admitted during discussions: 'I never have time to use these tools at home, because of my household tasks'. Many academic women acknowledged, 'I can't use ICT at home before having fulfilled my familial responsibilities'.

According to these women, time constraints constitute the major obstacle to their development of optimal use of available ICTs. The Internet does not help to reduce the burden of domestic work and family and social responsibilities of women. Thus, despite women's obvious enthusiasm regarding the availability of computers, the Internet and online resources, 'these tools cannot do the laundry and cook', as pointed out by a working woman.

Personal and professional development in ICT: between
renunciation and the desire for advanced performance

Among the respondents, the older career women use ICT tools to facilitate their work but have given up on taking full advantage of these technologies. During interviews some declared: 'because of my age, to have skills in the field of ICTs will not provide me with professional or personal benefits', and 'what we know of these tools is more than enough'. They do not seek to benefit from a wide range of ICTs and do not aspire to enhance their ICT use in their personal and professional lives. Thus, rather than a personal attitude of satisfaction, they have an attitude of renunciation. A small number (two) of these women were distrustful of ICTs and felt that 'ICTs have killed, among younger generations, the use of books, reading and culture and therefore they have allowed the emergence of generations who know everything and nothing'. In addition, we noticed that it was among these respondents that we found the women who were most recalcitrant in the use of online social networks.

In contrast, the young women (early or mid-career), who constituted the majority of female respondents among administrative staff and academics, all of whom were married with dependent children, sought enhanced performance through ICT 'by increasing my skills and deepening my knowledge' and 'greater ICT training'. These women believe that 'these tools are of great importance both personally and professionally'. However, time constraints constitute the major obstacle to their optimal use and technical mastery of the tools: 'I would like to see the day stretched into a day of 48 hours instead of 24 hours for doing all what I want to do and also to have full use of the ICTs'. As an administrative staff member put it: 'upon returning home after work, the broom replaces the computer'.

In this context our research has shown that, for academic women, the greater their number of children, the less their use of ICTs and the less time they spend surfing the Internet and accessing the Internet from the workplace (Ben Hassine 2011). They say that, as soon as 'we finish teaching, we have to rush home to be home in time to take care of our children and to accomplish the household duties'. Our research has also shown that women who married at an older age use, master and benefit more from ICTs than those who married young, because 'before we were married and had family responsibilities, we had more time to follow our interest in ICTs and to master them'.

These women want to fit use of ICTs into their lives because of all the benefits that they see could be gained, but they do not challenge the established social order in their homes or seek an egalitarian sharing of family responsibilities with their spouses. Instead of questioning the unequal roles that are socially and culturally established within the family and society, these women 'ask to be relieved by the university of some of their family responsibilities through the creation of nurseries and canteens to increase their time to devote to developing ICT skills and to realize their dream to be empowered in this field'.

In their case, the opportunity for access to the Internet from the workplace is inhibited by sociocultural demands on their time. Women's gendered roles prevent them from staying longer at the workplace (Mbambo-Thata et al. 2009). For these women, teaching, research and family responsibilities compete for their time (Mbambo-Thata et al. 2009). Family responsibilities and their teaching come before full use of ICTs.

As for female students and some young, single, early-career women from the administrative staff and academics, who have more time to access and use ICTs and who master these tools more than married women, most state that 'the Internet is a tool that contributes to expand my knowledge and possibilities, and facilitates also my studies or my work'. During group discussions two women called marriage into question, seeing it as 'an obstacle to the freedom of women'. However, they believe 'the status of single women in Tunisian society is less enviable than the situation of married women who obey norms and traditions', thinking that, unlike single women, married women enjoy a certain social respectability. However, one PhD student who seems to have decided to negotiate the equality of her rights in the private sphere with her future husband is 'inspired by my childhood experience of my parents (mother and father) who always shared domestic tasks'. Her intentions are also shaped by her desire to 'have a career in higher education and scientific research where I hope to acquire certain notoriety'. She seems to consider this incompatible with an overload of domestic responsibilities not shared with a spouse. She confessed: 'If I marry, I would not agree to serve my husband; and if he does not accept to share household chores with me, especially the cooking, he will go to eat at his mother's, or we will both go to a restaurant'.

A few very young women (single students) who grew up in open-minded and highly educated family environments that encouraged freedom and empowerment, and who had the same varied and diversified use of ICTs as men, acknowledged that 'my parents encourage me to use and to master ICTs because these tools help my learning and allow me to improve and deepen quickly my knowledge and then broaden my options'. These women envision themselves taking on various ways of gendered being and doing and becoming co-creators of new gender relations and realities, despite the risk of appearing marginal in their society.

Thus, apart from the older women and a few of the students, the majority of respondents dream of performance in the field of ICT without questioning the gendered stereotypes pertaining to domestic labour.

Dreams of performance while maintaining the stereotypes

To remedy the situation of inequality, most of the women respondents – who believe that acquisition of advanced skills in ICT will ensure their empowerment regarding ICTs – suggested that, 'in order to have some of our time made available some of our family responsibilities [child care] could be alleviated by our work places [by the creation of nurseries, kindergartens and canteens]'. They suggested also 'taking on additional training to strengthen our skills and increase our knowledge in the field of ICT'. They want to gain the self- and professional development that they see as possible with ICTs, but without questioning or unsettling the current gender roles and relations.

Some female academic respondents admitted during discussions that 'to do certain work tasks, using computers and the Internet, we are forced to have days so long that we feel exhausted'. These women believe 'these tools allow us to save time and therefore facilitate the achievement of our roles, not only professional but also our familial and social roles'. Instead of questioning their status and social condition, these exhausted women want their institutions to help them manage their multiple roles so as to have time to use ICTs and improve their effectiveness. Among these women few pointed to the non-egalitarian division of domestic work or raised the need for participation of male spouses in these and other social tasks.

Women's acceptance of their condition is a major obstacle to their emancipation

This research shows that availability of computers and the Internet does not mean equity of access to them or equally beneficial use thereof. It shows that even gender-sensitive ICT policy on its own does not ensure equally beneficial use; such policy and a legal framework for women's rights are not enough. This research also shows the strength and resilience of socially, culturally, historically and economically normalized, internalized and perpetuated gender relations.

Yet the Tunisian PSC constitutes a major legal gain not only for Tunisian women but also for society at large; in this legal framework the relations between spouses are defined on the basis of reciprocity of obligations and in terms of cooperation. However, the legislation in itself has not substantially helped society to overcome discrimination based on social interpretations (Chekir 2000, 2001, 2005).

Thus, neither the policy of widespread access to ICTs and of promotion of women's capacities in this area nor the PSC have been able to create a context for gender equality among professional university women. There is a gap between the national policy regarding women's rights and the development of ICTs and the practice of men and women in their daily lives and their relationships. Women's acceptance of their condition is a major obstacle to their emancipation from social and cultural norms that keep them from challenging the status quo and shifting their focus onto self-awareness and self-development. This prevents them from contributing to co-creation of their environment and the creation of their own selves.

In this context, at Tunis El Manar University access to and use and mastering of ICTs remains inequitable, despite the availability of the technologies and women's appreciation of ICTs, which, according to them, 'allow us to save time by quickly obtaining information'. Professional and academic women, with few exceptions, have internalized the traditional values that define gender roles and continue to prevail in Tunisian society and are even on the increase with the rise of Islamism.

Indeed, society produces and reproduces differences between women and men by prescribing family roles and statutes that limit women's room for freedom (Collectif 95 Maghreb – Egalité and AFTURD 2008). According to research conducted in Tunisia, there is relative consensus among respondents on existing gender roles (Collectif 95 Maghreb – Egalité and AFTURD 2008), allowing disparities to persist or be reconstructed, particularly in the private sphere, where division of domestic work remains at the expense of women who have to reconcile obligations between paid work and family life. The involvement of women in the public realm has not been accompanied by more involvement of men in the private sphere (Collectif 95 Maghreb – Egalité and AFTURD 2008). The patriarchal system of gendered inequality is firmly ensconced in the collective unconscious of most of those whom we interviewed, reflecting the degree of misogyny present within themselves and their society.

Who are the exceptions? They are young women who grew up in families that inculcated in them values of autonomy and freedom different from the traditional values prevalent in Tunisian society. Therefore, following in the spirit of those who developed the PSC, these young women feel and think differently from the majority of respondents and seem to live and act upon that way of thinking, which results in them making use of the ICTs they access, in order to co-create their living environment and their realities along those lines of thought.

The majority of women, however, by increasing their burden, deepen their sense of alienation from who they are, from what they value and believe in and from any sense of personal agency. This alienation arises from the inscription of oneself to the ideology of those who dominate, which leads to refraining from thinking of one's own condition. The ways of thinking and behaviours of those who are dominated thus serve the interests of the dominant group.

This alienation can be attributed to a woman's identification with an existence that is socially imposed (Chouala 2003). The setting of a rigid social hierarchy based on sex, referred to by Daly as the 'sexual caste system' (1972, 1973), prevents women from participating fully in the world. In this system women have no right to withhold their social and family roles because it is the 'duty' of the woman caste. This status of lower caste keeps women oriented by the norms, values and expectations of the dominant group and estranged from contemplation of their sense of themselves, their self-awareness and self-concept, contributing to their estrangement from contemplating what gender equality means and could look like – beyond being equally present in certain jobs and academic departments.

A striking example of this alienation of the self is the fact that women themselves believe that domestic work falls within the woman's role (Collectif 95 Maghreb – Egalité and AFTURD 2008). Thus, instead of claiming an egalitarian division of labour within the family, they aspire to be superwomen 'able to do it all': integrating enhanced ICT use within their lives while maintaining the gendered stereotypes pertaining to domestic labour. These women submit themselves to the performance standards of patriarchal society, where the stereotype of the housewife remains firmly entrenched as the 'caring' mother in the context of the heterosexual couple with children and work (Gaborit 2009). In this society the woman perceives herself and is perceived as 'significant' because she is essential to her spouse, children and work. She becomes effective only insofar as she is able to reconcile everything and meet everyone's expectations. Even the two respondents who called marriage into question, seeing it as an obstacle to women's freedom, found the status of single women in Tunisian society less enviable than that of married women who obey norms and traditions.

Thus gender stereotypes, which structure mental representations and define roles, activities, qualities and powers, contain and restrain the demand for and realization of gender equality, which would upset established norms and values. In this society women perceive themselves and are perceived as powerful when they are able to manage their three roles (family, social and professional) simultaneously and equally well.

At Tunis El Manar University the majority of women find themselves set within this portrait, which is drawn up for them according to the stereotypes of patriarchal society and which prevents them from evacuating the prejudices that surround them and contributing to a true revolution in attitudes. These women have internalized the values of the dominion and of male privileges and reproduce them.

The danger therefore exists that the use of ICTs evokes unrealistic expectations of what women are capable of and should be doing and in this way not only supports the existing gender inequality but also exacerbates it. The irony of these tools is that, while they may ease some women's access to further learning, they make it possible for women to increase their workload even more.

Conclusions

*Integrating ICTs into existing gendered relationships contributes to
stabilization of gendered relationships instead of transformation*

At the Faculty of Sciences at Tunis El Manar University, women's
experiences of ICTs are not divorced from their social context. The
results of this research indicate that access to, use of and benefit derived
from computers and online resources correspond with normalized gendered inequalities. Existing gender relations appear to be sustained in
the relatively new terrain of ICT access, use and technical know-how.
Therefore, instead of transforming gendered relationships, the availability of ICTs has contributed to their stabilization, allowing women to fulfil
their three or more normalized social, cultural and economic roles even
more efficiently.

In addition to doing more, these women have less time available for
self-realization, personal growth and development that generates self-
fulfilment and well-being. In this way their aspirations for ICT use can
be seen as contributing to the stabilization of gendered relationships
instead of to gender transformation.

There is thus a gap between the objective of the Tunisian policy concerning the development of ICTs, which is their expansion equally to
men and women to ensure economic development, and the benefits that
women actually experience. Indeed, in Tunisia, as in other developing
countries, ICTs have been included as an integral part of national agendas for social and economic development (Khalil et al. 2009; Kamoun
et al. 2010).

Generally the gap between the Tunisian policy of promoting women's
equality and the real social experience of the respondents is affected by
acceptance and perpetuation by women and men of the normalized social
and cultural relations of the patriarchal society. The PSC has remained
overpowered by social and cultural gender norms encouraged and legitimized by a traditional interpretation of Islam. Indeed, in spite of secularism displayed by the political regime and feminist state, exclusion of
part of the population from development and unequal distribution of the
benefits of economic growth between individuals and regions contributed to the emergence in the 1990s of a radical Islam that represented a
kind of refuge from and alternative to the experience of marginalization:
'Fundamentalism feeds off discontent' (Charrad 1997: 304).

Thus 'the Islamic fundamentalist movement in Tunisia acts in part
as the political voice of the disappointed urban poor, for whom national
sovereignty and the discourse of modernization failed to deliver the

promised goods' (Charrad 1997: 305). The message promoting, in the name of religion, a return to traditional values that consider women as objects rather than subjects spread from its initial base in poor urban zones with the help of the distribution of 'yellowish booklets' (Charrad 1997: 304) and using fear of the afterlife to gain followers. Hence, the fundamentalists have made progress, despite the government ban of their movement. Their speeches resonate in a society described by a politically active Tunisian woman as 'unquestionably the freest country for women in the Arab world. But the irony is that it is not women who fought for their rights in this country. It was the men who gave them to us' (cited in Charrad 1997: 309).

In this context of a mesh of various influences and forces, which path can be taken towards change?

The path towards change

Our study shows that most of the respondents live by the gendered traditional social norms as though there were no alternative ways of living. They perpetuate these norms themselves rather than open themselves up to experiencing a sense of being alienated from their own sense of self and self-determination. Women's acceptance of their gendered conditions and their abiding by traditional gender norms are major obstacles to women's emancipation and their potential to use ICTs to further their empowerment.

In this case the change must come from women themselves: their willingness to become active agents in the co-creation of their environment, especially in the context of the threat of radical Islam that is currently increasingly expressed in Tunisia, especially since the 2011 revolution. This preaches a model of society in which there is no place for women to be autonomous, independent and free to decide and act.

The few young women in our study who felt and thought differently and seemed to have another vision of being and doing – a vision of becoming co-creators of new gender relations and of a new social environment – constitute good examples that could point the way for other respondents. Indeed, it is these women who, in the face of the pressures of Islamic fundamentalism, will know how to defend the already guaranteed rights in the PSC and ensure their consolidation and strengthening.

Recommendations

This chapter's recommendations therefore focus on supporting and nurturing young women's gender awareness since this is the first step in an empowerment process. It is envisaged that such would be accomplished in the following ways:

- Establishment of a 'gender and development' centre at Tunis El Manar University that would, among other things, focus on issues such as the equitable sharing of tasks in the family and society and developing citizenship-education modules. Equitable sharing of tasks and equality of opportunities cut to the heart of the problematic of citizenship about which there is currently much talk in Tunisia, since the revolution.
- Development and certification of a 'gender and education for emancipation' curriculum for students, with the purpose of stimulating the capacity for critical reflection, as this would contribute to affecting the gendered roles of women and men in the workplace, the family and personal life.
- Encouragement of young, self-aware women who seem in charge of their lives as co-creators of their environment to organize themselves into a virtual network that would be open to all women of the University. As there are still many women in Tunisia who are not aware of their rights, this network would provide a space where information could be shared and disseminated and where ideas could be exchanged and popularized.

Note

1 The Personal Status Code is a series of progressive Tunisian laws promulgated on 13 August 1956 that aim at equality between men and women in a number of domains. It gives women a unique place in Tunisian society and in the Arab world in general, abolishing in particular polygamy, creating a judicial procedure for divorce and authorizing marriage only with mutual consent of both partners. This feminist policy unquestionably contributed to political modernization of the country.

References

Babnet (2005) 'PC familial: les différentes configurations existantes' [Family personal computers: the various existing combinations], 13 October, www.babnet.net/cadredetail-3201.asp, accessed 10 December 2012.

Ben Hassine, O. K. (2005) 'Participation des femmes tunisiennes au développement: Etat des lieux de leur intégration au marché du travail' [Participation of Tunisian women in development: current situation of their integration in the labor market], http://issuu.com/gracenetwork/docs/participation_des_femmes_tunisiennes_au_d_veloppem, accessed 19 February 2013.

— (2011) 'Is there a gender difference in access to and use of ICTs at the University of Tunis, Tunisia?', www.grace-network.net/research_tunisia.php, accessed 10 December, 2012.

Buskens, I. (2005) *Free Attitude Interview Manual*, http://issuu. com/gracenetwork/docs/fai__ final, accessed 10 May 2010.

Charrad M. M. (1997) 'Policy shifts: state, Islam, and gender in Tunisia, 1930s–1990s', *Social Politics*, 4(2): 284–317.

— (2001) *States and Women's Rights: The Making of Postcolonial Tunisia, Algeria, and Morocco*, Berkley, CA: University of California Press.

Chekir, H. (2000) *Le Statut des femmes entre les textes et les résistances: le cas de la Tunisie* [The status of women between the texts and resistances: the case of Tunisia], Tunis: Chama.

— (2001) 'Universalité et spécificité: autour des droits des femmes en Tunisie' [Universality and specificity: around women's rights in Tunisia], paper presented at the Round Table on Liberalism, Republicanism – Women's Rights, the Issue of the Islamic Veil, Ferrera, Italy, 21 November.

— (2005) 'Tradition et modernité dans la perception des droits des femmes dans les cultures de la rive sud de la Méditerranée: l'exemple du statut des femmes arabes' [Tradition and modernity in the perception of women's rights in the cultures of the southern shore of the Mediterranean: the example of the status of Arab women], *Jura Gentium*, 1(1), www.juragentium. org/topics/med/tunis/fr/chekir. htm, accessed 20 May 2014.

Chouala, Y. A. (2003) 'Galanterie masculine et "aliénation objective" de la femme: la légitimation feminine d'un "habitus androcentrique"' [Masculine gallantry and 'objective alienation' of the woman: feminine legitimation of an 'androcentric habitus'], www.polis.sciencespobordeaux. fr/vol1ons/arti8.html, accessed 9 June 2012.

Collectif 95 Maghreb – Egalité and Associations des Femmes Tunisiennes pour la Recherche sur le Développement (AFTURD) (2008) *Degré d'adhésion des Tunisiens et des Tunisiennes aux valeurs égalitaires (principaux résultats)* [Degree of Adherence of Tunisian Men and Women to Egalitarian Values (Main Results)], Tunis: Publications Collectif 95, pp. 1–23.

CREDIF (2000a) *Femmes et villes* [Women and Cities], Tunis: CREDIF, pp. 1–143.

— (2000b) *Budget-temps des ménages ruraux et travail invisible des femmes rurales en Tunisie* [Time Budget of Rural Households and Invisible Work of Rural Women in Tunisia], Tunis: CREDIF, pp. 1–192.

— (2000c) *Gérer son devenir professionnel: mode d'emploi, programme de soutien aux femmes cadres* [Manage Her Own Professional Future: User Manual, Support Program for Women Executives], Tunis: CREDIF, pp. 1–83.

— (2001) *Les femmes entrepreneurs en Tunisie: paroles et portraits* [Women Entrepreneurs in Tunisia: Words and Portraits], Tunis: CREDIF, pp. 1–179.

— (2002a) *Femmes et hommes en Tunisie en chiffres: observatoire de la condition de la femme en Tunisie* [Women and Men in Tunisia in Figures: Observatory of the Woman Condition in Tunisia], Tunis: CREDIF, pp. 1–104.

— (2002b) *Femmes et emploi en Tunisie* [Women and Employment in Tunisia], Tunis: CREDIF, pp. 1–161.

— (2003a) *Femmes et développement régional en Tunisie* [Women and Regional Development in Tunisia], Vol. I, Tunis: CREDIF, pp. 1–216.

— (2003b) *Femmes et développement régional en Tunisie: monographie par gouvernorat* [Women and Regional Development in Tunisia: Monograph by Governorate], Vol. II, pp. 1–376.

Daly, M. (1972) 'The women's movement: an exodus community', *Religious Education*, 67(5): 327–35.

— (1973) *Beyond God the Father: Toward a Philosophy of Women's Liberation*, Boston, MA: Beacon Press, pp. 1–225.

Gaborit, P. (2009) *Identités, rôles sociaux et politiques publiques* [Identities, Social Roles and Public Policies], Paris: L'Harmattan, pp. 1–342.

Gilligan, C. (1986) *Une si grande différence* [Such a Large Difference], Paris: Flammarion, pp. 1–270.

Hamdy, A. (2007) 'ICT in education in Tunisia', www.infodev.org/en/Document.434.pdf, accessed 22 December 2012.

Kamoun, F., J. Chaabouni, S. Tabbane and A. Ben Letaifa (2010) 'Tunisia ICT sector performance review 2009/2010: towards evidence-based ICT policy and regulation, volume two, policy paper 12', www.researchictafrica.net/publications/Policy_Paper_Series_Towards_Evidence-based_ICT_Policy_and_Regulation_-_Volume_2/Vol%202%20Paper%2012%20-%20Tunisia%20ICT%20Sector%20Performance%20Review%202010.pdf, accessed 10 December 2012.

Khalil, M., P. Dongier and C. Zhen-Wei Quiang (2009) 'Overview', in *Information and Communications for Development: Extending Reach and Increasing Impact*, Washington, DC: World Bank, pp. 3–18.

Lakehal-Ayat, N. (1978) *La Femme tunisienne et sa place dans le droit positif* [Tunisian Woman and Her Place in the Positive Law], Tunis: Dar El Amal d'Edition, de Diffusion et de Presse, pp. 1–67.

Mbambo-Thata, B., E. Mlambo and M. Mwatsiya (2009) 'When a gender-blind access policy results in discrimination: realities and perceptions of female students at the University of Zimbabwe', in I. Buskens and A. Webb (eds), *African Women and ICTs: Investing Technology, Gender and Empowerment*, London: Zed Books, pp. 67–76.

Ministère des Technologies de la Communication (2008) *Interaction femmes et TIC en Tunisie: rapport d'une étude réalisée par Actif Consulting & STARC Consulting en groupement solidaire et financée par la Banque mondiale* [Interaction between Women and ICT in Tunisia: Report of a Study by Actif Consulting & STARC Consulting as Joint Liability Consortiums and Funded by the World Bank], Tunis: Tunisian Ministry of Communication Technologies.

Murphy, E. (2003) 'Women in Tunisia: between state feminism and economic reform', in E. A. Doumato and M. P. Posusney (eds), *Women and Globalisation in the Arab Middle East*, Boulder, CO: Lynne Rienner, pp. 169–94.

OECD and Banque africaine de développement, Centre de développement de l'Organisation de Coopération et de Développement Economiques (2009) *Perspectives économiques en Afrique: notes par pays volumes 1 et 2, Volume complémentaire aux perspectives économiques en Afrique 2009 : Synthèse* [African Economic Outlook: Country Notes Volumes 1 and 2, Complementary Volume to the 2009 African Economic Outlook: Synthesis], Paris: OCDE.

Organisation Internationale du Travail (2011) *Études sur la croissance et l'équité: Tunisie – un nouveau contrat social pour une croissance juste et équitable* [Studies on Growth and Equity: Tunisia – A New Social Contract for a Just and Equitable Growth], www.ilo.org/public/french/bureau/inst/download/country_tf.pdf, accessed 19 February 2013.

Rabaaoui-Essefi, N. (2001) 'La condition de la femme en Tunisie' [The woman's condition in Tunisia], in *La condition de la femme au Maghreb et en Méditerranée* [The Condition of Women in the Maghreb and in the Mediterranean], Tunis: Association des Etudes Internationales & Union Européenne, pp. 1–381.

Ruedy, J. (1994) *Islamism and Secularism in North Africa*, New York: St Martin's Press, pp. 1–298.

Sinha, S. (2011) 'Women's rights: Tunisian women in the workplace', *Journal of International Women's Studies*, 12(3): 185–200.

Wilmots, A. (2003) *De Bourguiba à Ben Ali: l'étonnant parcours économique de la Tunisie (1960–2000)* [Of Bourguiba to Ben Ali: The Astonishing Economic Path of Tunisia (1960–2000)], Paris: L'Harmattan, pp. 1–148.

7 | Hiba's quest for freedom: ICT and gender-based violence in Yemen

ROKHSANA ISMAIL AND RADIA SHAMSHER
WAJED ALI

Introduction

The study on which this chapter is based explored how Yemeni women who experience gender-based violence (GBV) in their domestic lives have used information and communication technology (ICT) in an effort to stand up for themselves and create free and independent lives. Yemen is a traditional society where women are considered minors in their relationships with male relatives, as 'property' in relation to their husbands. Because of the culture of 'honour and shame', they cannot speak out freely. Divorce – even when the marriage is abusive – is not a simple issue. To illustrate how the use of ICT can help women in Yemen to stand up to domestic abuse and create a free and independent life, we present the story of Hiba, a woman from Aden, who we followed and supported over a period of two years.

Background: social context

Yemen was ranked last of 135 countries in the 2012 *Global Gender Gap Report* (World Economic Forum 2012: 358). Hiba is from Aden in South Yemen, and this is significant to her story. Aden is quite different from the rest of Yemen due to the fact that the city is an ex-British colony where the active role of women in daily life and in solving family matters was accepted in families and by the community at large as a matter of normal conduct (Al-Alas 2006: 9), in accordance with the inherited British norms. Also, after independence in 1967, when Aden saw strict implementation of the law of the Republic of South Yemen, little was changed in the domain of women's rights. The reason for this could have been the favourable economic conditions and equal citizenship rights that prevailed at that time; disputes relating to women's rights were resolved either by the judiciary or through family relations. The heritage of equality and equal opportunities for both men and women was maintained. This is evident in the laws that were issued, such as the Family Law of 1974 and others, in which women's social, economic, cultural and political rights were recognized (Manea 2010: 546): 'It would be appropriate to say that women in Aden had many opportunities and a supportive environment for empowerment, until the declaration of Yemeni Unity on 22 May 1990.'

After unification things changed for Aden as a result of bringing together North and South Yemen into one political dispensation. These two regions were vastly different in terms of cultural, socioeconomic and geographical aspects, and unification was a major blow to almost all advancements gained and achievements made by women in Aden. Furthermore, the unification coincided with two factors that contributed to the deterioration of the whole country from a political, social and economic perspective: the 1990–93 Gulf War, which caused more than 1.5 million Yemeni citizens to return home from Gulf States, and the civil war of 1994. The repatriate Yemenis brought with them thoughts, beliefs and practices that previously had not been prominent in Yemeni society, and definitely not in Aden. One of these was Wahhabism, which prescribed the exclusion of women from the public sphere, their place and work being confined to the field of managing the household and child-rearing, having to wear the black body-covering dress known as the full *hijab*, early marriage for girls[1] and restrictions on women speaking up as women's voices are regarded as 'blemished' (Shamsher 2006: 17).[2]

Incidences of physical, sexual and verbal violence against women escalated, clearly indicating the increasing constraints on and male control over women's lives (Shamsher 2006: 19). It has to be noted, however, that even so family law in South Yemen gave women more scope to fight GBV. This is important, because, although GBV also occurs in the South, having a good law in place that protects women's rights gives women the strength and the motivation to stand up for themselves.

Methodology

In order to gain an understanding of the way Yemeni women coped with the escalating GBV and to advise policy-makers as to what could be done to support women and change their situations, we conducted action research over the period May 2010–June 2012 that comprised cycles of exploration and intervention.

We worked with thirty-four women in total. We used two non-directive, controlled in-depth qualitative research methods that guided our data collection and data analysis: free attitude interviews (Buskens 2005) and the transformational attitude interview (see Chapter 22). As interventions we created and broadcast radio and television programmes designed to raise awareness about women's rights and GBV. These were developed with the cooperation of non-governmental organizations[3] in Aden that deal with GBV. We also produced a play on CD and various workshops and television programmes, all showcasing the rights women have according to the Yemeni constitution.[4]

To convey what we learnt in this two-year period we have chosen to tell Hiba's story; this story of her life and the choices she made using information communication technologies (ICTs) for her empowerment enable us to share many aspects of women's struggles in Yemen, highlighting how a woman in such conditions can make good use of ICTs.

Using the free attitude interviews and transformational attitude interviews in conjunction allowed us, together with Hiba, to reach into her mind and soul and become acquainted with her sufferings, answering questions such as, 'Who is Hiba?' and 'What is she suffering from, and what is she dreaming of?'. Many other questions relating to her life and situation revealed themselves at various points on this journey. Using these methods created the space for Hiba to go deeply into recognizing and understanding her feelings and to pay attention to her fears, weaknesses and strengths; these methods also created opportunities for us to be attentive to moments of silence, confusion and contradictions, the goal being to get to moments of truth.

What our intervention meant for Hiba

The research interventions were designed to reinforce Hiba's (and the other research participants') desire for change and their subsequent actions during the various stages of their journeys. Over a two-year period we continued to meet with Hiba and continued our in-depth interviews. Our intent was to understand her struggles, thinking and decisions, and contribute to her own reflection on and understanding of the changes she was undertaking and how she was empowering herself, starting from her determination to escape from a life of violence with her husband. She found support in our interventions while embarking on this new path: 'Your programme on radio and TV was very useful for me, to give me more power to continue my life depending on myself.'

Facts and data revealed and spoken about on our television and radio programmes were certainly indicators of the current situation of violence against women and GBV in Aden, providing chances to open direct dialogue with the community and raise this critical issue. We never felt embarrassed or shy dealing with audiences and listeners, who appreciated our participation revealing violence against women and GBV. This was the first time the culture of shame and the belief that the voices of women are 'blemished' had been so publicly broken. While our media programmes focused on issues that concerned the whole of society, the messages presented in the workshops raised awareness that ICTs are important tools that can be used by women and for women in their stand against domestic violence.

Hiba's story

Childhood, marriage and asking for a divorce

Hiba comes from a middle-class family and was born in Aden in 1987. Growing up, Hiba experienced a context of family relations based on mutual respect and understanding between her father and her mother. However, her mother's sudden death when Hiba was seventeen years old created an unstable and complicated situation for the whole family, especially for her. She had to leave school in order to take responsibility for looking after her father and the household.

The main problem for Hiba was that her father couldn't cope with the death of his wife and started to take his anger and agony out on her, treating her violently and abusing her verbally. He placed the whole responsibility of the household on Hiba, who was the only other person in the house because her other sisters were married.

Hiba accepted the first marriage proposal that came her way, from a man from Sana'a in northern Yemen, in order to get away from the psychological pressures she faced at home. She said:

> My father persuaded me to marry a man from Sana'a, where I was seriously shocked after a couple of months – my husband started treating me violently; it was beyond my expectations! My husband treated me as though I'm a piece of furniture, thinking that he can do whatever he wants.

Suffering her husband's daily abuse, she used her mobile phone to take pictures of her physical wounds in the privacy of the bathroom. She needed this evidence of her abuse because she wanted to request a divorce: in Yemen only men have the right to grant a divorce. Women can merely request a divorce, and in order for their request to be taken into consideration in court they need to be able to prove that they were harmed by their husbands.[5] So Hiba used the photos she took with her mobile phone to prove the physical harm her husband had inflicted on her.

In doing this she broke an unspoken rule: sexual relations between a husband and wife are a private matter in all Muslim and Arab societies. When something is amiss, this should not be spoken about or revealed. Yet Hiba documented with the camera built into her mobile phone the evidence of her husband's brutal beating on her thighs. Doing this was not easy for Hiba: she had to overcome the deeply internalized cultural commandment of keeping private what should remain private. Her act was also risky socially: her community could have taken her 'coming out with her abuse' in the wrong way and stigmatized her for breaking the cultural code of silence and privacy. Her urge to be free from her husband, however, was so strong that she could face even this.

With the help of her husband's brother, Hiba was able to flee to Aden with her three-year-old daughter, Hanan. However, awaiting her was a police warrant accusing her of kidnapping the child; no doubt it was her husband who had informed the police. The pictures that Hiba had taken using her mobile phone proved her husband's abuse, and she could therefore plead the legitimacy of her request for a divorce at the Aden Court. Hiba was granted a divorce and guardianship of her daughter. However, Hiba's husband rejected the decision of the court in Aden and appealed to the Sana'a Court, practising his right as a man in the sense that only he can grant a divorce and nobody else.

Hiba's husband subsequently kidnapped Hanan and took the child back to Sana'a, where he now lived with a second wife. While the child was staying with him he took great efforts to impress upon the child that her stepmother was her real mother, and that Hiba ('the one in Aden') was the 'auntie'. Hiba gave us more hints of her suffering as a mother:

> It was during Ied Al-Fiter when he called the family asking to see his daughter. As a father, I felt that he has the right to see her, especially given that it is a festival day. I never imagined that he would be using tricky methods showing his daughter how he feels sad and desperate not able to see her every now and then. After a couple of hours I felt worried because I know his ways of his cheating. I informed my husband's brother about my worries; he calmed me down but he himself later on took an action towards informing the police station of the whole story, where the police discovered that he had left to Sana'a with Hanan. It was a big shock for me – I seemed not to have learnt my lessons yet about this man's devious behaviour.

Kidnapping is common in Yemen by people who feel that they are above the law. Hiba's case was, however, already known to the police station in the Malaa district where she lives. The moment she found out about the kidnapping of her daughter, she got her family and her husband's relatives involved and managed to get Hanan back.

Building an independent life: the request for divorce continues
In order to earn an income, Hiba started developing her skills in handicrafts, using her mobile phone to market her products and trying

to manage the challenges of daily living as a single parent in order to be able to afford to meet at least the most important needs of her daughter and herself. To earn a more reliable income and continue to maintain and build her and her daughter's independent future, Hiba developed her computer skills by taking a one-year course. This allowed her to get a job with a monthly income of US$200, which enabled her to try for her divorce again, seeking Al-Khula'a. Al-Khula'a is a *shariaa* act by which Muslim women can free themselves from domestic violence committed by their husbands, such as beating or insulting. The wife pays compensation to the husband to free herself with the dowry given to her by her husband upon marriage. This dowry is often transferred in gold or gold jewellery. The husband is then obliged to give the woman her divorce. Unfortunately for Hiba she had already given her dowry back to her husband so that he could restart his commercial business; he had convinced her that when it was on its feet he would return the money. When she gave him her dowry she had felt that she could not ask him for a receipt, because she saw this as a sign of mistrust in him and their marriage.

While waiting for the court verdict, Hiba started to create a new social life for herself using ICTs to connect with people she could relate to:

> I'm benefitting during my working hours using e-mail, Facebook, communicating with my friends, exchanging with them my feelings and sufferings, at the same time getting advice from them, sharing my problems, encouraging me to continue through the Internet to get information on cases similar to my case.

The Internet also provided Hiba with a great deal of support in terms of getting information related to her marital status and problems. She said, 'Talking to women on the net helped me a lot; some of them became my best friends, and I hope that one day we can meet.'

She ended by saying:

> I found that the Internet is very useful to get information about taking care of children. It saves me time and money; using this tool I do not have to get books and information from other sources. I can enjoy my time chatting and sending jokes, cards and e-mails to friends, which I choose online.

Hiba discovered through chatting on the Internet that she is not alone; many women find themselves in similar situations of experiencing violence and seeking divorce, and online networks of mutual support and sharing of important information have arisen. Hiba has also spread her social networks beyond her immediate circles; accessing information and advice, and finding new friends has made the Internet more than a means to meet her needs for material and social survival. Finding intimacy and camaraderie so 'close by' through the Internet when cultural norms isolate women makes ICT very pertinent for women in Yemen.

Hiba continues her quest to get a divorce

Hiba's court case is still pending. The fact remains that, should she lose her case asking for Al-Khula'a, her husband would be able to get her back as a second wife. 'Discrimination against women in matters concerning marriage, divorce and child custody, according to the Personal Status Law (No. 20 of 1992) and its amendments, clearly stipulates that a wife must obey her husband by deferring to his choice for their place of residence' (Manea 2010: 15).

At the end of 2012, Hiba approached the Higher Council of the Judiciary for help. In the aftermath of the Arab Spring revolution, many changes took place within Yemeni society; notable was the appointment of two female judges in the Higher Council of the Judiciary. Our intervention continued in the form of the television and radio programmes that focused on GBV issues, which were presented by us and in the form of workshops presented by non-governmental organizations. All this may have encouraged Hiba to take her request for a divorce to the highest authority in Yemen.

If Hiba is able to get her divorce this will mean a true victory, not only for her but also for many women. During the past decade Al-Khula'a has been purposefully neglected as an option for women in the Personal Status Law, due to the differences in culture and education between the North and the South and the strict religious, conservative mindset of the judges appointed in this period.

Still not free ...

From a subordinated woman Hiba has grown into a self-confident, independent woman with the courage to face her reality with a new vision of life. In addition, obtaining a job paying US$200 per month made Hiba realize that she was quite capable of getting her child back and looking after her.

Even so, Hiba is still afraid of the future: she is aware of the fact that her husband wants her and the child back, not because he wants to love and care for them but because he considers them his property and wants to punish her for leaving him: 'I received many calls from my husband threatening to kill me if I do not come back to him with my child. I sleep with a knife under my pillow ... I need to get a divorce.' She realizes that the legal system does not protect her because of the shortcomings in the Personal Status Law and the force of old traditions, and she dreads having to return to her husband as his second wife.[6]

Discussion

Exceptional as she was in her courage and determination, Hiba's case has shown that women in Yemen can use ICT to defend themselves against GBV and create new selves and new realities. The conflict between her dreams and her daily reality sparked her journey of change. She was able to succeed by using ICTs in various ways and overcame various barriers. As mentioned by Maltzahn (2010), privacy has always been a double-edged sword for women, because women coming out publicly break the cultural code of silence and might face stigmatization. Equipping herself with the evidence of her abuse, Hiba challenged the culture of women's shame and isolation of which she was part and pursued her freedom nonetheless.

Hiba also had to overcome economic barriers, as 'women's economic rights and opportunities in Yemen are undermined by social barriers as well as deficiencies in the state's ability to implement and coordinate its economic development efforts' (Manea 2010: 557). The constraints Hiba faced spanned both her private and social spheres: 'The guardianship of a man on a woman in Yemeni community exceeds the private scope of a family to the general scope which is evident in standardization in public functions and public life' (Ismail and Al-Saem 2010: 149).

Buskens (2010: 20) mentioned that 'ICT can be instrumental in enabling women to empower themselves economically and otherwise; to connect and communicate across physical, social, cultural, ethnic and religious boundaries; to draft new identities for themselves; and to challenge the environments that are coherent with their "old selves"'. We can see how Hiba was confronting both her old environment and her old self in her journey towards freedom and dignity.

Hiba's personal development using ICT reflects the conclusions of Unwin (2009: 375), who indicated that 'it is possible to use ICTs to support and empower people to become better educated, to live healthier lives, and to gain fairer incomes'. Hiba's life story also speaks to the experience that, as Mosedale (2005: 244) argues:

> Empowerment is an ongoing process rather than a product. There is no final goal. One does not arrive at a stage of being empowered in some absolute sense. People are empowered, or disempowered, relative to others or, importantly, relative to themselves at a previous time.

We, however, also agree with Gurumurthy (cited in Spence 2010: 71), when she states that the ability to harness technology is political. It involves a shift in power relations that reflects women's needs, interests and aspirations. Through her personal journey of empowerment, Hiba challenged the masculinized political landscape in Yemen.

Even given all the positive and empowering aspects of ICT, there is a limit as to what ICTs could do for Hiba, even while she put them to optimum use. The real alteration that would make a difference in her life is a change in the Personal Status Law. The current situation in Yemen is very clearly described by Manea (2012: 3) as follows: 'Traditional rules, prevalent cultural attitudes that accord women a low status in the family and the community, and State-sanctioned discriminatory law together limit women's rights and opportunity.'

The question that remains is thus whether we have the collective political will as Yemeni people to work together to deliver such initiatives. This will not only allow processes of real women's empowerment but also free ICT to deliver on its promise to contribute to development, so that the least advantaged can share in the benefits that so many people around the world now take for granted.

Conclusion

While An-Naim (1990: 30) recognizes the difficulty in applying universal values to cultural norms, because each culture has its own context, he establishes that 'there are two forces that drive human behaviour, namely the will to live and the will to be free, which imply and augment each other. What is life without freedom? How can one safeguard one's life when one is not free? These two forces drive not only every person but also every culture and tradition.' We should thus, in our striving towards women's empowerment, not leave control over the arrangement of issues such as poverty and welfare policies in the hands of the masculinized state. The dilemma we are facing here is that male guardianship over women is a fundamental concept that drives Muslim communities and shapes their cultures to the degree that patriarchy is all-pervasive (Hussein 2011: 35).

The interrelationship between political, statutory and customary laws and culture is quite explicit in Yemen. The tribal legacy has imposed its normative system on politics and law. Yemen has a dual legal system, which reflects the inability of the state power to impose the rule of law and a system of justice.[7] Aleem al-Soswa, a Yemeni feminist and the first female Minister of Human Rights, emphasized this notion by raising the slogan that 'women's rights are human rights are Islamic rights', denying the split between secularism and Islamism

(Sunder 2003: 30). Moreover, the lack of female judges, prosecutors and lawyers discourages women from turning to the courts. Given the social discrimination experienced by women, they hesitate to approach male legal consultants, particularly on issues such as abuse or rape. Instead, women often rely on male relatives to go to court in their place, or turn to them to solve their problem rather than taking the matter to the judiciary (Hussein 2011: 36).

Most women will not be able to do what Hiba did: taking her case to court and standing face to face with a judge. In the current situation it is very complicated to raise the question of changes in the Personal Status Law of 1992. However, as researchers we must not lose hope that the activities resulting from the 2013 National Dialogue Conference, which include a focus on women's issues,[8] may lead to reforms. Hiba's case has convinced us, however, that there can be no effective legal reform without actual societal and institutional reform in Yemen.

Acknowledgements

Thanks to the field researchers, Dr Nadia Sallam Haider and Dr Farial Manaa Algaber, who assisted us with conducting in-depth interviews. Thanks also go to the non-governmental organizations that assisted us: the Yemeni Women's Union – Aden, the Al-Aidroos Association for Eliminating Poverty and Empowering Women, the Arab Foundation for Supporting Women and Juvenile Issues (www.afswj.com) and the Yemeni Psychological Association.

Notes

1 There is no minimum age for marriage currently. For example, using the Personal Status Law of 1992, the marriage of Nugood at the age of nine or ten years to a man twenty-two years older than her was condoned.

2 Women's voices are *awra*: this means 'blemished' and it implies that women's voices should not be heard.

3 These organizations were the Yemeni Women's Union – Aden, the Al-Aidroos Association for Eliminating Poverty and Empowering Women, the Arab Foundation for Supporting Women and Juvenile

Issues and the Yemeni Psychological Association.

4 It is clearly noted in Item 32 of the Yemeni constitution (amended 2002) that the state 'shall provide the facilities and opportunities necessary to enhance the welfare of women to enable them to realize their full potential and advancement; the state shall protect women and their rights, taking into account their unique status and natural maternal functions in society; women shall have the right to equal treatment with men and that right shall include equal opportunities in political, economic and social activities;

... women shall have the right to affirmative action for the purpose of redressing the imbalances created by history, tradition or custom; laws, cultures, which are against the dignity, welfare or interest of women or which undermine their status, are prohibited'.

5 Article 59 of the Personal Status Law stipulates that a man may divorce his wife at will, without providing a reason, yet a woman seeking a divorce must resort to a court if she wishes to obtain one and can only do so on very limited grounds and with solid proof. On applying the Khula, which is supposed to support a woman's will to terminate the marriage contract in exchange for her financial rights, the legislator allows the divorce on condition of the husband's approval. Again, the legislator is responsive to the patriarchal norms dominant in Yemen and not even to Sharia law. At the level of tribal law, divorce is one of the core issues that is now allowed to be solved by arbitration.

6 The issue of polygamy is one of the most complicated and sensitive problems in Yemeni society. The Personal Status Law (No. 20 of 1992) and its amendments, article 12, paragraph 1, states: 'polygamy is permitted for the man up to four if the capability of justice between the four is guaranteed, otherwise one only is enough'.

7 No progress has been reported on implementation of the Convention of the Elimination of Discrimination against Women in Yemen. Women's access to identity and travel documents continues to depend on the permission of male guardians, and the Personal Status Law remains discriminatory in its unequal treatment of husband and wife in their family relations.

8 The National Dialogue Conference, supported by United Nations agencies, was held in the period March–September 2013 under the auspices of the Yemeni Presidents' Office. The conference participants, of which 30 per cent were women, focused on, among other things, a new constitution in which women's rights will be included.

References

Al-Alas, A. (2006) 'Position of Yemeni women in Aden during the British colony', paper presented at the Workshop on German Arab Universities Dialogue, Oldenburg, 26–30 May.

An-Naim, A. (1990) *Towards an Islamic Reformation: Civil Liberties, Human Rights, and International Law*, Cairo: American University in Cairo in arrangement with Syracuse University Press.

Buskens , I. (2005) *Free Attitude Interview Manual*, http://issuu. com/gracenetwork/docs/fai__ final, accessed 20 May 2014.

— (2010) 'Agency and reflexivity in ICT4D: research – questioning women's options, poverty, and human development', *Information Technologies & International Development*, 6: 20.

Hussein, D. (2011) 'Legal reform as a way to women's rights: the case of Personal Status Law in Yemen', *International Journal of Sustainable Development*, 3(6): 21–46.

Ismail, R. and N. Al-Saem (2010) *Gender-Based Violence in Yemen: Quantitative and Qualitative Analysis*, Sana'a: United Nations Population Fund.

Maltzahn, K. (2010) 'Argentina: strategic use of ICT as a response to violence against women', www.genderit.org/es/node/3119, accessed 23 July 2010.

Manea, E. (2010) 'Yemen women's status – new', in S. Kelly and J. Breslin (eds), *Women's Rights in the Middle East and North Africa*, New York: Freedom House, pp. 545–76.

— (2012) *The Perils of Yemen's Cunning State (NOREF Report)*, Oslo: Norwegian Peacebuilding Resource Centre.

Mosedale, S. (2005) 'Policy arena – assessing women's empowerment: towards a conceptual framework', *Journal of International Development*, 17(2): 243–57.

Shamsher, R. (2006) 'Women's status during the period 1967–1990', paper presented at the Workshop on German Arab Universities Dialogue, Oldenburg, 26–30 May.

Spence, N. (2010) 'Theory, gender, ICTs, human development, and prosperity', *Information Technologies & International Development*, 6: 69–73.

Sunder, M. (2003) 'Piercing the veil', *Yale Law Journal*, 112: 1401–11.

Unwin, T. (2009) *ICT4D – The Technologies: Identifying Appropriate Solutions for Development Needs*, Cambridge: Cambridge University Press.

World Economic Forum (2012) *The Global Gender Gap Report*, www3.weforum.org/docs/WEF_ GenderGap_Report_2012.pdf, accessed 1 July 2013.

TWO | **Developing critical voice in and through safe ICT-created space**

8 | ICT in a time of sectarian violence: reflections from Kafanchan, northern Nigeria

KAZANKA COMFORT AND JOHN DADA

Introduction

This chapter is based on a spontaneous qualitative study of the way women used mobile phones, in combination with social networks on the ground, to sustain individual, family and community resilience during the 17 April 2011 sectarian crisis that engulfed our communities in Kafanchan, Nigeria.

When the political crisis struck,[1] the Fantsuam Foundation (FF), the organization that we'd founded ten years previously, was approaching its peak of achievement. It had grown into the leading rural development organization in Kafanchan, with its services spread out over ten chiefdoms of Kaduna State, serving a population of over 1.5 million. Next to the government, the FF is the largest employer in Kafanchan. This highly visible presence was one of the reasons that a large number of displaced women and children took refuge here during the crisis.

Loud sounds of gunshots coming from various directions throughout the night marked the sudden political crisis that erupted in the small town of Kafanchan as a result of a disputed presidential election. At dawn news reached us that people were being killed, both Christians and Muslims. As we stood outside our home feeling frightened and confused, we saw a lot of people coming into our small village. Most of the women and children started coming towards our house, so we had to leave the gates of our compound, which was the FF compound, open for them from around 7:30 a.m. Many were still in shock, fearful and confused, and feeling helpless. We spread out mats and chairs so that people could sit on the floor in the compound. We got our older children to start preparing breakfast for the first set of arrivals of around sixty women and children with a few men. By afternoon, as we tried to prepare lunch, more people had arrived. By evening the number had increased to about two hundred.

The women seeking refuge with us soon started using their mobile phones to call friends and distant relations. I remember one of the women in the sitting room was making calls right through the night. It was difficult to get regular and honest information during this period. The security uncertainties and the poor information flow from authorities created a heightened sense of fear and made mobile phones prized possessions.

The mobile phone is the predominant ICT in Nigeria. There were 148,161,358 connected lines by April 2013 ('Wiring Nigeria' n.d.), making it the fastest growing mobile phone market in Africa (Africa Business Pages n.d.). This high mobile phone penetration made it a significant means of communication in the post-election crises. The country has poor telecommunications infrastructure and experiences frequent quality-of-service problems (ITU News 2011; 'Wiring Nigeria' n.d.), a higher literacy rate among men than women ('National literacy main report' n.d.) and an existing rich oral culture. The last two factors make mobiles the preferred communication technology, especially among rural illiterate women.[2] The fact that only 60 women out of the 155 at the refuge centre had their phones with them may have been a reflection of the haste with which they escaped from their homes. With barely enough time to escape from their homes in areas overtaken by fighting or arson, the only possession some of the women could salvage was their mobile phone and this became a lifeline to information, emergency help, food, medicines, protection, remittances and networks (Njeru 2009).

What was remarkable, in hindsight, as we take stock of those difficult days, was that more within the FF compound and among the two hundred refugees did not go terribly wrong. Blind hatred for the opposing side was accepted behaviour during the crises. Anonymous SMSs and phone calls were being used to spread rumours of impending sectarian attacks. In the Kenyan experience blogs and SMS were used to fan ethnic hatred (Zarro 2012). The mandatory mobile phone registration service, which would make tracing such calls possible, had yet to be implemented in Nigeria at this time. These inflammatory SMSs could have originated from women or men from either of the warring factions. While security agents said that some of the SMSs were the work of pranksters and should be ignored, rumours at the FF refuge were 'frequently perceived as truths' (Collender 2010) and such rumours took precedence over government or broadcast media accounts. In these times of conflict ICT, mobile phones especially proved to be a double-edged sword that could promote unity or exacerbate the fault lines of tribes and religions.

This chapter therefore seeks to understand how our spontaneously formed refuge of women, children and a few men in this time of crisis had the capacity to resist the divisive destruction of the sectarian conflict.

What actions, values, characteristics and attributes of our FF refuge, our guests and ourselves as the founders and hosts made this possible?

Methodology

The study and learning experience took place during this critical and politically unstable situation within a context of limited resources and urgent humanitarian needs. In-depth group discussions, informal groups and one-on-one discussions informed this study; however, participant observation was the most informative process. Supporting a group of traumatized and vulnerable adults and children requires thinking on one's feet to determine and deploy available resources optimally. It was during such encounters that the discussions and observations would take place. Close to 150 women and men were interviewed in this way.

Weaving in and out of the roles of participant and observer, while supporting traumatized refugees, was demanding: while discussing needs, fears and issues, we were watching ourselves and observing the discussants.

Elements that helped ground and guide us in this time of upheaval were the values and practices we had imbued in the FF since its early days. The organization maintains a studied political independence and religious neutrality in the implementation of its programmes. These values make it impossible for sectarian interests and other biases to feature in its services. We see this as a prized value that makes FF accessible to all its clients. Therefore its reputation for equity and fairness may be another reason for the steady influx of displaced persons to the organization; in the circumstances, we saw their recourse to the FF as an endorsement of this stand.

Taking a ground-up approach, the FF remains focused on recognizing the needs of its communities, as determined by them. The community is assisted to focus on the concrete steps that are required to meet those needs, irrespective of the external (national and global) circumstances that may not be favourable to them. The FF's role is to stand with the communities to address those inequity issues within their reach while advocating on their behalf for those issues that are patently outside their control. It is this understanding and unwritten pact, between the FF and its host communities, that informed our reactions to the politically motivated communal disaster of April 2011. Our mission and how we work are grounded in understanding and appreciation of the homegrown traditional values of non-violent communication (Rosenberg 2003: 9).

When the FF was established, the founding team explored the various indigenous social-change processes and challenges that already existed within the Kafanchan social milieu. Kafanchan was an unusual blend of tribes, religions, economic attainments and political inclinations, all working within a depressed rural economy. It was the awareness of these realities that informed the design of the projects and programmes, ensuring that they served the identified needs of the population.

Non-violent communication is an age-old tradition among the Kafanchan communities, and it is a responsibility assigned to elders. This communication is largely orally mediated and face to face. It has evolved over the years and elders (females and males) are especially respected because they are regarded as repositories of communal history and arbiters of issues that require historical context.

It was instructive that elders' voices were not evident in the Kafanchan crisis. The elders' voices are traditionally used to prevent outbreaks of violence through negotiation, needs identification, clarification and authentication of claims. However, this traditional role has been largely neglected, and the FF found itself in the role of applying this approach across the sectarian divide. In the elders' absence, we were determined to 'stay connected to [our] compassionate nature under even the most trying circumstances' (Rosenberg 2003: 8).

Findings: the role of communication

The influx of displaced persons into the FF can be seen as an expected response based on the mutual trust and respect that have developed between the organization and its host communities. For the traumatized, close-knit communities of Kafanchan, and especially for those who have been beneficiaries of the multi-faceted interventions of the FF, the organization provided a community atmosphere that engendered safety, trust and a spirit of sharing. Taking refuge at the FF was an affirmation of their trust in the organization. The refugees were further united by a sense of infringements of their rights to self-determination as equal citizens.

Women who fled their homes with their children in the dark could not move with confidence in search of safety. In addition to the danger and fear they faced due to the conflict, traditional restrictions on women's physical mobility that are rooted in social norms,[3] customs and family responsibilities affected their ability to chart their escape routes during the violence. This was even more confounding for Muslim women who were in *purdah*.

In spite of the constraints and distress, shared interests were rallying points and drew people together for rational discussions and analysis on how to sustain the communities. Discussions among many of the clusters of women at the refuge often centred on conflict prevention, resolution, peace-building and post-conflict governance, focusing on the preservation and continuation of their communities: 'It is not possible that the mere loss of an election by one of the political parties has been the cause of all the violence we suffered.' 'We must insist that politicians play by the rules, and get disqualified when they break the rules.' Although there were disagreements on culpability and the causes of the violence, this did not lead to a break-off of discussions, as was observed among the few males in the refuge.

There was a consensus that the conflict was entirely preventable, and that, although women were hardly consulted in the run-up to the crisis, they and their children were not spared its consequences. 'My son and his friends had no business getting involved in all these troubles.' 'Why do men fight wars where there can never be a winner?' 'Our neighbours have been at this war long before us, and up till now there is no peace, why do we have to repeat the same mistakes?' 'The politicians have set us against each other while they have escaped with their families. I haven't seen any of the politicians injured or killed in this battle, why can't our men see through this deception?' There was also a concern about the urgent business of ensuring the survival of their dependants (the elderly and children): 'My husband insisted on protecting our house, and now look what has happened to him, he is dead, and I am left alone to look after our children and our aged parents.' 'Our farm is very far in the bush; I and my children should be busy clearing the land before the rains arrive, but look at where we are.'

The women at this refuge were not there out of their own choosing; each person came with their experience and entrenched positions. They were a diverse population with differing ideas of what constitutes the values of community service and common good. The whole panoply of human emotions was on display: anger, desire for war, altruism, withdrawal. There was a minority of women, for instance, who would boast of their male relatives who had sustained bullet wounds: 'Unless there is bloodshed, those people will never accept that they are not superior to us in any way. My husband is at the forefront of this battle and I fully support him.'

Some of the discussants in the clusters tended to attribute the fundamental causes of the crises to poverty and social inequity, while the men tended to hold tenaciously to their perspectives based on perceived religious and ethnic superiority. As one of the women observed, 'if our men were to succeed in killing off all the men from the other tribe and religion, how does that create job opportunities for them, reduce the incidence of home burglaries, improve the state of our schools, hospitals or repair our roads?' The men sometimes described the actions by the women, in the politically charged and unstable environment, as betrayal or foolishness. Although some scoffed by saying, 'these women think these issues are so simple?' they had no ready response to the 'simple' queries of the women.

Women at the refuge said they used their phones to track other displaced family members, to mobilize remittances, to confirm the safety of business associates and to reach across to families and friends on the opposing side. They used SMSs and calls to mobilize support, to negotiate safe passage with marauding youths and community elders, to buy food with phone credits and to spread information about outbreaks of violence.

Through phone conversations with friends and relations located in other cities with access to the Internet and radio, especially BBC World Service (which regularly broadcasts in the main language spoken in Kafanchan, Hausa), the women became better informed about possible flashpoints and they used their networks for approximate mapping of danger zones. When we tried to trace the sources of external news in the refuge, such as about the arrival of security forces, we were referred to certain women, who would usually say they got the news through phone calls from their contacts within or outside the security services. They would often quickly disseminate such news to their friends and contacts within and outside the confines of the refuge. In this way, the technology helped to improve the individual and communal responses to the tragic events.

For us as participant observers trying to remain sufficiently observant in order to understand the needs that were being expressed both verbally and non-verbally in a crowded refuge space, the events had moments of anxiety, exhaustion, anger, diffidence, elation, trust and reassurance. We had to cope with the heightened emotional, intellectual and physical demands of a new application of our leadership role. While our individual needs for psychosocial support had to be subsumed to the needs of the two hundred refugees, the daily e-mail contact with the outside world, within and outside Nigeria, reinforced by Skype chats and phone calls (locally and internationally), helped us to feel supported, to remain focused and to transmit a sense of hope to the members of the refuge.

Soon after the height of the violence, the women who were interviewed said they used mobile phones 'to confirm if she is still my friend'. The conflict's destruction of mutual trust required the gentle, gradual but persistent reaching-out strategy of the women. The mobile phones allowed them to reach out to grieving friends and families without the intrusion of personal space while offering reassurance of continuity of pre-crisis friendships and bonds. The distance offered by the mobile phones helped the women to check that their friends still had the space, interest and will to re-establish severed contacts and start the process of rebuilding old trusts and interdependencies.

The Kafanchan communities were awash with dangerous weapons during the crisis. Unconfirmed reports said both men and women were running guns and making quick profits. Only the security agents would have the details of such activities in the run-up to and after the crisis. This lack of public information was partly the cause of rumours about the identity of the gun-runners, and this fuelled the distrust prevalent in the communities, adding another dimension to the need to use mobile phones as a first step 'to confirm if she is still my friend'.

As normality slowly returned to the estranged communities, it is significant that only women had the freedom to go across the invisible dividing lines between the warring factions. The mutual suspicion between men on the opposite sides made them feel unsafe. The old habit of going to 'greet my neighbour' took on a new meaning after the crisis. To go and 'greet my neighbour' now meant going across the 'enemy lines', and, with unconfirmed reports of secret and reprisal killings, anyone attempting to go and 'greet' the neighbours immediately aroused attention, first concern about the safety of such an action and second suspicion about the genuineness and motive of such a visit – why visit 'our enemies' at such a time? The first women to take such steps attracted the sanction of their families, and were often derided as 'foolish', 'feminine' and 'cowardly'. It was considered a betrayal to think or talk of restoring old relationships with those now on the other side.

Discussion

When mobile phones became lifelines in the Kafanchan crises, their use brought to the fore the determination, commitment and passion of the users. The mobile was no longer an inert object; it assumed a crucial role in the life of its users, conveying their physical and emotional deprivation and how their personalities rose to meet these challenges. The fluid security situation demanded constant review and evaluation, which were facilitated through the unofficial communications received through the mobile phones, including rumours, hate messages and genuine news. Mobile phones, with their capability for wide dissemination, thus had the potential for inflammation of an unstable political situation beyond all local control, starting with the FF refuge centre itself. But such a dire scenario did not happen. Why?

Why was it that the majority of the women at the refuge insisted that the sectarian conflict was irrational and argued that the causes of their harrowing experiences could not be resolved through further violence? That these women opted for a medium- and long-term view of the crisis is probably not surprising. Women in similar crisis situations in Angola, Liberia and Uganda (Institute for Inclusive Security n.d.) have been strategic in promoting long-term peace in their communities. The women are closer to the deprivations of daily life in Kafanchan: lack of water, poor roads, inhospitable hospitals, poor quality of education in the schools and lack of reliable grid electricity. Their focus is on meeting their own, their families' and their community's needs.

The survival of the social networks of those women who advocated a long-term solution was initially dependent on the use of mobiles, and later followed up with their daring face-to-face contacts. Rather than women's social networks and interdependencies – their means of social security – being shattered in this time of crisis, these electronic lifelines were put into the service of reducing the dismantling and damage brought to bear on these networks and support systems, and subsequently some members of the community were able to coalesce and recuperate, and even move forward when it became feasible to do so. Such rebuilding of networks and support systems would have been unaided by this avenue for communication in the pre-mobile phone era, when divisions and the destruction of community cohesion could not be mitigated by virtual support networks.

However, central and critical to the entire incident is the FF: its history, location, services and approach to engagement with its clients. The flow of refugees into the FF compound is a logical expression of the relationship that has developed over the years, between the organization and its host communities. The intensive interactions that happened within those spaces, at that critical period, are a continuum of mutual trust, compassion and respect that has been nurtured as the FF focused on clarifying, understanding and responding to needs – rather than analyzing and justifying who is right and who is wrong – in the fulfilment of its mandate of eliminating poverty (Rosenberg 2003: 9). The approach was embodied differently by each of us – Kazanka, John, our guests and the institutional identity itself. However, as we each responded differently to particular felt, witnessed, acknowledged and understood needs, we kept our focus on maintaining, sustaining and rebuilding what it takes to meet individual (including our own), family and community needs.

Conclusion

Although some of the people at the refuge were strangers to each other, they had been brought together by a communal catastrophe into a shared space, the FF refuge, where everyone felt safe. The most obvious unifying factor was their fear and sense of disempowerment: fear of the violence they had witnessed and experienced, sense of loss of rights to life and security as citizens. If there were any mutual suspicions, fear or disapproval of their new 'neighbours', this was not apparent. The ready access and acceptance the refugees received at the FF compound were constantly acknowledged. For those harrowing days, the FF represented a measure of continuity in their lives. The subsisting relationship between the organization and the refugees had an added value to it.

Although the FF had built a reputation for itself as a rural development champion, provision of leadership in a crisis situation was a skill we had to learn at short notice. Our approach to providing local leadership 'grounded in our natural state of compassion' (Rosenberg 2003: 13) in other spheres of rural development in peace time probably made this challenge easier to cope with. Recognition of the social-resilience processes that were apparent in the FF refuge during the crisis is now informing a new mode of rebuilding the peace of Kafanchan. Evidence is being gathered concerning the significance of the roles played by our organization; by some women who similarly took the approach of understanding and responding to needs by providing secret shelters and food in their attics for their at-risk male neighbours, in the face of rampaging weapon-wielding youths; and by those women who stood in front of angry youths and demanded that they drop their weapons and stopped them from engaging in reprisals. The traditional African value of respect for elderly persons is also being explored through an Elders Forum that deliberately includes women as members. The potential of elders' voices as a conflict-resolution strategy remains one of the issues that is being taken forward in order to build communal peace in Kafanchan.

Amid the crises caused by the sectarian conflicts, we have also discovered the type of interpersonal communication and mediation efforts that can bridge religious and tribal divides, and, when used wisely, ICT can accelerate their beneficial impact.

Recommendations

On the basis of our research we have come to the following recommendations:

1. The potential of women's networks to act as peace-building bridges between and among communities involved in conflicts should be recognized so that women can be engaged proactively.

2. Reactivating traditional conflict-resolution strategies, such as encouraging the peace-making role of elders, should be explored in conjunction with training in non-violent communication for women and youth leaders.

3. Since the Kafanchan communities are still experiencing occasional outbursts of violence, peace-building should be a regular feature of all development activities of organizations which are working in the region.

4. It would be good to engage a critical mass of people who live in conflict-prone communities in non-violent conflict-resolution skills such as non-violent communication and the types of communication and mediation mode that have developed in the FF.

Since mobile phones have been used to such positive effect in complementing and augmenting peace-building communication and mediation efforts, we argue that the role of ICT be further explored in relation to the above recommendations.

Notes

1 Nigeria's recurring cycle of violence triggered by ethnic and religious divisions can be traced to its pre- and post-colonial experience, which reinforced ethnic and religious identities as prerequisites for access to state resources. It was in 1914 that the northern and southern protectorates were amalgamated into the country that was named Nigeria, motivated by colonial rather than local interests. With a huge diversity of cultures (about 370 ethnic groups), three of which were dominant – the Hausa/Fulani in the north and the Yoruba and Igbo in the south – the union went into recurrent crises from 1962 to the present day, stagnating the country's potential for steady growth and development.

2 Nigeria's population of 162.5 million is made up of 49 per cent females (about 80.2 million girls and women). Nigeria's human development indicators show that 54 per cent still live in poverty and 42 per cent of Nigerian children are malnourished. These averages have not been desegregated for women and girls but poverty and malnutrition are considered to be worse for them. Therefore, any discussion about Nigeria's development must give due consideration to girls and women because the roles they play can have far-reaching consequences for human development and conflict mitigation.

3 For example, in October 2012, 1,226 Nigerian Muslim female pilgrims were denied entry into Saudi Arabia because they did not have approved male chaperons (Sahara Reporters 2012).

References

Africa Business Pages (n.d.) 'The market for mobile phones in Africa', www.africa-business.com/features/mobile_phones_africa.html, accessed 25 May 2014.

Collender, G. (2010) 'Crowdsourcing and rumour: the double-edged sword of ICTs in conflict situations', presented at ICT: Africa's Revolutionary Tools for the 21st Century? Edinburgh, 5 May.

Institute for Inclusive Security (n.d.) 'Why women: women are a powerful for for peace. Here's why', www.inclusivesecurity.org/why-women/#.U4GVxvldXIx, accessed 25 May 2014.

ITU News (2011) 'Nigerian Communications Commission: delivering broadband for development in Nigeria', June, www.itu.int/net/itunews/issues/2011/05/25.aspx, accessed 25 May 2014.

'National literacy main report' (n.d.), www.nigerianstat.gov.ng/uploads/latestRelease/de4f17834ea0c57a9e1f440d029aebaa460863d0.pdf, accessed 26 February 2012.

Njeru, S. (2009) 'Information and communication technology (ICT), gender, and peacebuilding in Africa: a case of missed connections', *The Peace and Conflict Review*, 3(2): 32–40.

Rosenberg, M. (2003) *Nonviolent Communication: A Language of Life*, 2nd edn, Encinitas, CA: PuddleDancer Press.

Sahara Reporters (2012) 'Saudis threatened deportation of 400 Nigerian female pilgrims "without approved chaperones"', 25 September, http://saharareporters.com/news-page/saudis-threatened-deportation-400-nigerian-female-pilgrims-%E2%80%9Cwithout-approved-chaperones%E2%80%9D-%C2%A0, accessed 25 May 2014.

'Wiring Nigeria' (n.d.), www.columbia.edu/itc/sipa/nelson/newmediadev/Nigeria%27s%20Infrastructural%20Challenges.html, accessed 25 May 2014.

Zarro, A. (2012) 'Africa's silent revolutions: what the headlines missed. An interview with Charles Onyango-Obbo', *The Forum: Society for Internaional Development*, 13 July, www.sidint.net/content/africas-silent-revolutions-what-headlines-missed-interview-charles-onyango-obbo, accessed 25 May 2014.

9 | Disconnecting from and in the public sphere, connecting online: Young Egyptian women expand their self-knowing beyond cultural and body-image dictates

MERVAT FODA AND ANNE WEBB

Introduction

The starting point for my research[1] was my interest in understanding the reasons that lead some young Egyptian women to feel ashamed of their body and to prefer to be unnoticed and out of sight, even in relation to their family and close friends. I wanted to understand why some young women over-eat or under-eat and are less active than is healthy and desirable. I also wanted to understand why access to online communication plays such a meaningful role for these young women.

While learning to eat and live healthily (from my perspective as a nutritionist) is one important step (Hassan et al. 2011), the importance and power of changing one's self-perception and sense of autonomy became increasingly apparent to me. I was particularly concerned to see how women isolated themselves due to name-calling and pressures put upon them to change their weight and behaviour. Was it that the young women's acceptance of and attachment to norms and values of their own culture were working against them and their sense of self-worth? How was their lowered sense of self-worth contributing to their harmful eating habits and dissatisfaction with their body image (Hatata et al. 2009: 42), and their attachment to online connections?

Seeing the contrast between my sense of self – having followed my chosen interests and career – and the missing sense of potential among the young women was striking. Recognition of one's own worth leads to seeing oneself as worthy of visualizing and aspiring to reach one's own dreams. Aspiring to attain a particular vision or goal means that we see ourselves as capable and deserving of not only shaping our own life and future but also contributing to and shaping the future of our family, community and society.

So I designed and conducted a research process with twenty young women to bring to the surface their inner reasons for feeling unworthy and ashamed, and to introduce and model different ways of seeing oneself and one's options, of connecting with others and of together reaching greater self-understanding, self-knowing and self-valuing.

Cultural influences

A number of influences seem to play a significant role in these young women's lives and their sense of themselves and their futures. A central lesson taught to girls is never to talk about feelings and not to let anyone know your emotions – neither family nor friends. If you share your feelings, others will not respect you. Furthermore, thinking about oneself is considered selfish; instead you should give and give to be a good daughter, wife and mother. So women get used to not thinking about themselves; they learn to need and desire to satisfy others – family, husband, friends, even neighbours. In addition, in Egypt food is the centre of every social event, and special occasions and family gatherings always offer large amounts of starchy food. Egyptian young women have been taught that they should accept and appreciate whatever parents and relatives offer to them, including large amounts of food, to be good girls.

Among middle-class young women troubled by their body image, these behavioural 'terms of recognition' for respectable young women require that they 'subscribe to norms whose social effect is to further diminish their dignity' (Appadurai 2004: 66) by increasing their sense of marginalization. Carefully adhering to what is considered appropriate female behaviour and keeping one's feelings to oneself and accepting what one is offered, including food and behavioural guidance and controls, do not prevent girls from experiencing depression, a poor quality of life, an absence of their own sense of direction, low self-esteem or body dissatisfaction. According to Appadurai (2004: 63), for those whose self-determination is undermined, 'one of their gravest lacks is the lack of resources with which to give "voice", that is, to express their views and get results skewed to their own welfare'.

Research methodology

The twenty young women who took part in this research were obese, overweight or very slim post-graduate students working at the National Research Centre in Cairo, and undergraduate students who were daughters and/or relatives of female staff working at the same institute. Some of the young women were concerned about their binge eating, while the mothers of the others were mostly concerned about their daughters' under-eating. They were all using various ICTs.

In-depth individual interviews were conducted to consider what could influence the women's behaviour and eating habits. Questions about their relations with their parents and their online communication were given close attention. The interviews were followed by group discussions and sharing of life stories. The group discussions were intended to provide a safe space for the young women to break the taboo against sharing feelings and speaking about themselves. My decision to bring the young women together to speak as a group with similar experiences was based on my own experience. Having grown up in the same cultural context, I too had learnt to keep my feelings to myself. However, recently I had experienced very different listening and sharing through my involvement in the GRACE project. I noticed that, by talking and listening to others whom I trusted and loved, I could understand myself better. I learnt that when you listen to yourself and when you speak directly and honestly you can find understandings and solutions by yourself too. For example, it took me a long time to understand why I was not able to resist eating, why I chose food I knew was unhealthy, why I stopped all my sports. As I learnt to be more self-aware of who I am, of my experiences, interests and values, such challenges became less difficult to understand and less challenging to deal with (Newhouse and Orr 2014). Through this process I have developed a firm belief in the centrality of knowing and being oneself if one is to take control over one's own life and future. It became important to me to act on this experience and understanding in my own context, with young women whose full selves and potential were hidden from themselves and others.

My research process used the Egyptian cultural practice of 'to be together is to enjoy together' and solve our problems together, but in ways that counter how we were all raised. Instead of adhering to social taboos, silences were broken and experiences and emotions shared. I completely avoided the blaming, judging, critical, unheard experience of their youth and replaced it with a safe space to speak from the heart. To gain the trust of the young women, I offered support through listening well (Ciaramicoli and Ketcham 2000) and understanding the feelings, emotions and experiences they shared as one who recognizes their situation, rather than as one who advises or judges, in whose presence they would have maintained their silence about their feelings.

Through the processes I introduced I hoped to strengthen the young women's capacity to have and to cultivate 'voice' – to know and express themselves so as to improve their sense of self, their well-being and their capacity to aspire (Appadurai 2004: 63) to lives they have reason to value (Sen 1999). With this capacity enhanced, they could explore and use their own abilities to a greater extent, attaining greater self-determination. As noted by Sen (1999: 18), 'having greater freedom to do things one has reason to value is (1) significant in itself for the person's overall freedom, and (2) important in fostering the person's opportunity to have valuable outcomes'.

During the research the young women used the Internet communication tools they already depended upon for a sense of connection with virtual friends who didn't know them (chat rooms, online discussion, e-mail), as well as websites and blogs to gain various perspectives on issues that concerned them – nutrition, body image, their lack of autonomy, communication, disconnection and self-doubt. They were encouraged to use these same mediums to access information that would show them different ways of communicating, to see how women share about themselves, feel about themselves and listen to each other, and to increase their self-reflection, self-awareness and nutritional self-awareness. They began to connect with each other online and offline and share about themselves in what became a trusted and reinforcing in-person and online community.

Dream drawings (see Chapter 22) were used several times as a way for the young women to become self-conscious of what is important to them. In some cases it became apparent that their initial visions for their future were the dreams of others for them, or were intentions to meet the expectations of others. Over time the young women could identify all the steps that could lead to their own dreams becoming part of their reality and could discuss the obstacles that they face. I recognized from my own experience that being conscious of one's own dreams is a key element in being less affected by what others think and more affected by finding ways to reduce barriers and expand oneself to encompass those very dreams. This capacity to aspire to reach one's dreams gives one a focus that goes beyond the attachment to and acceptance of norms, or removes oneself from these norms, to a place of engaging one's own future.

Research findings: what we learnt together

All the young women who participated were unhappy with their body image and had tried many ways to lose or gain weight. From the research process it became apparent how the young women's eating and communication choices were connected to how they felt about themselves, their feeling of being alone and the experience of not really knowing themselves or their capacities. Many felt unworthy, not good enough, ashamed, ugly or even hated by others.

Family influences: confidante or critic

I realized – from my own experience as well – that family has a strong effect on how young Egyptian women feel about themselves, the decisions they make and how they see their future. I noticed that during the dream-drawing discussions some of the participating young women had no dreams for themselves and their life, while the others did not know how to go about trying to reach their dreams. The well-learnt expectation of girls to not think of themselves or for themselves means no time is given to visualizing, let alone aspiring to reach a future of their design. This absence of autonomy is apparent even in their everyday decision-making. One of the young women explained her feelings with tears and said, 'I am not able to buy any clothes by myself, I could not choose because always my mother selects good things for me, it is different from my friends, maybe old fashioned but good, as my mother said.' She added that her dream was to go shopping with her friend only: 'I wish to choose but I am scared to pick something that is not beautiful and my mother hates it.'

A second aspect of family influence that became very evident was the confidante role filled by the young women's father or mother. This person was often the only one with whom they could talk freely and openly, feel strong and self-confident and perhaps question and discuss the norms that frame their social lives in a cultural milieu that looks down upon women's sharing of emotions, feelings, personal interests and perspectives. Often this was the only person who would really listen to them with empathy. Most of the young women in this research had lost this close person, due to death, long absences or divorce of their parents.

Marwa, an only child, described her mother's death as leaving her feeling fearful and without a trustworthy family member: 'My father is so busy, he hates my movies, my favourite music … we are so different, he can't enter my life … my house is empty, cold and my mother's death took all the happiness from my life.' This loss left the young woman with no one to turn to. The young women turned to the Internet, which they identified as their favoured source of companionship in the absence of their confidante.

The young women find themselves between the contrasting influences of their family's advice, their friends' perspectives, their online chats and what they see in the media, and this increases gaps in understanding between them and their family. Contrary to the images of beauty conveyed in the mainstream media, some mothers believe girls who are overweight are the most beautiful and slim girls are unattractive and will never marry. Mothers urge girls' acceptance of what they see as a valued cultural norm, and push them to eat more to become overweight and beautiful. Some fathers believe the same and advise their sons to marry a heavy woman. There are also young women who see extreme slimness as beautiful, although this is considered unattractive by many. In both cases women's appearance is responded to by hurtful name-calling shrouded in humour, highlighting the contrast with and benefits of the online spaces, where women can hide from all eyes, avoid social activities and chat and enjoy the experience of being invisible and free to describe themselves and their ideas as they wish to be known.

Disconnecting from and in the public sphere: connecting online

One of the young women gained thirty kilograms after her father's death and described her only joy as eating while chatting on the Internet: 'Whenever I feel alone I run to the Internet to get some comfort from the unknown people behind my screen.' To remain true to their mothers' teachings to keep their feelings out of view, the young women hide themselves behind electronic screens to chat freely with people they don't know, to find the comfort and the pleasure of sharing that they miss when disconnected from the parent they depended upon for mutual caring and sharing. Here the young women can express their own feelings, ideas and thoughts instead of only those that are acceptable to the norms and values for women in their society. With their outward appearance hidden, they avoid and escape the discriminatory treatment they experience when visible in person, and avoid social and cultural pressures.

According to one young woman, her best friends are food and the Internet: 'I enjoy eating when I am chatting, food is the only joy, I go out to eat and meet friends to eat.' She said that, beyond a few friends,

> I love people but I am trying to avoid them; I prefer to be with myself, with the Internet I can ask and discuss whatever I like with girls and boys without shame because they could not see my body and during my chat for hours every night, I enjoy eating but I don't think about how much I have eaten, I am happy chatting so I eat.

Enjoying the freedom of making their own choice, many of the women would consume large quantities of junk food when they had the chance to do so.

In public some of the women would take steps to avoid being noticed. The highly educated young women remain silent during official meetings with colleagues, hoping to avoid others looking at them. After the meetings they turned to their online connections to get their voices back. Here the women fully engaged, chatting with new people who have never known them in person; their thoughts, feelings and interests were less curtailed by social conditioning and expectations, and this seemed to give the young women a sense of being valued and valuable for who they were, although they still kept themselves physically hidden. One of the young women said: 'The Internet and joining different Facebook groups is so important and I am always free and open without fear or responsibility whenever I chat with people who don't know me.'

Learning to trust, share and be visible

During the group discussions it was a great relief for the women to realize that their problems are similar to those of some other young women of the same age. We all experienced a wonderful sense of freedom. I encouraged the young women to get together and share, speaking about things they *like* about their body, they like about themselves on the inside, or things they like about another member of the group on the outside and on the inside. They were surprised by how many things they liked and others liked about them and how great they felt after such sharing.

To open the door, to start becoming visible, the young women helped one another learn how to design a personal website page, and they shared it with a close group of people they were familiar with. They started to chat online with those they knew – other women in the research, including myself – to share with, listen to and advise each other. I also introduced various ways of being by encouraging the women to use their Internet connections to increase their knowledge of other cultures. Observing different people and customs revealed the aspect of cultures influencing each other, and that nothing remains stagnant or is impermeable, including how our own culture situates women.

I noticed that the young women in the group were not shy and could express themselves freely if I or one of the young women started a discussion; if one person started to talk about herself, her problems and feelings this encouraged the rest to speak and also to describe their feelings freely. We could do crazy things together that we were never able to do alone or in a different context, such as play games, dance, sing and tell jokes. The young women could search within themselves, listen to themselves and share with and listen to each other to find their own sense of truth and their own beauty, and transfer this into self-awareness, self-love and self-confidence. Describing their problems reduced their sense of being alone, as did listening to others who had succeeded in overcoming similar problems with parents or friends.

After some time the young women started to put less emphasis on the interpretation of external appearances and more on their inner strengths and nature and on the beauty of being and feeling a complete person.

They found themselves shifting from feeling uncared for, alone and seeking invisibility to increasingly caring for themselves and being prepared to become visible and show a self they take pride in. They became more comfortable with sharing from this position of self-knowing, seeing themselves for more than their stigmatized body image and lifting themselves out of the limiting and regressive expectations of 'good girls' and self-denying invisibility. This recognition permits them to move beyond their loyalty and attachment to the discriminatory beliefs that inhibit them and beyond their previous need for invisibility, potentially pushing the highly limiting boundaries of social acceptance, particularly for Egyptian women.

Over time, even after the research process was completed, I kept in close contact with the young women. The participant who dreamt of choosing her own clothes started to do so all the time. She even chose her own university programme, which differed from what her parents wanted her to study. Two other women who had remained very quiet in public, and had expressed how they tried to remain unnoticed, became trainers on human resources courses. One woman who was nervous and expressed jealousy and hatred towards her sister during our meetings, while sitting next to her ('I do not like my sister because she is the favourite of my mother, I hate her'), became calmer, and even her mother thanked me for the positive changes she saw in her daughter. Several young women told me how they had begun to trust people and to be more open with others. They seemed to be gaining more control over their lives, more independence and a sense of connection with themselves.

What it means: building greater self-knowing, self-valuing and agency

Becoming self-aware

What I saw in the research process itself was that as it was designed along the lines of the familiar cultural practice of 'to be together is to enjoy together', it had resonance with the young women and they felt mobilized to benefit from this space (Appadurai 2004: 67). The process and its familiar but altered terms of engagement created an opportunity for the young women to start learning to care for and about themselves and to share with others who experienced similar issues in relation to how they felt about themselves and their place in society, and how they had come to cope with both. Together they shared the growth, happiness and benefits experienced from speaking up for themselves, opening up to others and feeling listened to, understood, respected and admired. This sort of sharing is not practised as part of our sociocultural norms but, from my own experience and the responses of the young women, it is apparent that knowing yourself and being yourself give you a clearer sense of your own capacity to direct your own life and your future.

The importance of getting together and the way the women enjoyed sharing is also understandable, given the value of building and gaining a sense of self-approval, connection and sense of self in order to be strong enough to withstand the forces of social judgement and social determination and to find one's own way of being one's full self. Through the in-person forms of communication, the dream drawings and use of ICT spaces, the research process created an alternative social environment in which the young women could gain perspective on their own status and aspire to different ways of expressing and respecting the self. If invited to see life from a different perspective, and to communicate about life in different and unconventional ways, norms may not automatically slip into place. With increased space or openings for individual reflection, one can contemplate one's own dreams and even how to progress towards them – what Appadurai (2004) identifies as the capacity to aspire, and which entails a growth in a sense of agency, to lead a life one has reason to value (Sen 1999).

Understanding and growing out of harmful social adherence

For these young women, who grow up in a context in which there is plenty of socially defined and expressed judgement of how and who they should be, their safest and most respected avenue is to loyally adhere to cultural norms. The young women did so, having a 'fairly deep moral attachment to norms and beliefs that directly support their own degradation' (Appadurai 2004: 65) as individuals with capacities and dreams left under-developed.

From this perspective, their various preferences – whether these were to seek virtual companionship and express themselves freely or to take the opportunities they found to eat or not eat how and what they liked – seem more understandable. Using food and ICT resources in this way gave them a degree of the comfort and autonomy they craved without breaking or challenging the criteria for social approval. Their way of using ICT mitigated their suffering without taking issue with the social norms that contributed to their silencing, disconnection from themselves and their society and desire for invisibility. In this way these women's technology use sustained a detrimental status quo for them.[2] 'How ICT is integrated [into our lives] is influenced by social, cultural and economic circumstances and relations, and therefore also by existing inequalities' (Webb 2012).

What also became more understandable due to and during the process of the research was that the young women could attain other types and forms of comfort, autonomy and a sense of worthiness through an increased sense of connection with themselves and each other. While the online connections they had previously developed provided them with a sense of connection, intimacy and comfort that they had been missing in their in-person relationships, these online connections met their needs as they had previously understood and accepted them, within the cultural and social norms and values of their upbringing and environment, which motivated them to keep part of their physical selves hidden online, just as they had kept aspects of themselves hidden offline. Through the research process the young women began using ICT resources to explore beyond the boundaries they were accustomed to, including the perhaps previously unrecognized boundaries on their self-empathy, self-knowing and aspirations. They acquired different perspectives and ways of communicating, sharing about themselves, feeling about themselves and listening to each other.

Social implications of self-knowing

With increased self-acceptance the young women could benefit differently from both their online communication with those they don't know and from those they came to know well and trust in person through the research process, including themselves. When they no longer felt looked down upon, ashamed and ugly, but instead worthy of trust, love and respect and of being listened to (by themselves and by others), there was no longer a need to hide. Coming from this perspective, how they saw themselves participating in their own future and with the world changed. The young women could apply their newfound sense of being worthy for who they are to their relationships, both online and offline. It was apparent that knowing yourself and being yourself give you a clearer sense of your own capacity to direct your own life and your future. Changing how they related to themselves in the world – in their homes, schools, society and online – released them to varying degrees from their embeddedness in the social and cultural gendered norms and dimensions of their society that had previously reinforced or sustained their need to hide.

Without addressing and contesting social relations that are detrimental to women, particularly women who feel marginalized by society and unworthy, the same social norms and forces will also occupy online spaces (Webb 2012). This research process made evident how, by increasing their self-valuing and potential to visualize and act upon their own aspirations, the young women could also benefit from more reinforcing online relationships that did not require that they hide and feel ashamed of their appearance.

With this increased understanding of the interconnectedness of social, cultural and within-themselves influences on the young women's sense of their potential and on their capacity to shape their own and their community's future, a pressing challenge is how as families and as a society (Lerner et al. 2000) to equip young women with the means to grow their self-awareness and recognition of their agency. Both are needed if women are to benefit from online and offline spaces from positions of strength. As noted by Jenson (1989: 196), 'the price paid for the absence of a critical consciousness about gender in discussions of communications and technology is the reproduction of old patterns of power and privilege'. It seems there is a clear need for such understandings to be integrated into policies and practices that strengthen capacities of families and social institutions to recognize and enhance the strengths of all young women, such that their potential for positive contributions is not wasted and missing (Lerner et al. 2000: 17) in the development of Egyptian society and culture.

Notes

1 The research informing this chapter was designed and conducted by Mervat Foda and is presented from her point of view.

2 The recent study 'Facebook use predicts declines in subjective well-being in young adults' (Kross et al. 2013: 5) raises relevant questions, noting: 'Rather than enhancing well-being, as frequent interactions with supportive "offline" social networks powerfully do, the current findings demonstrate that interacting with Facebook may predict the opposite result for young adults – it may undermine it.'

References

Appadurai, A. (2004) 'The capacity to aspire: culture and the terms of recognition', in V. Rao and M. Walton (eds), *Culture and Public Action*, Palo Alto, CA: Stanford University Press, pp. 59–84.

Ciaramicoli, A. and K. Ketcham (2000) *The Power of Empathy: A Practical Guide to Creating Intimacy, Self-Understanding, and Lasting Love*, London: Piatkus Books.

Hassan, N. E., S. T. Zaki, S. El-masry, M. A. Mohsen and E. Elashmawy (2011) 'Impact of balanced caloric diet and physical activity on body composition and fat distribution of obese Egyptian adolescent girls', *Macedonian Journal of Medical Sciences*, 4(1): 17–24.

Hatata, H., M. Awaad, M. El Sheikh and G. Refaat (2009) 'Body image dissatisfaction and its relationships with psychiatric symptomatology, eating beliefs and self esteem in Egyptian female adolescents', *Current Psychiatry*, 16(1): 35–45.

Jensen, S. C. (1989) 'Gender and the information society: a socially structured silence', *Journal of Communication*, 39(3):196–215.

Kross, E., P. Verduyn, E. Demiralp, J. Park, D. S. Lee et al. (2013) 'Facebook use predicts declines in subjective well-being in young adults', *PLOS One*, 8(8): e69841.

Lerner, R. M., C. B. Fisher and R. A. Weinberg (2000) 'Toward a science for and of the people: promoting civil society through the application of developmental science', *Child Development*, 71(1): 11–20.

Newhouse, D. and J. Orr (eds) (2014) *Aboriginal Knowledge for Economic Development*, Black Point, NS: Fernwood Publishing.

Sen, A. (1999) *Development as Freedom*, New York: Anchor Books.

Webb, A. (2012) 'ICT in a gender inequality context', *ICT Update: A Current Awareness Bulletin for ACP Agriculture*, http://ictupdate.cta.int/en/Regulars/Q-R/Une-inegalite-hommes-femmes-seculaire, accessed 20 May 2014.

10 | Teenage girls' sexting in Cape Town, South Africa: a child-centred and feminist approach

JOCELYN MULLER

Introduction

In the space of a decade, new media have revolutionized youth culture. With the convergence of radio, television and computer solutions, electronic media and information and communication are gradually becoming common (Lenhart 2009). Use of new technology for communication among young people has produced a new social phenomenon: 'sexting'.

In recent years, sexting – sending sexually explicit video, texts or picture messages using instant messaging via digital platforms – has become common practice among young people. While the texts are not inherently coercive or harmful, use of the technology is not neutral in a patriarchal society: gendered roles may be amplified through new technologies (Hasinoff 2012).

This chapter is based on a study into how girls in Cape Town, South Africa, used sexting on the MXit platform (at the time, in 2009, this instant-messaging platform was more popular among teens than Whatsapp or BBM). MXit is a instant-messaging programme developed in South Africa that allows users with mobile phones to communicate with each other instantaneously from anywhere, at any time, and at a fraction of the cost of normal SMSs.

Adolescent sex and sexting

Advances in digital photography and distribution technologies enable people to create and distribute images of their sex acts. When young people do this it can legally be classified as pornography, even when consensual. The law makes no exception for youth who create sexually explicit images of themselves for their own sexual pleasure. In South Africa they are liable to be charged as 'sex offenders' under the Film and Publications Act, legislation that is (in theory) designed to protect them from predators. As yet the Constitutional Court still needs to confirm a High Court judgment that upholds the right of South African adolescents to consensual sex among peers aged fourteen to sixteen years.[1]

This will be an important advance in children's rights to sexual pleasure and exploration.

At the same time, however, these same children may have to navigate sexual experiences that are both consensual and legal when physically consumed but still illegal to visually record under South African law. The fact that the age at which one can consent to sexual self-representation will differ dramatically from age of consent for embodied sexual activity points to the fact that legal responses need to catch up with technological advances. For teens it will be difficult to understand how the presence of a mobile camera will turn sexual acts into a crime.

The South African context

South Africa is a particularly sexist country. The hierarchy of patriarchy is not only grounded in male domination of females but also in adult domination of children. For young girls this is a double-edged sword. It is thus essential to examine sexting within the context of societal power relations.[2] The aspects I want to discuss are misogyny on the Internet and in society, the sexualization of women, the age of consent for sex and sexting, and socio-sexual anxiety around female sexual freedom.

Misogyny on the Internet and in society

With newer technologies, new forms of violence emerged, especially among those who absorbed the technologies first – our youth. Violence prevalent in society is easily transmuted into the digital world, giving rise to so-called 'cyber cesspools'.[3] A study by the Centre for Justice and Crime Prevention (Burton and Mutongwizo 2009) reveals that 31 per cent of participants interviewed experienced some sort of mobile bullying on school premises, whereas 42.9 per cent experienced it outside. However, dominant media debates often conflate consensual sexting with cyber-bullying (Hinduja and Patchin 2011).

Given the messages in society, one could contend that culturally you are 'normal' if your sexuality is based on domination/subordination and on objectifying female bodies; at its extreme, this induces a rape culture.[4] We have seen violent outbursts among young people, with young girls the most susceptible to violent sexual crimes like those committed against Thandeka Mandonsela, Anene Booysen and Jyoti Singh Pandy.[5]

Commercial sexualization of women

In our consumerist society, corporations rely upon and reproduce hyper-sexualized images of women and girls to sell products and create brand loyalty. Pervasive objectification of women and girls contributes to subordination of females, to the extent that many have given up control over the way they relate to their bodies and their sexuality to the 'male gaze'. This gaze has been internalized to the extent that it has been normalized as self-objectification (Gapinski et al. 2003). In the digital age, one may say the media has created the space for and become complicit with conscious, deliberate or explicit conspiracies to commodify sexualization of girls for profit (Heldman 2007).

Socio-sexual anxiety around sexual freedom for girls and women

It is important to consider that girls' sexting may evoke 'socio-sexual anxiety' in society.[6] According to McFadden (2002), 'the intensity of this anxiety is generated by the fact that there is an extremely intimate relationship between sexuality and power' – a connection that is manifested through the media, legal and policy responses to girls' sexting. This response is nothing short of a 'moral outcry' – a term Cohen (1972) uses to explain the clampdown (on young girls and boys) to restrict and control girls' sexuality by the media, government and reform groups with sufficient means to lobby for their conservative interests.[7]

Methodology

At the start of the study (2009) there were no known discussions on sexting that began with the subjectivities of young girls; very little was known about what sexting means to young people, and even less about how these online interactions influence their concepts of sexuality. In this light it was crucial to interrogate the concepts and assumptions that characterize mainstream understandings of sexting as a problem, and perhaps narrow the gap between adult discourse and young people's lived experiences.

This study approaches sexting from a children's rights perspective, acknowledging rights to privacy, to sexual exploration and to sexual desire and pleasure. In the research the girls were given the opportunity to contribute their own perspectives grounded in a girl-centred critical acknowledgement of their sexual rights. They spoke about what they did and reflected on what happened while sexting. As a separate but integral aspect of the research design, they also explained what they wanted to experience as young women while developing their sexual selves and sexual agency, and how they saw sexting as part of striving for gender equality and, within that, for sexual equality.

Underpinning the approach was the understanding that interactive dialogue facilitates critical reflexivity in research participants, a process Freire (1970) described as 'conscientization', and that it was important to take a feminist stance from the onset, recognizing links to personal, social, political and sexual dimensions of well-being. Through dialogue a critical awareness arose that revealed how the girls shaped choices, decisions and actions and how their doing, being, relating, knowing and becoming created their gendered identities (Nussbaum 2011); agency and voice became lived experiences in and through the research process itself (see Chapter 22).

The research took place from November 2009 to December 2012 among female teenagers who self-identified as coloured, black and white, from the Cape Flats and the Southern Peninsula in Cape Town. Four principal research techniques were employed: individual interviews (free attitude and transformational attitude interviews; see Buskens 2005a, 2005b and Chapter 22), focus-group discussions, visioning exercises and participant observation.[8]

Findings

The findings will be presented in two parts: the girls' experiences and perspectives of sexting, and 'sexuality vision mapping'.

Sexting experiences and perspectives

The girls felt that most sexting is about healthy exploration and expression of sexuality embedded in wider systems of friendship, courtship and social bonding. Sexting via MXit has become a centrepiece of sexual life among young people – not only as a place where the social interaction that precedes sex occurs but also as a space for sexual activity. There are many reasons why children engage in sexting: seeking popularity, flirting, pursuing and/or securing a relationship, revenge and even as a form of safe sex. The conversations brought up the themes outlined below.

A space for sexual exploration and agency When asked about MXit compared to face-to-face communication, the girls said they thought MXit makes 'getting hooked up easy! And fast!' Use of MXit also freed them up, as one girl said: 'Personally, I'm more sexually aggressive on MXit'; she used more sexually suggestive texts and images than she would in 'real life' – 'but this doesn't make me a sex fiend either!' She said she didn't see anything wrong with sexting – and enjoyed it.

Online communication enhances privacy and control 'I can interact with others when and where I want, even in school!' – girls do not have ask parents' permission to use their mobile phone or suffer the embarrassment of being overheard. The mobile telephone also lowers the threshold for social interaction and allows immediate, direct, personally controlled access to peers – unlike the traditional telephone: 'You can say and do things without the usual concerns of face-to-face communication, being shy or "my big zit [pimple]"!'.

Everybody does it '[I've sext] a few times', said one girl, 'just between my boyfriend and I. I sent pictures of myself to him, and he to me. Everybody does it.' 'The boys sext too', one girl said with amusement. In return, they expect pictures. 'They use it for sexual pleasure', she said, giggling. Another remarked: 'Adults have no idea! It's so common, we all do it!'; she even shared sexually suggestive images and texts that had been sent to her with friends. Another said: 'You have to do it if you want to get hooked up!'

There has to be trust Sexting doesn't just happen 'out of the blue' – it is preceded by flirtatious texts, texting sex and flirtatious images. 'I have to trust him first!', one girl exclaimed. Another concurred: 'it took him a while to convince me – he was constantly begging "please" – he needed them for when we were apart. Eventually I said yes, ok. I couldn't just give in! And then I sent him a picture of my breasts.' Sexting is a 'normal' part of relationships, with 'stages' of sexting: from suggestive texts to filming of sexual acts, all dependent on sexual self-confidence and/or confidence in the relationship, perhaps to be interpreted as trust. 'I wouldn't do it if I hadn't been in a relationship', another girl later said, 'I wouldn't just do it for any one either.'

From intimacy to pornography? The girls emphasized that it is not as common as adults believe for images to be passed along to friends, but it does happen. One remembered an unsavoury experience: 'Everyone had seen the photo, not only everyone in my class but also some from schools in the area. One girl called me a porn star.' Another said: 'Some boys just want you to send a photo to show their friends, to pretend that you slept with him, when you didn't.' 'But is this pornographic? I think not!', exclaimed another. The girls supported a move to increase young people's rights to defend themselves against abusive and unwanted mobile inter-action when deemed appropriate.

Rights to sexual pleasure and desire Unfortunately most adults seem to fail to take into account the fact that young people, especially girls, have sexual desire: 'My parents will be shocked to hear, I know. But it's not just adults who have sexual desire and want sexual pleasure.' Perhaps, I was told, one should consider the fact that the girl might want to enjoy sexting for herself too. Perhaps online spaces create opportunities for girls to subvert gendered roles of intimacy? Their sexual pleasure and desire are constantly ignored in favour of the view that young girls engage sexually in order 'to please boys'. Said one: 'Why is it that adults think that? I have a right to have orgasms too.'

How to celebrate my body? The girls were emphatic and concurred with a participant who said, 'I like my body, I like being a girl, not a boy.' Another added, 'I love being a woman. I want to celebrate this. And my body too. But how? I don't know how.'

Protection or judgement? 'Unfair ways' in which girls are treated were mentioned: 'it is the girls, not boys, who are being labelled' and judged by peers and broader adult society for engaging in sexual exploration and expressing desire – rather than a simultaneous focus on both girls and boys. At the same time the girls expressed concern about the child pornography laws and potential for these to be applied indiscriminately to all sexual texts and images produced and distributed by those under eighteen, even when consensual.

Mapping a script for girlhood sexuality

Exploration of what was important for the girls regarding their sexuality started with a dialogue on feminist thinking on sexuality. This was followed by a visioning exercise where the girls were encouraged to:

- 'dream' the ideal situation where they could nurture their sexual selves;
- question to what degree their perspectives and experiences were influenced by patriarchy in their various environments (intrapersonal, interpersonal, family, community, society and beyond);
- endeavour to look beyond those patriarchal realities in assessing what sexting could mean for them.

The girls agreed to the following vision statement on sexuality: 'Girls' sexual well-being means celebrating Womanhood! as a critical agent – it includes the right to pursue sexual pleasure and desire while respecting the sexual Rights for one's Self and the Other' in pursuit of a partnership model for sexual equality. This 'definition' emerged from a discussion on:

1. finding out what 'womanhood' means – to celebrate my femininity in the way I think, feel and act that upholds my values and body integrity;

2. 'self' as a potential agent of change in my personal life and social milieu by developing critical reflectivity and critical agency in negotiating and resisting dominant ideas of sexuality in society;
3. understanding the 'right' to sexual pleasure and desire as expressed in the Children's and Human Rights Acts;
4. advocating for critical sexual agency that encompasses having ownership of one's body and sexuality, including measures to ensure freedom from unwanted sexual activity and sexual coercion;
5. fostering a new model of sexual equality between sexual partners 'in relation and mutuality' that encompasses the personal and political;
6. ensuring child-led participation for new forms of collaboration with adults (including the legal and policy fraternity), away from the top-down approach to a 'partnership' model as a response to sexting;
7. developing a platform for interactive dialogue via digital platforms to create new and better ideas on sexuality among girls (and girls and boys) through positive images and texts as a way of changing attitudes among young people.

Discussion

Sexting appears to be important for girls for many reasons. They use it to validate their opinions and determine the appropriateness of their attitudes and behaviours in their peer group; it is part of their sexual development, and they use it to find out 'how' to celebrate their budding womanhood and developing bodies. MXit enhanced opportunities for self-presentation, for communicating one's identity to others and for self-disclosure – like when discussing sex.

However, listening to the girls expressing how they would like to experience their sexuality and comparing this with their experiences and perspectives about what actually happens while they are sexting reveals discrepancies. Emphasizing 'womanhood' as enacting a developing self and being free and yet protected in using the new technology, the girls discussed persuasion by boys and risks of having their trust and intimacy abused, discomfort about not being understood by 'adults' (their parents) and being unsafe under the current legal system.

Is female agency possible in a patriarchal society?

Coercion does appear to be a feature of sexting relationships; subtle as it may appear to be, girls are pressurized by boys and boys by each other. Kelly (1987) contends that subtle, systematic forms of coercion, pressure and sexual harassment are underlying elements of the most violent forms of sexual violence; a woman does not have to experience physical force in order to experience sexual violence; sexual violence occurs on a continuum.

Girls who sext often get trapped into a cycle: coercion (to which they submit on the gendered basis of power and control), then shame for their actions, followed by fear of exposure if betrayed by the boy. Gill (2003: 104–5) has argued that the contemporary sexing-up of culture involves a 'deliberate *re-sexualization* and *re-commodification* of bodies' and the 'sexual subjectification' of women in ways that reinforce conventional ideas of female attractiveness and desirability for men. Yet this hyper-sexualization of girls cannot exist without hyper-sexualization of boys (Albury and Lumby 2010; Egan and Hawkes 2010) – they reinforce each other. Therefore, girls respond to boys' coercion to sext. Perhaps sexting is an adaptive preference – an unconscious action of girls conforming to limited choices in a patriarchal society. Or perhaps it is counter-hegemonic, challenging notions of the 'charmed circle' of patriarchy (Rubin 1984).

Objectification theory presented by Fredrickson and Roberts (1997) focuses on the effects of living in a society where objectification of women (and increasingly girls) is the norm. According to this notion, girls and women internalize the male gaze and tend to view themselves through this lens as a result of pervasive sexual objectification, normalized as self-objectification. They are living what Du Bois (1903) termed 'double consciousness', a sense of always looking at one's self through the eyes of others. Yet perhaps the girls are actually expressing agency of the 'charmed circle' and the moral panic is about those on the outer limits of sexual practices?

Digital literacy

For young people to harness the full potential of the digital era in ways that nurture and empower them, a certain kind of digital literacy is required. It is imperative that young people are encouraged to be both critical thinkers and creative producers of an increasingly wide range of messages using images and texts – even sexting. Such digital literacy would strengthen individual capacity to use communication for change in the personal and social milieu, promoting a democratic knowledge society. In this regard, reframing consensual sexting as media authorship may be the approach that is more respectful of young people and their needs. Expanding the definition of media production to include sexting highlights the importance of rights to privacy and consent for authors of social media content (sexting included), and would make it possible to hold youth accountable for their actions in a way commensurate with the emerging nature of our networked society (Hasinoff 2012).

Emotional literacy

Along with digital literacy, a certain kind of emotional literacy is also required. Although the self is often framed as primarily private, young people are framing their personal identity in the digital age differently (Attwood 2006). Sexting in particular demonstrates the need to look at the self in relation to other people, within cultural forms and moral norms, in the making of the self. Here, the construction of self can be thought of as a central mechanism through which the individual and social world intersect. This makes it imperative for girls to become 'emotionally literate'. While digital platforms have increasingly created opportunities for 'virtual' connections, they have also perhaps created increasing disconnection for girls. What is the basis of these online relationships? Do they really reflect what girls want? Do the girls themselves know what they really want? Can they, in the current sexist climate, actually find out what they want?

Towards a visionary discourse and methodology

Because of the sexism inevitably inherent in common thought, research theory and method have to be grounded in a visionary discourse that points towards a post-sexist future, in a manner similar to how the research participants contributed to this study. When given the space for interactive dialogue, the girls spoke. Such a space is key to uncovering and confronting hidden aspects of the self that are complicit with and perpetuate the role of a 'victim' of sexting. Critical reflexivity requires a shift in consciousness; holding up this inner personal mirror may set in motion a process of change, a journey of empowerment that requires training – theoretical and practical, personal and political. Critical reflexivity becomes a tool for guiding a girl towards a healthy exploration of her own sexual pleasure and desire (Fine 1998). Perhaps critical reflexivity holds potential for developing young people as critical thinkers and agents, developing a cadre of critical citizenry?

The girls linked female sexuality with sexual pleasure and passion to love. Love is the glue in a partnership of mutual sexual pleasure, away from isolation and alienation into community – into connection. In a world where positive expressions of sexuality are common ground, two people will choose those sexual practices that affirm and nurture mutual growth. At the heart of such a human existence would be a commitment to grow away from domination in relationships. Emphasizing an ethics of mutuality and interdependency, mutuality would be the norm.[9] Such an endeavour seems unrealistic given the current pervasiveness of sexism and misogyny, yet it is imperative to hold this vision as a theoretical and hence methodological yardstick to give meaning to research in this field (in much the same way as a definition of health guides research theory and methodology in medical research).

Conclusion

There is a discrepancy between the joy and the freedom the girls expressed about their use of sexting and the responses sexting is receiving in the legal world and the world of adults and educators.

New forms of culture such as the Internet evoke anxiety because – like feminism itself – they help destabilize old power structures and obscure boundaries between public and private. The Internet has become the flashpoint of struggle between those who view access to information as a means to political, social and economic participation and those who wish to restrict that access. The inflammatory focus on sexting as pornography can be seen as a drive to control the Internet by groups interested in restricting girls' sexuality.

Perhaps one should consider Heldman's (2007) view that self-objectification has negative effects in the political realm, and that Wolf (2012) – who explores how the vagina affects a woman's wider sense of well-being, affecting creativity, imagination and sexual agency – is also correct. While being internally focused and engaging in constant body monitoring, how can girls observe the external environment and assess what is happening politically? Ultimately, women's sexual well-being would indeed threaten the gendered status quo in the current political democracy, and would have serious implications for our future political world. Politically minded and active girl children who understand the forces that shape politics and media, and know how to articulate and fight for what they believe in, are not in the interests of the powerful.

Unless South African society faces its own anxiety about female sexual agency, it will be difficult to heed the call of McFadden (2002) to 'shake off the shackles of patriarchy' and yield to the wildness within (those who heed this urge being described by Estes (1992) as 'women who run with the wolves') so as to feel 'the surge of power and clarity that comes with the revelation that one is beautiful' – and challenge women globally to link sexuality to joy, pleasure and self-love. And yet this is what the girls who participated in this study seem to point towards.

Recommendations

Sexting needs to be examined in a more nuanced way, foregoing prosecution versus non-prosecution for a more situational approach encompassing educational initiatives and appropriate legislative frameworks, always ensuring the rights of the child and the well-being of the child are being upheld and not compromised. This will help us to create a cultural context that fosters sexual agency and in so doing promote the sexual citizenship of girl children. The focus on a discourse of laws aimed only at protection serves to undermine and restrict conceptualizations of childhood sexuality and makes the idea of children's sexual agency unthinkable and unattainable.

From a legal perspective, however, thinking through what consent means requires immediate attention. At the moment, consent appears to be applied inconsistently across a spectrum of interventions related to the legal rights (national and international) of the child, indicating an inconsistent approach to children's emerging autonomy and agency. This disconnection between the law and use of technology by consenting adolescents generates problems for policy, education and legal systems. Failing to clarify consent thus amounts to criminalizing sexuality among children when they use ICT.

To enable legal authorities to distinguish between cases where images and messages are sent voluntarily and between two consenting parties from instances where the distribution was malicious, non-consensual and/or widespread, responses to sexting should consider:

- any significant age differences between the participants;
- the extent and nature of distribution of the images/texts;
- consent and the presence of abusive or coercive behaviour (subtle/overt);
- the nature and extent of prior incidents of sexting;
- the level of understanding by participants of the potential harms of sexting.

Fuelling much of the debates around children and texting is the fact that children's, especially girl children's, sexuality is constructed as dangerous and socially unacceptable and therefore in need of adult intervention. A perspective on girls' sexuality that is grounded in an acknowledgement of their sexual agency would appreciate the intricacies of the relationship between their emergent sexual agency and political efficacy. Exploring how such an approach to developing critical citizenry among youth can be integrated into approaches to sexting among consenting teens would be life-affirming for teenagers but also an exciting prospect for social change in society as a whole.

Notes

1 In the Teddy Bear Clinic case the High Court declared some sections of the Sexual Offences Act unconstitutional, a decision still to be confirmed by the Constitutional Court, which upholds the right of South African adolescents to consensual sex among peers aged fourteen to sixteen years. See Sapa (2013).

2 Foucault (1978) says resistance is as much a part of power relations as repression, and that it pops up in irregular ways, e.g. sexting perhaps reframed as resistance.

3 'Cyber cesspools' are those places in cyberspace devoted to demeaning, shaming and harassing individuals; in short, violating their dignity, e.g. Outoilet (see Gontsana 2013).

4 A poll in 1999 of 1,500 schoolboys in Soweto showed most thought 'jackrolling', or gang rape, was 'fun', and 25 per cent of young men from Eastern Cape and KwaZulu-Natal admitted to having raped someone (Burton and Mutongwizo 2009).

5 I am referring here to three particularly vicious and violent sexual crimes: the rape and disembowelment of fourteen-year-old Thandeka Madonsela in Soweto in March 2013; the gang rape and killing of seventeen-year-old Anene Booysen in February 2013 (found with parts of her intestines next to her in the dirt at a construction site); and the case of Jyoti Singh Pandey, who was attacked in December 2012 by six men who raped her repeatedly and bludgeoned her with an iron rod.

6 A phrase coined by McFadden (2002) to describe anxiety and fears expressed in society surrounding the freedom of girls (and women) to enjoy sexual pleasure.

7 A moral panic is an intense feeling expressed in a population about an issue that appears to threaten the social order.

8 The study started with semi-structured interviews with staff and members of the Children's Movement. Later a focus-group interview was conducted with members of the organization, girls between ages eleven and fifteen years. The girls were recruited through referral from community workers with links to the Children's Movement and came from a range of schools on the Cape Flats. From the themes that emerged from the preliminary analysis of the first focus-group interview, it became apparent that girls who had personally had experiences with sexting should be recruited for in-depth interviews. This was particularly necessary in terms of the research approach of respecting girls' agency and subjectivities. This became possible a few months later, after substantial networking with friends, relatives and colleagues. With the help of a key informant I was able to conduct two focus groups with five adult women, each at the home of one of the participants. These focus groups resulted in another refinement of the interview questions. The data analysed for this chapter come primarily from these five in-depth interviews and focus-group interviews with young adult women (over the age of eighteen) willing to discuss their girlhood sexting via MXit.

9 The Stone Centre model focuses on human 'desire for connection'. In this model both members of a relationship as well as the relationship itself change while interacting with each other. The relationship is also shaped by a 'web of others' composed of 'the family, the culture, the historical context and the larger world' (Shem and Surrey 1998).

References

Albury, K. and C. Lumby (2010) 'Too much? too young? The sexualisation of children debate in Australia', *Media International Australia*, 135: 141, 147.

Attwood, F. (2006) 'Sexed up: theorizing the sexualisation of culture', *Sexualities*, 9(1): 77–94.

Burton, P. and T. Mutongwizo (2009) 'Inescapable violence: cyber bullying and electronic violence against young people in South Africa', Centre for Justice and Crime Prevention, CJCP Issue Paper 8.

Buskens, I. (2005a) *Free Attitude Interview Manual*, http://issuu. com/gracenetwork/docs/fai_ final, accessed 20 May 2014.

— (2005b) 'Transformational attitude interview', www.grace-network. net, accessed 10 September 2008.

Cohen, S. (1972) *Folk Devils and Moral Panics*, St Albans: Paladin.

Du Bois, W. E. B. (1903) *The Souls of Black Folk*, Avenel, NJ: Gramercy Books.

Egan, R. D. and G. Hawkes (2010) *Theorizing the Sexual Child in Modernity*, New York: Palgrave Macmillan.

Estes, C. (1992) *Women who Run with the Wolves: Contacting the Power of the Wild Woman*, London: Rider.

Fine, M. (1998) 'Sexuality, schooling and adolescent females: the missing discourse of desire', *Harvard Educational Review*, 58(1): 29–53.

Foucault, M. (1978) *The History of Sexuality*, Vol. I, trans. R. Hurley, New York: Pantheon.

Fredrickson, B. L. and T. Roberts (1997) 'Objectification theory: toward understanding women's lived experiences and mental health risks', *Psychology of Women Quarterly*, 21: 173–206.

Freire, P. (1970) *Pedagogy of the Oppressed*, New York: Herder and Herder.

Gapinski, K. D., K. D. Brownell and M. LaFrance (2003) 'Body objectification and "fat talk": effects on emotion, motivation, and cognitive performance', *Sex Roles: A Journal of Research*, 48: 377–88.

Gill, R. (2003) 'From sexual objectification to sexual subjectification: the resexualisation of women's bodies in the media', *Feminist Media Studies*, 3(1): 100–6.

Gontsana, M.-A. (2013) 'Controversial youth website dodges censorship', *GroundUp*, 22 May, www. groundup.org.za/content/ controversial-youth-website-dodges-censorship, accessed 2 June 2014.

Hasinoff, A. A. (2012) 'Sexting as media production: rethinking social media and sexuality', *New Media & Society*, 15(4): 449–65.

Heldman, C. (2007) 'The beast of beauty culture: an analysis of the political effects of self-objectification', paper presented at the annual meeting of the Western Political Science Association, Las Vegas, NV, 8 March.

Hinduja, S. and J. W. Patchin (2011) 'High-tech cruelty', *Educational Leadership*, 68(5): 48–52.

Kelly, L. (1987) *Surviving Sexual Violence*, Cambridge: Polity Press.

Lenhart, A. (2009) 'Teens and sexting: how and why minor teens are sending sexually suggestive nude or nearly nude images via text messaging', http://pewresearch. org/assets/pdf/teens-and-sexting. pdf, accessed 11 July 2013.

McFadden, P. (2002) 'Sexual pleasure as feminist choice', *Feminist Africa*, 2, http://agi.ac.za/sites/agi. ac.za/files/fa_2_standpoint_1.pdf, accessed 11 July 2013.

Nussbaum, M. (2011) *Creating Capabilities: The Human Development Approach*,

Cambridge: Harvard University Press.

Rubin, G. (1984) 'Thinking sex: notes for a radical theory of the politics of sexuality', in C. S. Vance (ed.), *Pleasure and Danger: Exploring Female Sexuality*, Boston, MA: Routledge, pp. 267–319.

Sapa (2013) 'Child sex law ruling explained', *ENCA*, 27 May, www.enca.com/south-africa/child-sex-law-ruling-expected, accessed 10 July 2013.

Shem, S. and J. Surrey (1998) *We Have to Talk: Healing Dialogues between Men and Women*, New York: Basic Books.

Wolf, N. (2012) *Vagina: A New Biography*, New York: Harper Collins.

11 | Of browsing and becoming: young Yemeni women enhance their self-awareness and leadership capacities

ZAHRA AL-SAQQAF

Introduction

Integrating gender issues in the curriculum at bachelor level is currently being discussed at the University of Aden. Advocates of integrating gender issues into the university curriculum state that Yemen's sustainable development and women's well-being and empowerment cannot be attained without raising people's gender awareness and adopting a gender perspective in policy-making and planning (Women Research and Training Center 2008). Gender awareness helps individuals, especially women, to understand the power within and 'recognize through analyzing their experiences how power operates in their lives, and gain the confidence to act to influence and change this' (Williams et al. 1994). Recognition of this power within helps women to perceive themselves as able and competent and raises their sense of responsibility and self-esteem.

Amartya Sen (1999), in his book *Development as Freedom*, emphasizes women's agency as central for development in any country. He argues that, while improving women's well-being is important, enhancing their agency is just as critical. According to Sen, the empowerment of women is one of the main issues in the process of development, and can take care of many issues that society faces. Accordingly, empowered women who take actions to change can make more sustainable contributions to the lives of women and the whole society.

This research aimed at exploring the possibility of raising women's gender awareness and establishing and/or enhancing their self-empowerment through Internet use, reflection and discussion. Raising women's gender awareness in this context involved women increasing their understanding of the structures of gender roles and relations, becoming able to identify problems arising from gender discrimination and realizing ways in which women and men participate in the development process and how they are affected by and benefit from it. The process involved participants' verbalization of their lived experiences of Internet use, their gaining of critical and analytical perspectives while using the Internet to read about gender issues and their reflecting on, contemplating, sharing and evaluating the process.

Analysis of women's consciousness-raising (Sowards and Renegar 2004) emphasizes that women's telling of their stories allows them to recognize the connected nature of their personal experiences, be exposed to new ideas and situations, become connected together and find role models to identify with. While activating her critical and analytical thinking on gender issues, the individual makes connections between herself at the intersection of gender and society, including consideration of her privileges and oppressions, thus gaining awareness of the impact of social systems on the self and the interconnection between the individual and social and political structures. The individual realizes then that she cannot be separated from the social and political structures within which she lives.

Awareness of the connectedness of the individual and social and political structures results in new understanding and knowledge of the self. Self-knowledge, which includes recognition of the power within, as stressed above, increases capacity for individual agency and personal change. From this perspective, individual transformation is a process of interaction between the self-aware individual and her society, which may manifest as action for social and political change.

The research approached self-empowerment as both an individual and collective process that evolves from the individual's understanding of her own power in her own context. It is 'an individual process' in that it is governed by individual differences related to the individual's readiness to nurture aspects of self-empowerment or let those evolve to make the process happen. This is a personal, inner process in which the individual's thoughts, emotions, aspirations, assumptions, needs, worries, dreams and frustrations interact and integrate in relation to her own context to produce her own understanding of her own power.

Empowering the self entails individuals' struggle to attain economic self-reliance and their self-confidence to have a voice, to choose for themselves, to make decisions and act and to have control over their own individual life. On the other hand, the research understands women's empowerment as a collective process through which to attain women's participation in all aspects of life: acquisition of skills, decision-making capacity and equal control over resources. In the atmosphere of collective female empowerment, the individual female self learns, internalizes, derives and withdraws empowerment into herself, and in the struggle for self-empowerment the individual female herself paves the way for and contributes to other women's empowerment.

While empowering the self, the individual finds herself in a space where she is participating and sharing with other women in shaping the future and opening up opportunities for women. As Kamua (2010: 200) puts it: 'empowerment is both an individual and collective process. The self is a critical part of the collective and each drives and supports each other.' The process of female empowerment – individual and collective – generates development, betterment, justice, care and love for the self, family, other women and the whole society.

Research methods

Ten female students aged between twenty-two and twenty-five years who were completing a bachelor degree in English at the Faculty of Education, University of Aden, were interested in participating in this research after being given a comprehensive idea of the topic and objectives of the research. The research created an educational situation in which the Internet as an unlimited source of knowledge was used by the ten participants to raise their gender awareness.

The participants received training in the free-attitude interview (FAI) (Buskens 2005) and then conducted fifteen collaborative action inquiry cycles during the period January to May 2010. According to Buskens, the FAI is a non-directive, controlled, in-depth interview, a qualitative research technique in which the interviewee is free to talk about anything she feels like, as long as it is within the framework of the starting question. The interviewer summarizes, reflects, stimulates and asks questions for clarification. It can be used in a two-person interview as well as in group discussions.

The participants and researcher acted together in the research process as fellow learners. In every cycle each research participant and the researcher chose a certain topic related to gender issues and searched the Internet to collect data on it, and then each participant wrote a report on that topic and another report on the process itself (what she felt and thought while using the Internet, what she discovered about herself and a description of the search journey, process, changes in her ideas, self-evaluation, self-image, self-perception, etc.). Each participant gave a presentation on the two reports. The full group then held discussions of participants' reports. The presentations were taped and then transcribed and circulated at the next meeting. Thus, every time there was a search (action) leading to a reflection leading to an evaluation leading to a contemplation. This process continued in spiraling cycles of increasingly heightened self-awareness and reflexivity, and this generated data for the research.

The FAI techniques, reflections and contemplations helped the participants to reach deep insights and become aware of the change and development they were experiencing. It also helped to enhance a sense of intimacy among them, such that each young woman easily, willingly and comfortably told her story. The FAI techniques influenced the way in which the research participants gave their presentations as well as how they listened to each other.

The reflective parts in their presentations, which in the very beginning were more about their contemplations of and questions on the themes they read about, gradually and smoothly turned into self-discovery and self-revelation. Each presentation became more like an FAI, with the presenter as the interviewee and the other ten listeners as the interviewer asking questions for clarification and not asking the more challenging 'why' questions. This technique created a sense of respect and intimacy among the participants that gradually grew at each meeting.

Some of the young women opened up to themselves and the group easily, right from the third meeting; some did so in the middle of the research; and some did so towards the end of the process. Regardless of when each was ready to reveal her inner self, each one willingly, in a process of self-awareness, talked about her dreams, worries, problems and points of weakness and strength.

Findings

The research participants searched the Internet and read about a variety of gender issues that were of significance and interest to them, such as gender-based discrimination in education; gender-based violence; honour crimes; female genital mutilation; early marriage; polygamy; the status of divorced women, spinsters and widows; women's political positions in elections, parties and parliament and the use of electoral quotas for women; women journalists; status of Yemeni women before and after Yemeni Unity; women in Islam; leading and politician women; the *hijab*; inhumanities of women to women; women's illiteracy; and many other topics.

Being engaged in a collaborative action research, the participants' individual contributions were intertwined and various pieces of knowledge (sometimes contradictory) were connected, helping the evolution of critical thinking on gender issues. In addition, the ongoing reflectivity deepened understanding and analysis of individual experience in relation to the group's experiences. Each participant's reflective awareness illustrated her understanding of her own specific context and of the forces within her gendered being that mobilize or immobilize change and development in her life.

The research participants' telling of their stories of using the Internet and their increasing self-awareness and reflexivity revealed how self-empowerment was constituted and enhanced. In their individual contexts, self-empowerment meant having the courage to express oneself, making choices, taking actions and assuming power in some aspects of their lives. Self-reflexivity enhanced the participants' awareness of how their values and experiences affected their choices, expression and actions.

In the following story, for example, the participant emphasized her awareness of the change that had happened within her:

> I did not enjoy girls' interests nor did I like what other girls usually like, such as going to weddings and parties, visiting friends, going shopping and so on. I found myself in things that boys are usually interested in, like electronic games, using a computer, camera, mobile, also riding a bicycle, playing football, basketball and fixing and maintaining broken equipment. After the eighth cycle of my Internet readings in this research, I noticed the change that happened in me. I now feel self-confident in being a girl, and more self-confident when I do things that boys do because I feel that I/the girl can deconstruct the belief that girls do not have the strength to do such things; which is in contrast to the past when I was doing things because I wanted to be like a boy.
>
> What I have never thought of, and it never came to my mind, was how women are very powerful, how they are great human beings. [The] Internet has provided me with a lot of images of wonderful women – famous and unknown – and given me information about their lives in more detail which I could hardly find anywhere else. Internet searches and readings provided me with international images of powerful women, so the circle of characters that I learnt from has widened. I came to know about a great number of empowered women who I dreamt to be like. They have become like role models for me. I can follow their steps in order to reach the high position I dream of. Before, I thought that empowered women are only those who work in big companies as managers or those who have a lot of money and they are always aged and not young, but now I think that even without position and money, as a young woman, I can be empowered as long as I have the qualities of a powerful woman (being self-confident, self-respecting, self-articulating, never gives up, and stands up for what she believes in) and age is not a problem as long as I behave in a good, rational way.

In the next excerpt one participant tells of discovering her voice and recognizing an inner source of strength while using the Internet:

The majority of websites I visited ask the visitors to send comments. This gives a reader like me the impression that her opinion is valuable and can make a difference, so I get the courage to participate when I dislike an article or agree with it. There is some inner voice that tells me that my opinion is important even if it is only one sentence. When I do this I feel that other people may like my comments, and I enjoy this sense and feel I am someone special.

In this reflective piece the participant's self-articulation mingles with her self-consciousness; one led to the other as she used the Internet to read about gender issues. Her sense of self-appreciation is evident:

Every time I find information that is new to me, each single piece of information which I need or look for either for my study or other purposes, I feel as if I own the world and I am powerful; I am the only one who could find it, even though it is available for every one and someone else has written it. I feel like I am the only one who discovers it and as if it was hidden under something and I have removed this cover and got it. These feelings of happiness and delight make me self-satisfied. I feel I did my duty towards myself and I got what I deserved after a long time of working. Even if I feel pains in my eyes and back; after I find it I feel I still have energy and power to complete my search and reading and all my pains are removed. This enjoyment and satisfaction make me proud of myself and love who I am. In these moments I feel all my psychological states are in harmony. All my emotions, power, organs, and senses get together enjoying the success, and I forget my weaknesses and every negative point in me. I feel like I am a complete person [where there is no such person]. With this recurrent feeling, I touched my sense of self-confidence and self-trust.

Here a participant shows how she changed her perspective on barriers preventing her from attaining her dreams and future goals while using the Internet, through reading stories of other women's empowerment as she simultaneously contemplated and reflected on her own context and gender relations. In this way she recognized her inner strength and determination:

One of my dreams was to travel to pursue my higher studies in some foreign country. I knew for sure that I would have to face the rejection of my family, so I gave up even the idea of travelling. When I read through the Internet and knew a lot of stories about women who insisted on reaching to their goals despite all the difficulties and hardships, I got the strength and determination to hold on to my dream. I believe now that I can persuade my family, get their approval, and make my dream come true despite all the difficulties that I will have to face.

In the following excerpt from a participant's presentation she explains her own definition of self-empowerment, which she formed while using the Internet and contemplating her past lived experiences. A sense of responsibility, which she describes as 'duty', and motivation for collective action are apparent:

I came to understand that I really have empowerment because I can say yes or no. I can decide on the thing that I really want, I can accept or refuse any offer of marriage, I can say my opinions, my ideas, and this is a power I have but did not pay my attention to before. Reading through the Internet has awakened my awareness to that kind of empowerment and made me feel its existence inside me; I really felt it. It helped me also understand that I have been using it correctly as one of my points of strength. I did not know before that empowerment could be in very small things that we do in our lives. I came to realize that I have empowerment because I am in the place where I want to be, I do what I really like to do, because I am ambitious, I plan for my future and try to draw it as I want, not as others want. Even if my dreams did not come true, the most important thing is that I dreamt of them as I wanted.

Whenever I face barriers and difficulties I do not stop working to attain what I want, on the contrary I always try to face and overcome them and create new ways for myself. I believe tomorrow is better and never give up when I want something, even if I try a hundred times. I came to realize that I had empowerment in all those moments when I looked at life with a new set of eyes after I failed in something, when I thought of positive things despite all the problems and difficulties. When I realized that I have all this power while some other people do not have it, I felt that it is one of my duties to help those others, at least help them to be heard. I feel now that it is my duty to be one of the makers of change for the better in everything I take part in.

Positioning the female self in the collective global context of women and the impact of this experience is clearly expressed in this excerpt from a participant's presentation:

My eyes opened on facts and issues that were very important to me, and many questions have arisen in my mind which I may never ask loudly even to myself. I think these questions were already there; I knew them, read about them, but I did not bother myself to think about their answers or to discuss them even with myself. I used to see what I was in life and other women (our position and our sufferings) as our destiny, the destiny of any woman, a normal aspect of a woman's life. What I had seen was a very small number of women in my surroundings. But now with the Internet, I have seen many women everywhere from different cultures and in different fields of life, working, helping, sharing, learning, affecting, etc. These images have changed my traditional image of women.

The following excerpt from a participant's presentation illustrates her growing self-awareness, described in relation to her concern about women's suffering:

As I was searching for a topic each cycle, contemplating and reflecting on it and then we got together and discussed it, I didn't feel while reading or discussing it that I was doing it for the sake of knowledge only, but I felt that there was an internal power and desire directing me into picking certain topics that were related somehow to me. Doing that over and over again, I came to realize that my passion in women's issues has developed and got bigger than ever. Using the Internet was a releasing zone for me. It opened my eyes to different aspects and types of repression that women suffer around the world.

Discussion

The stories of the research participants displayed how using the Internet to read about gender issues in combination with reflection, contemplation and group discussion contributed to the participants' self-awareness. During the research process each participant had an internal dialogue with herself while exploring gender-related issues on the Internet; then in discussions with other participants she co-constructed/reconstructed new meanings in relation to their reflections and her own. When the research participants communicated knowledge of their experiences in group discussions, they allowed their perspectives to be transformed, being open to including others' views that extended, challenged or validated their own. Reflexivity functioned as a bridge between their internal and external worlds. The group's reflecting from various perspectives – all having their own ideas and practices that included many aspects of themselves – captured and highlighted in the research process enriched the individual experience of each, and the research process became a vehicle for personal growth.

It was through self-awareness and self-articulation that the participants were able to make positive shifts in self-perception, self-concept and ways of thinking. Their awareness of the change they experienced and how it happened made that a change in thought, which led to a change in the perception of what is possible for women. The Internet provided the young women with many images of 'others' to identify with. They received a source of motivation for female empowerment through the images of empowered women and women who were struggling and striving to empower themselves. Thus a process of self-discovery and self-definition happened.

Moreover, reading critically about gender issues resulted in understanding the structure of gender relations and roles and the complexities within this structure. This understanding helped each participant to deconstruct and analyze her own specific context and understand the forces that mobilize or immobilize change and development in her life. Consequently the young women gained in self-confidence and readiness to make decisions and take actions, especially to fulfil their own dreams. In becoming so, they disrupted in their own mindsets, and as a group, the derived image of the ideal passive, dependent woman, which they had internalized from their sociocultural context. While using the Internet, the individual women felt that they were part of the whole global female context and escaped the limits and restrictions of their immediate external and internalized environment.

When the young women used the Internet comfortably, they experienced the intricate relationship between being and doing. In using the Internet they became more aware of the existence of inner resources for knowing, and discovered the existence of their sources of strength, which led to a shift in their self-concepts, self-esteem and self-appreciation. Buskens (2001: 24) identified and analyzed this intricate relationship between being and doing in 'Fine lines or strong cords? Reflections on being and doing in the quest for quality in qualitative research': 'very often we realize that our being embeds our doing. Our being seems to form the parameters for our doing, as if we can go as far with our doing as our being can carry us'.

The participants used the Internet to seek knowledge and were comfortable in participating in various Internet activities. They felt appreciative of themselves, their minds and their voices. The increased sense of self-appreciation, which embedded self-respect, self-love and self-care, motivated them to seek a more fulfilled life and developed a sense of responsibility towards themselves, other women and the whole of society.

Optimistically speaking, this collaborative research process helped the participants to build and enhance leadership capacities: innate qualities (for the individual) and collective qualities (for the group). The individuals have become visionary and inspirational, having autonomy, independence, aspiration and initiation, and able to make decisions and take responsibilities. On the collective level they developed the capacity and skills to become engaged in courageous conversations, listen to feedback and provide feedback that may lead to improvements. They learnt to identify strengths and weaknesses and realized the importance of setting collective goals and being committed to getting them done collectively. These young women have come to know their way and are keen to show the way to others.

Conclusion

This research combined four elements (Internet use, gender awareness, self-reflexivity and group discussions) in its exploration of the process of self-empowerment. The research participants' use of the Internet to read critically about gender issues helped them to raise their gender awareness. Self-reflexivity and group discussions helped them to produce authentic critical knowledge of the self in relation to their individual lived realities and the experiences of other women, and were the research tools that captured their self-awareness in words. They understood the nature of the gendered social structure, and relations and forces within this structure that mobilize and immobilize the change and development in a female's life. Positioning the female self within the global female context enhanced individual empowerment, as the women saw themselves, their possibilities and capabilities in relation to women exploring and asserting their own agency and creating better situations for women.

From the narratives and images of empowered women in other contexts, they found images of 'others' to identify with and discovered new aspirations for female empowerment. Gaining in self-confidence and personal ambition, these young women started cherishing their own dreams and disrupting the derived image of the ideal passive, dependent woman. Feeling comfortable in using the Internet, they became appreciative of themselves and motivated to seek a more fulfilled life for themselves, other women and the whole society.

Being engaged in collaborative research helped enhance a sense of collective commitment to envision a better reality for the whole society, as well as for each individual participant. Enhancing elements of self-empowerment and collective empowerment introduced and developed capacities for leadership.

Information and communication technology (ICT)-based education and gender awareness can affect the way of thinking of young women. Analytical and critical thinking on gender issues and aspects of development and the potential for betterment of life in Yemen clarified for these young women the need for and benefits of women's participation in and contribution to all aspects of life (political, economic, social, educational etc.). Consequently they respect and appreciate women's participation, which will help in disrupting the image of the ideal woman in their mindset as being passive and dependent. This redefinition of the roles and capabilities of women by women themselves shifts their sense of being – their self-concepts, self-esteem and self-appreciation – and subsequently shifts the parameters of their doing.

Recommendations

The research recommends that:

1. the ICT policy and master plan of the Ministry of Higher Education and Scientific Research to integrate ICT in education is implemented as soon as possible in all institutions of higher education;
2. gender issues are included and integrated in the curriculum at bachelor level in Yemeni universities;
3. girls are encouraged by their families to use computers and the Internet to research in depth the gender issues included in the curriculum.

References

Buskens, I. (2001) 'Fine lines or strong cords? Reflections on being and doing in the quest for quality in qualitative research', keynote address at the Quality in Qualitative Research in Education Conference, Johannesburg, 25–27 June.

— (2005) *Free Attitude Interview Manual*, http://issuu.com/gracenetwork/docs/fai__final, accessed 20 May 2014.

Kamua, J. N. (2010) 'Empowerment through interventions for women's collective agency', *Development: Gender and Empowerment*, 53(2): 99–201.

Sen, A. (1999) *Development as Freedom*, New York: Alfred A. Knof.

Sowards, S. K. and V. R. Renegar (2004) 'The rhetorical functions of consciousness-raising in Third Wave Feminism', *Communication Studies*, 55(4): 535–52.

Williams, S., Seed, J. and Mwau, A. (1994) *Oxfam Gender Training Manual*, Oxford: Oxfam.

Women Research and Training Center (2008) *A Guide in Integrating Gender Concepts in the Curriculum of Bachelor Level* [in Arabic], Aden: Aden University Printing and Publishing House.

12 | ICT in the search for gender freedoms: Jordanian university students think, talk and change

ARWA OWEIS

Women in Jordan, as in other Arab countries, live in a patriarchal society that views them as second-class citizens of lesser status and lesser value than men. Often, women perceive themselves as wrongdoers of deeds they had nothing to do with, or guilty of crimes they did not commit – crimes of being women, of being born with the wrong gender. Womanhood is their perpetual challenge.

Women live their whole life trying to prove to the world and to themselves that they are as worthy as men, and continue this struggle under adverse situations and oppression throughout their lives. This life-long disheartening journey strips them of their self-respect and instead implants doubt, shame and feelings of inadequacy. It limits their positive experience, distorts their view of themselves and thwarts their interest in understanding themselves and exploring options for changing the status quo.

The link between gendered images in the environment and the degree to which gender-based violence (GBV) is acceptable has been extensively documented (Haj-Yahia 1997, 1998, 2000; Hassouneh-Phillips 2001; Oweis et al. 2009; Gharaibeh and Oweis 2010). In my research and advocacy work around issues of domestic violence and violence against women I noticed that often women are party to their own abuse, and often act as agents of their own disempowerment. GBV is a sensitive topic, and the concept of women co-creating this to a degree is easily misconstrued. Without abdicating men's responsibility in these issues and definitely not falling into the trap of 'victim blaming', I realized that, for GBV to come to an end, women themselves would have to learn to take responsibility for the way in which they are treated.

In my research project I therefore endeavoured to explore how women could learn to take responsibility for their own empowerment. Because of the hopes vested in information and communication technology (ICT) I decided to investigate how ICT could assist women in such a journey.

Kavanaugh (1999) investigated the relationship between computer networks, social networks and civic engagement and found that ICT (especially e-mails and list servers) reinforced and extended social networks. Users in this study indicated that ICTs facilitated strong ties, promoted trust, bonded social capital and provided intensive daily contact for support and mutuality within homogeneous and exclusive communities.

As I work at a university, I decided to do the study at the campus. This would not only allow me to have more intense and frequent contact with my research participants but also would enable me to get a sense of how such empowerment work could be integrated into teaching and learning for female students at the Jordan University of Science and Technology (JUST) and other Arab universities.

Research methods

I conducted in-depth qualitative research over a period of one year at JUST. Participants included nine second-year female master's students from JUST and one doctoral nursing student from the University of Jordan. In addition, two nursing faculty members from JUST participated in the study. I used this convenient sample for ease of access and communication with the participants.

Several participatory research methods – e-mails, focus-group discussions, free attitude interviews and the transformational attitude interview (Buskens 2005; see also Chapter 22) – were selected to create an empowering dialogue between and among the participants, and to define and explore the concepts of self-knowledge and awareness, empowerment, self-love and self-abuse. These participatory methods not only facilitated getting to know the participants, to prepare them for and to stimulate their reflections, but also allowed all of us to document our experiences adequately.

Because of the convenience, privacy and accessibility of e-mails, we created an e-mail list and used it as a space for reflecting on self-knowledge and awareness. The participants were asked to document their reflections as often as they needed; they were allowed to correspond and interact via the list or not, without judgement or coercion to participate. I moderated and participated in the flow of e-mails and the correspondence, commented on the reflections and initiated some of the discussions. This participatory process of reflection, sharing and corresponding continued throughout the research.

During this research I considered myself as an active respondent and saw myself as a co-creator of the meanings. My personal journey of empowerment was unquestionably a catalyst or contributor to the social change I witnessed in the respondents, and vice versa. Seeing them take on their issues was a great source of inspiration for me.

Results

Becoming aware of who we are and what we want

In this research we used face-to-face group meetings and e-mail correspondence to create a new social space for us. In his most well-known work, *The Pedagogy of the Oppressed*, Freire (1998) indicated that a person who does not think (and think critically) about his/her social reality but simply accepts it is thereby participating in the world in a way that has been organized for him/her by others. If being human means exercising freedom, this is to be less than human. To reflect 'the normal life laid down for one in this society is not freedom and then to change nothing does indeed render the reflection superficial, mere vaporizing empty thoughts' (Freire 1998: 47).

Women in this study described the importance of obeying the social and cultural norms and expectations for their survival. For example, one of the women I interviewed indicated that, 'I had to accept the husband selected by my father to be accepted by my family.' Another woman said, 'I had to accept my family's decision not to study engineering because I was a woman and women cannot be engineers according to my father.' She continued, 'I even had to go to a nearby university selected by my father while my brother was sent abroad to become an engineer despite his low-grade-point average compared to mine.' She also expressed her obligation to accept the discrimination between her and her brother: 'I could not protest or show any objection toward sending my brother to study abroad; I had to pretend that I was happy for my brother and celebrate his achievements, while I was heartbroken and hurt by the discrimination.'

Women I worked with in the research process discussed how their society and their family treated them and raised them to believe that they are powerless followers – that the reason they exist is willingly to serve the well-being of the men in their family. They learnt to be helpless and hopeless; they accepted or were forced to accept their exclusion from being a member of the family who can contribute or participate in family decisions. Discussing and reflecting on the role of society in oppressing women allowed participants to discover and realize that this dynamic causes women to lose their self-respect and self-love, and to live their lives dealing with feelings of shame and worthlessness as a consequence of exclusion.

For example, one of the participants noted that she now realizes that putting up with the stress that comes with denying herself is a type of self-abuse and her own particular contribution to the way she is abused. On self-denial she stated the following: 'I try to make everyone around me happy, work hard to make them happy, and do my best to comfort them, and I ignore my needs and feelings, by being happy only when others are happy.'

Another woman shared her insight about her responsibility for allowing oppression: 'I am often afraid of rejection, therefore I am reluctant to do things differently than what is expected and then I regret it; this is another way in which women contribute to their own oppression.'

One participant explained how intimidation is a method of manipulation and abuse:

> People around me, especially my mother-in-law and my mother, are
> pushing me and are trying to convince me to become pregnant again
> to have a boy, and if I reject or do not agree with them they become
> mad and think that I am stupid. This makes me feel that my rights
> were breached and that I am allowing others to interfere with my life.

She further explained that she felt guilty and ashamed about not respecting their wishes, and at the same time saw herself as guilty of self-abuse.

One of the participants burst into tears during one of the face-to-face interviews because she discovered that she was in graduate school because she wanted people to talk about her success and achievements, and not for her own self-development and personal growth: 'Dr, I am nothing, I have done nothing; all this is all a lie, I am here for no reason', she said, and left the room.

Women indicated that, when they obey the rules and social expectations, they are described as acceptable, honourable beings, and when they maintain the honour of their society they can be celebrated and feel proud. Yet women need to work hard to maintain this social functioning. During the process of reflecting and discussion we discovered that, by striving to live up to the social expectations and the approval we were seeking, we were tolerating and creating various forms of abuse and discrimination. This was a shocking discovery for most of us. As one of the participants described:

> I have been following my parents' advice to stay with my husband
> although we are not happy together, but they forced me to tolerate
> him for my daughter's sake and because they do not want to see me a
> divorced woman. Now I realized that they were pushing me to accept
> my situation and live a miserable life, and this too is abuse.

We realized that we felt betrayed, and yet we also realized that we had had that feeling of betrayal all along because this is the way it is in a male-dominated society. But to face this fact was painful, especially when we discovered that not only have we been abused but also we have played along with it – we could have done something, and we did not. Perhaps we never thought that we could, or maybe we built insensitivity to ourselves into our lives so that we did not have to think about how we are living our lives.

When we shared and compared our stories with each other, we started thinking about the interrelationships between the dominant social structure and the social roles of women. We realized the price we have been paying for not understanding this dynamic. It may not be our fault that we have been following the social rules because we have never controlled our destinies; we have been controlled by our parents and other actors in our society. However, now we believe that much can be done and needs to be done. Each one of us has her own ways of dealing with her situation. Maybe we will not leave our immediate environment, but we can work towards modifying it and change the way we live in it.

Sharing our emotions and experiences and telling stories about ourselves helped us to generate solidarity and discover our identities, and provided us with more possibilities to improve our lives, reframe our existence and wake up out of limited self-understanding. As one of the participants said:

> I did not think that I could love my husband because he was imposed on me and I had to accept him despite the fact that he was limping. I felt that I married a man who is less complete, and I felt that people never respected me because I agreed to marry such a man, and the feeling of shame haunted me all the time. I really could not love him or see the other side of him! ... but now I cannot tell you how much I love him, after I discovered that these emotions were brought up in my relationship with him because I was dealing with the shame that was part of me as my self-image developed in relation to my parents ... it is like I woke up and now I feel his love ... because I changed the way I look at him, he has changed too. The other day and for the first time in five years, he took me shopping and we left the children at home alone – I mean for the first time I go shopping without my children and shopping for me, it felt really great.

The power of our ICT-enriched space

As time went by, and the more we interacted and communicated with each other, a sense of connectedness, belonging and coherence was developed and created, allowing us to engage in dialogue and to share our emotions, stories and experiences without embarrassment, shame, self-blame or fear of judgement.

This research was very delicate in the way we disentangled and reconstructed our lives, especially when we discovered that we were able to discuss issues of being abused and abusing ourselves. We were able to embrace new identities and forge new and empowering relationships built on trusting and nurturing connections. One participant, describing her experience, said, 'knowing that I have a private space that I can use whenever I like comforted me because I can express myself more easily and instantly'. She continued: 'Being able to instantly share my feelings and thoughts through the e-mail list allowed me to safely confess to you about my unstable relationship with my husband because I trust that you will not judge me; you will support me and will give me your opinion.'

Another described how the e-mail list and the conversations that went on created a sense of continued connectedness and togetherness that became stronger with every instance of sharing, because of the relative freedom granted from time and space. The dialogue and e-mail discussion of our personal stories generated new forms of knowledge, awareness and agency in relation to our being and doing. Said one participant:

Exchanging, sharing and reflecting on my own experiences, like being abused as a child and accepting to marry the first man that proposed to me even if I was not completely convinced that he is the right man, so I can leave my parents' house and live away from their control and abuse and judgement and avoid seeing my mother's humiliation, helped me to understand more, not only about women's issues and what they go through, but also about my own life and what I have been through. Now I feel safe and feel better when I share my stories with my friends.

Another participant indicated as follows:

You know I have not felt like this for a long time ... I feel really vulnerable and I thought I am over my vulnerability and shame ... you opened a forgotten wound. I really want to cry ... my heart is pounding, I am restless and confused, and I am angry. I want a relief ... maybe a little support if I can really share my story ... stories ... talking to you maybe is the only thing I can do to express my feelings – why I am so afraid, vulnerable and weak. I go back with my memories, when I was a little girl who could not use her mind to solve her problems but whined about her situation. Actually I am not sure why I have to say this – I am also feeling guilty about even thinking about how I feel, like I do not want anyone to see my weakness.

One participant described how the link and connections provided by the shared spaces helped her to develop self-knowledge and awareness, and enabled her to reflect on her own life and how to better understand her social context:

> opening my e-mail on a daily basis means freedom to me; I cannot wait to open my e-mail and I am always eager to find out what is going on with each of us ... My e-mail is the space and place where I can be myself and talk freely with you: no barriers, no shame, and on top of that, when you share with me your life experiences I understand my own experiences – at least I do not feel I am alone. See, even our doctors tell us their life struggles and express their feeling of vulnerability with us, and this is great ... it does not mean that if you are well educated as a woman you are immune to feeling sad, unhappy sometimes. I thought that successful women do not have any worries; I was wrong, now I understand.

Another participant indicated that 'through this engagement in this e-mail group and reflecting on my life I was able to travel to work outside Jordan. My parents would never let me travel alone because I am a woman, but now I did it.'

This long process of discussion, analysis and reflection in which we all participated allowed us to hear ourselves and to be heard; it opened up a new venue for collective learning and making critical life decisions. As described by one of the participants:

> I did not think that having only my parents as my reference for advice limited my abilities to make decisions regarding my life. Without being engaged with this empowerment group I would never take the decision to file for divorce, and I would never stand up for my right to rent an apartment and live with my daughter alone. My parents would never allow me.

ICTs – mainly the e-mail list – were thus used as a liberating space and platform for exploring women's issues, relevant relationships and social issues; especially useful was that many times participants did not have to deal with their friends' immediate reaction. This space felt more alive and real for all of us than many of the other spaces we live and work in. This new environment became a change agent that we all wanted to live in, because it was more authentic and more respectful of who we all are. It was like a womb of creation where we recreated ourselves in our co-created space that had something of all of us in it.

Discussion

Brown (2010) discusses the power of fear, shame and vulnerability in preventing people – especially women – from sharing, connecting and reflecting on their own feelings, thoughts and experiences. She also describes how striving for social and cultural approval and acceptance are driven by fear, shame and vulnerability. She recommends sharing struggle stories that are loaded with shame and fear with someone who has earned the right to hear it, who can genuinely relate to what one is experiencing, feeling or thinking – a person with whom one can connect at the right time, sharing the right issue.

The Internet, with its availability and accessibility, brought with it expectations for empowerment. It was presumed to help individuals become more autonomous and to enable them to better shape their own lives in meaningful ways through networking, knowledge-gathering, making their voices heard and resisting their status quo (Wheeler 2008). In terms of how these processes affect women's lives, Young (2002) described ICTs as multi-dimensional tools whose power is based on their capacities to link places and connect people. She also believed that women can harness and exploit that power to their own purpose.

Using e-mail as well as face-to-face discussion allowed us to share multiple sources of knowledge – including our own stories, experiences and understandings of social norms and values – in addition to discovering empathy. It also allowed us to share a space for creative thinking and using our imaginations to create a picture of our lives that we had not seen before (such as getting divorced, working abroad or being satisfied with only daughters not sons).

It could be that the norms of connection, trust and freedom that circulated in our discussions and dialogues were different from the patriarchal, oppressive and suppressive social norms in that they fostered the power of knowledge gained through the e-mails and face-to-face network discussion. This in return could help women become more autonomous through fostering their individual ability to exercise critical judgement and to free themselves from dominant beliefs, norms and desires.

When we co-created the e-mail list we also needed the face-to-face meetings to ensure that what we had created was real and would continue. We needed to validate how we felt about our sharing, especially when we shared something that we had been hiding for some time. We needed to see this in each other's eyes, because we were not sure how we might feel about the stories we had shared. If someone regretted the confession, she wanted to see how others looked at her; if the others were supportive and understanding (which was the case most of the time), she would feel good, and would encourage others to share, assuring them that they would not be judged.

With time the relationships became tighter and stronger, and the use of e-mail became almost spontaneous. It was used by all of us at all times, and we all became sensitive to each other's feelings. Often when we read the e-mails and felt that the sender would be feeling bad, we would call each other on the phone and try to comfort her and help her to understand the situation better. This process raised our consciousness and improved our life in terms of the way we react, interact and respond to our environment.

We discovered the importance of having our own dreams, desires and needs, and each of us started her own journey towards realizing her dream. One got the divorce she wanted, another travelled to the Gulf to work, yet another decided to raise her two daughters without trying to have another pregnancy, another got married after she thought she never would at her age and another changed her mind about working abroad.

The use of ICT such as the e-mail network we created proved to be a worthwhile venue to forge empowering and trusting relationships through connecting, sharing and listening to previously unrecognized experiences. This enriched our understanding about the complexity of our everyday life experiences. The process of self-reflection and dialogue with the intent of gaining more self-understanding is desirable and ICT makes it possible in a way that respects the complexity that such sharing inevitably entails.

Nurturing our agency, we expanded our sense of personal responsibility to how we interact with our environment, and this led us to explore new choices and possibilities and create new realities. Jordanian women's perception of themselves as limited, helpless and inadequate can change when they take the opportunity to think, talk and share in order to more fully understand themselves and their environments as expressions of oppression.

Co-creating an open space of reflection to explore the social and cultural norms they live and think in will improve women's understanding of themselves, their realities and their perspectives – and this may free them up to reconsider their options and life choices.

References

Brown, B. (2010) *The Gifts of Imperfection: Let Go of Who You Think You're Supposed to Be and Embrace Who You Are*, Centre City, MN: Hazelden.

Buskens, I. (2005) *Free Attitude Interview Manual*, http://issuu.com/gracenetwork/docs/fai__final, accessed 20 May 2014.

Freire, P. (1998) *Pedagogy of the Oppressed*, trans. M. B. Ramos, 20th anniversary edn, New York: Continuum.

Gharaibeh, M. and A. Oweis (2010) 'Why do Jordanian women stay in an abusive relationship?', *Journal of Nursing Scholarship*, 41(4): 376–84.

Haj-Yahia, M. (1997) 'Predicting beliefs about wife beating among engaged Arab men in Israel', *Journal of Interpersonal Violence*, 12(4): 530–45.

— (1998) 'Beliefs about wife beating among Palestinian women: the influence of their patriarchal ideology', *Violence against Women*, 4(5): 533–58.

— (2000) 'Wife abuse and battering in sociocultural context of Arab society', *Family Process*, 39(2): 237–55.

Hassouneh-Phillips, D. (2001) 'American Muslim women's experiences of leaving abusive relationships', *Health Care for Women International*, 22: 415–32.

Kavanaugh, A. (1999) 'The impact of computer networking on community: a social network analysis approach', paper presented at the Telecommunications Policy Research Conference, Alexandria, VA, 27–29 September.

Oweis, A., M. Gharaibeh, A. Al-Natour and E. Froelicher (2009) 'Violence against women: unveiling the suffering of women with a low income in Jordan', *Journal of Transcultural Nursing*, 20(1): 69–76.

Wheeler, D. L. (2008) 'Empowerment zones? Women, Internet cafés, and life transformations in Egypt', *Information Technologies and International Development*, 4(2): 89–104.

Young, G. (2002) 'Feminizing cyberspace: rethinking techno-agency', in J. L. Parpart, S. M. Rai and K. Staudt (eds), *Rethinking Empowerment: Gender and Development in a Global/Local World*, London: Routledge, pp. 79–94.

13 | Scheherazades of today: young Palestinian women use technology to speak up and effect change

VERA BABOUN

Introduction

The GRACE Palestine research is inspired by the wisdom, compassion and eloquence of the mythical character of Scheherazade, the main character in *One Thousand and One Nights*. Scheherazade volunteers to marry Shahrayar, the King of Persia, who had taken up the habit of marrying a virgin each night and beheading her the next morning. Scheherazade tells a story each night to enchant and educate the king, who after one thousand and one nights (and three sons) realizes he loves her and hence proceeds to make her his queen. This puts an end to the era of beheading women.

Figuratively speaking, Shahrayar represents all the oppressive patriarchal power that women face, with beheading being symbolic of the elimination of and control over women's lives, voices and choices. Many women are beheaded while they are still alive, prevented from fully speaking their mind, truth and needs. Scheherazade, having prepared herself thoroughly for her self-chosen task, selected her methodology of resistance carefully: her story-telling and the medium she uses allow her to speak her truth to her oppressor unencumbered and in her own way. As such she is a powerful archetype of a heroine who ventures out into patriarchal space to face an unknown fate and, in doing so, creates a new and liberated reality for herself and other women.

Nowadays, more than ever, it seems to be almost impossible for women in Palestine to venture out into such a space and create the liberation they seek. Here, women live the reality of gender discrimination and social discrimination that come with political occupation, forming a near-complete stranglehold on their potential for personal growth and social expansion. As Palestinians they live in confinement: the reality of the Apartheid Wall and checkpoints, detention, land confiscation, house demolition, mobility restriction and spiralling military transgressions. The spaces they can move in are restricted and this cannot but highly affect women's 'psychological, economic, health, educational, professional, and social well-being' (Shalhoub-Kevorkian 2010: 5).

As women living in a patriarchal country, they also suffer from gender discrimination in the domestic, public and legal spheres. Although Palestinian Basic Law asserts that 'all Palestinians are equal under the law and judiciary' (Article 9), women in Palestine live in a state of inequity and social injustice due to the discourse of patriarchal power, conservative cultural codes, unquestioned religious laws and the lack of effective political will to enforce gender equity and equality. Additionally, growing conservatism and fundamentalism in certain areas of the Territories, in response to the increasing intensity of the Occupation, thwart any possibility Palestinian women and girls would have to engage change for the better (Chaban 2011). A considerable number of Palestinian women thus resign themselves to silence, making their suffering (already kept hidden to various degrees because of the political reality of the Occupation and the social reality of living a secluded life as traditional Arab women) even more invisible (Shalhoub-Kevorkian 2010).

Hence, many women, unaware as they are of their own capacities, voices and self-worth, are not able to conceptualize or voice what they are dreaming of and envision the reality they would like to experience. It should thus not come as a surprise that Scheherazade became a powerful symbol, inspiration and role model for a group of young Palestinian women who were given the opportunity to explore how they could use ICT for their empowerment. The GRACE Palestine research team was grounded in the understanding that women have the capacity to gain awareness and use their voices to achieve a better life for themselves and other women.

Since the days of Scheherazade the increasingly global world of this post-modern era has been thoroughly transformed by the way ICT's effect on the ways people live, work, know and relate. Considerable ICT initiatives have been conducted for the development and empowerment of the marginalized, unvoiced and poor. Women, often excluded from full participation in their countries, professions and areas of livelihood because of sexism and gender discrimination, have, to various degrees, been able to use the spaces opened up by ICT for their development and empowerment (Buskens and Webb 2009). Young people are often 'first adopters' of new technology and this appears to be true in the case of ICT as well (Halewood and Kenny 2007). The inventiveness, dynamism and eagerness of youth, if adequately guided, can initiate progress at all levels. Accordingly, young people in general and young women in particular might become the catalysts of the very changes they attempt to manifest by raising their voices to share their concerns, perspectives, dreams and genius, prompted by resilience forged through the self-awareness that often accompanies oppression and disempowerment.

The young women who formed the GRACE Palestine research team designed, in an iterative way, an action research process aiming to investigate how ICTs could be used to enhance gender awareness and agency. In this process they strengthened their self-expression and learnt to strategically and effectively speak their truth to power, whether the oppression was found inside or outside themselves and whether it was psychological, social, political or communal.

Research context and methodology

The twenty-one female students at Bethlehem University came from various academic majors, scholastic years and residential locations, including the southern part of Palestine, refugee camps, rural and urban areas of Bethlehem Governorate, Hebron and the Eastern Arab part of Al-Quds. I acted as the principal investigator; more than ten of the participants were not my students but they attended Bethlehem University. The research undertook to investigate how through the use of ICTs the participants could:

1. become conscious of the gender discrimination and inequality prevailing in the Palestinian context;
2. enhance their abilities to freely articulate and share their stories, experiences and concerns;
3. improve the effective organization of their thoughts to precisely and convincingly express themselves;
4. develop their technical capacities to use ICTs as a space to traverse socio-political boundaries.

The research comprised two stages designed to investigate and assess these objectives:

1. Raising gender awareness: participants attended gender-awareness sessions (November 2009–February 2010).
2. Finding our voices ourselves: participants designed and conducted three radio talk shows titled 'Voices of grown up women' and created the GRACE Palestine short film titled 'The Journey of GRACE Palestine' (February–May 2010).

The research adopted a participatory methodology for collection, documentation and analysis of the data. The research data were collected using qualitative participatory methods such as open-ended, semi-structured interviews, face-to-face group discussions and story-telling sessions. The students worked with Excoboard (a social e-forum), designed and presented the three radio talk shows and developed the short film. The face-to-face sessions were video-taped or recorded through the Livescribe paper-based computing platform. Excoboard automatically recorded the participants' online interpersonal interaction. The radio talk shows were publically posted, uploaded and transcribed into a textual document, and the film was publically posted on YouTube (www.youtube.com/watch?v=KeLD-kXuseE). All documented material was analyzed using a qualitative thematic content analysis, which was led jointly by the participants and the principal investigator.

Raising awareness

The awareness-raising stage was designed to explore the young women's awareness of their gendered experiences and inequalities and how ICT could contribute to the understanding and articulation of these. We engaged simultaneously in face-to-face communication and online communication (Excoboard) with each other. During the face-to-face sessions, we engaged in general discussions on gender issues and in gender storytelling sessions, and we did two transformatory attitude process exercises (see Chapter 22).

We had several spaces to work with and in: the face-to-face sessions were conducted in one of the classrooms, we used media digital tools such as audio CDs and DVD documentaries and we browsed the Internet to gather information. As sharing of stories, discussions and the writing on Excoboard unfolded, the young women learnt to trust the research setting as supportive, private and trustworthy. They became more expressive and let go of some of their fear.

In this stage, the research investigated which medium of communication was the 'richest' for development of the participants' gender awareness, enhancement of their expression capacities, interpersonal communication and information acquisition. Our study revealed that face-to-face sessions had a 'richer' effect on the participants' interpersonal relational communication and information acquisition. According to Media Richness Theory (Blau and Caspi 2010: 2), face-to-face communication is considered the richest medium for it is the 'most efficient way to convey complex messages'. This finding proved relevant in our research. Although these young women lived in abusive contexts to various degrees, they were not necessarily aware of the discriminatory and oppressive nature and ramifications. For example, continuous face-to-face discussions on specific complex issues such as gender-based violence in Palestine enhanced the understanding of the participants of its nature, types and consequences as well as the resistance mechanisms in their personal lives. Various ICT tools, including an audio CD (Bila

Quyood and Yalla Nehki's *Without Restrictions, Let's Talk*, produced by the Palestine News Agency on issues pertaining to gender issues in the socio-cultural context) and a DVD documentary (*The Golden Pomegranate Seeds* by the Palestinian women director Ghada Tirawi featuring four young Palestinian girls who speak out about their abusive, incestuous experiences), helped to facilitate this process. Razan pointed out that the ICT tools facilitated 'our learning process considerably; [they] presented the information in exciting and memorable ways since it is visual and auditory'. The audio CD included forty interviews on gender issues conducted with experts, legal professionals and Palestinian citizens who are not experts or legal professionals in gender. Each participant was provided with a copy of the CD to listen to in off-set sessions. Mary reflected on the flexible potential of ICT in her learning process in the sense that she could '[listen] to the interviews at her time of leisure, whenever she wanted, with whomever and whenever'.

In this first phase we also watched *The Golden Pomegranate Seeds* documentary; this enabled the students to witness in a very direct and personal way the abusive situations and dynamics that Palestinian women are living with and the difficulty they have in learning to break the silence and speak up. As part of the documentary's closing statement, one abused young woman said: 'Never remain silent. Speak out your abuse even to the vacant air.' Ghada, who comes from a divorced family, wrote on her Excoboard: 'Their words challenged my silence. I was afraid to voice my experience, but as I watched the documentary, I said: If they can do it, I can do it!'

The documentary instigated the start of the story-telling sessions. By receiving the approval of the participants to video-tape their story-telling sessions, we were able to document the process for data analysis and assess the participants' growth in their communication and expression. The story-telling methodology was adopted to allow participants to hear their actual words when sharing their abusive experiences. Letting them choose their own words to express their own realties is 'considered voice therapy or words therapy' (Shalhoub-Kevorkian 2003). Ghada bitterly narrated her dilemma of being known as a daughter of a divorced mother, which carries enormous weight in an Arab community. Dalia narrated her dilemma with her body and look (wearing glasses due to weak eyesight, having acne and being overweight) in an environment that is focused on beauty. Suzan narrated hers of living in a very conservative and patriarchal family where all her movements and choices are controlled, while Mary narrated how in her family she was degraded as a girl for being a girl. She wrote on her Excoboard: 'I encounter verbal abuse from my old aunt. I have never even thought a misogynist could be a woman! She keeps saying: "I hope all *el-bannat* [girls] in our family die. You are one of them Mary."' In her story-telling sessions Mary explored her verbal and emotional abuse further.

It transpired that the combination of ICT tools we used (CDs, DVDs, video-taping) had a transforming effect. Some participants changed their attitude towards the cultural code of staying silent in the face of abuse and overcame feelings of personal embarrassment. For example, while collecting material to produce the GRACE Palestine short film, three participants gave their approval to include their personal stories in the film, which was posted on YouTube: Ghada and Mary included their video-taped narratives, and Dalia posted her image. As Ghada pointed out on her Excoboard: 'I am released and liberated. Let the whole world know my story of disturbed childhood.' Their words, language and voices changed from being 'a decorative description' of their abuse to more of a 'human vision, ideology, and philosophy' (Etel Adnan cited in Shalhoub-Kevorkian 2003: 395), used powerfully to heal their own and other women's wounds 'with the atomic strength of their words'. As Etel Adnan writes: 'These little energies [words] are similar to atoms, in the sense that they contain tremendous power' (cited in Shalhoub-Kevorkian 2003: 395).

Excoboard: a haven for liberating voices

During the awareness-raising stage a private Excoboard account was registered under GRACE Palestine for sharing comments and reflections; Excoboard thus remained a private space. Twenty-two topics were posted during the gender awareness-raising sessions and story-telling sessions and the students reflected and debated. The Excoboard table included 343 posted replies and 2,742 registered views. According to our understanding, as a synchronous online communication medium, Excoboard had a richer effect on the participants' intertextual interaction, responsive interpersonal communication and development of their technical and expression capacities.

Allowing many actors to exchange comments with others as if in face-to-face discussions, the Excoboard synchronous medium provided equal opportunities to participants to voice and express themselves, especially benefitting the more introverted participants. Introverts expressed themselves significantly more freely over Excoboard than in face-to-face discussions – and started to adopt the offline behaviour patterns of extroverts. There was more active participation in online than offline discussions. Enas pointed out: 'At home, university, or any public place, I tend to remain silent. I think I have been always shy. I always was afraid to express myself in order not to be criticized, rejected, or scrutinized.' Her active participation on Excoboard reflected how she mobilized her self-expression and self-knowing. Excoboard functioned as a personal and private space where the students could openly and yet discreetly share their problems and stories and where they could practise speaking the way they felt like without fear of judgement and condemnation.

Excoboard provided them with the opportunity to experience a degree of autonomy of expression and sharing that their home environments and the university grounds did not offer them. Nadine made it clear that 'I always feel safe in our Excoboard discussions. I can share whatever I want with girls who are just like ME, who understand Me and would never judge Me.' The capitalization of the first-person 'ME' started to appear in the last stages of her participation on Excoboard. The manner of communication among the participants enhanced Nadine's understanding of her self-knowing and self-agency. As Willis states in *Youth and Information and Communication Technologies (ICT)*, informal cultural practices are undertaken because of the pleasures and satisfactions they bring, including a fuller and more rounded sense of the self, of 'really being yourself' within your own knowable cultural world. This entails finding better fits than the institutionally or ideologically offered ones, between the collective and cultural senses (World Youth Report 2003: 313).

Since textual interaction on Excoboard entailed the writing and reading of comments, the participants' writing capacities and thought organization became more effective. As the awareness stage developed, participants gained more concise and convincing self-expression. Simultaneously, through the online synchronous interaction the participants experienced a 'co-figurative' media culture where 'peers' learnt from each other and organized a versatile understanding of their daily realities as young Palestinian women. Namir pointed out that, 'Step by step we got to know each other more and more, share our feelings deeper and started making change in each other.' This was important to our research context since the participants came from an Arab Palestinian culture where people converse with one another face to face and live in a close-knit local environment. Their initial learning came from a 'post-figurative context', where 'socialization occurs as knowledge and traditions are passed down from the older to the younger generation' (World Youth Report 2003). To start learning from each other and give that learning the authority to confirm themselves in their experience of themselves was thus a substantial change.

TABLE 13.1 Actual participation in face-to-face sessions and Excoboard.

	Number of participants			
	L	M	H	Total
Face-to-face sessions	6	9	6	21
Excoboard	3	10	8	21

Face-to-face measures: L (6–12), M (13–19), H (20–26); Excoboard measures: L (1–10), M (11–19), H (21–30).

To assess the effect of ICT on enhancing the ability of the participants to freely articulate and share their opinion, stories and concerns, we measured the actual participation and quality of contributions in each research medium, which included the face-to-face sessions and the Excoboard. For measurement of actual participation we used three rating measures: L (low), M (medium) and H (high). The rate of each measure differed for the two mediums, and rating measures in each medium depended on the actual participation of each participant (Table 13.1).

In the face-to-face sessions six participants were fairly quiet and tended to carefully reflect on their thoughts before speaking or participating. The numbers for their participation were low and, content-wise, although their contributions were relevant to the discussion, they were expressed concisely and without elaboration. Nine participants had a medium rate of participation and six had a high rate of participation; content-wise their contributions were relevant to the discussion and expressed with elaboration and zeal. For Excoboard three of the eight who received the highest rate for participation were among the six who measured low in their face-to-face participation. The levels of their contribution were measured by the mode of their interaction. They raised questions, instigated critical points, continuously replied on others' posts, commented on all the posted topics and actively commented on the reflection topic. The other three participants who received a low rate in the face-to-face participation also received the lowest rate of participation on Excoboard. We conducted a word count to measure the contribution level of each participant and the time spent on Excoboard. The three who received the highest rating had word counts of between 3,200 and 3,500 words, while the word counts of the ones with a low rate varied from 580 to 660 words. In general, use of the Excoboard succeeded in enhancing the young women's communication, as it seemed to create an equal playing field of expression and reduced the fear of encounters.

Addressing the public: sharing and celebrating

In this stage of the research we intended to enhance and assess the ability of the participants to strategically use their awareness and enhanced voices to address the Palestinian public realm through three radio talk shows. The students formed three groups of seven members each, and took a month to prepare themselves for the shows. They selected '*Aswat nisa' saiidat* [Voices of grown up women]: a gender triplet' as the title of their radio talk shows. Broadcast in 2010, the three talk shows raised three controversial issues, including gender-based violence, women's financial independence and the stories of abuse that Palestinian women of today need to narrate in order to bring about a change. The students took the lead during this stage of the research and were keen to assess whether they were able to, in Said's definition of speaking truth to power, 'carefully weighing the alternatives, picking the right one, and then intelligently representing it where it can do the most good and cause the right change' (cited in Selby 2006: 45).

For their pre-talk preparations the first two groups adopted similar methodologies. Participants Googled for information, collected statistics, recorded random short interviews with staff and students at the University and conducted weekly meetings. The interviews were the most important output used in their preparation, which boosted their self-confidence immeasurably. As Lina pointed out: 'To interview others entails a sense of authority; you feel that you are aware and you seek for more.' Each group conducted twenty interviews, analyzing them and integrating their findings into discussion topics in preparation for the talk shows.

The interviews revealed that male students on campus are convinced that imbuing men with gender awareness would decrease gender-based violence in Palestine. Interviews also revealed that female students support the financial independence of women while the majority of male students do not since it has a direct effect on the gender hierarchal relationship. The students opened their talk shows with these findings.

Prior to their talk show, the third group analyzed the plot, theme and characters of an Egyptian film titled *Ihki Ya Scheherazade* (Speak Out Scheherazade) 2009 by Yusri Nassrallah. They started their talk show referring to this film, which revolves around a woman reporter who presents a television talk show titled *End of the Evening and Beginning of the Day*. Every time, this programme would host a woman who is subjected to oppression in its various forms (assault, exploitation, beating) to show what ails women in societies that consider women as tools for sexual pleasure and reproduction.

According to our findings, the radio talk shows and the short documentary enhanced the participants' gender awareness by boosting their collective and individual voices, facilitating attitude change and augmenting self-confidence and self-expression. In our analysis, we considered the quality and quantity of individual participation in the talk shows. During their talk show the interventions of the first group were relatively short but well expressed and presented. Two of the participants who had been characterized by the groups as having introverted personalities actually made eight interventions each. Daisy, who hardly participated in the face-to-face sessions but was the most active on Excoboard, commented that 'the experience of the radio talk show was very challenging and out of the box. The entailed responsibility liberated my voice.'

The third group, which focused on abuse of women, received the highest number of calls from listeners. Their intervention was highly developed, analytically presented and confidently articulated. Even though Mary, who has a nasal voice, was reluctant to participate at first, she registered eleven interventions and excelled in the quality of her participation. She pointed out: 'It is true that I have a nasal voice, but it is full of energy and confidence. It is a voice that is actually listened to.'

To celebrate their newly found voices, the students posted a short film on YouTube. 'The film was about our new born selves,' Nadine pointed out. To narrate their story, each participant posted her image and a personal quote. The majority of the quotes included a verb or a noun that represents utterance: 'Women have to learn to say no', 'speak up', 'express' and 'raise our voices'.

Conclusion

The study affirmed that ICTs can be used as tools to enhance the technical and expressive capacities of young women, and, in conjunction with each other, these tools can form an efficient medium to raise and facilitate young women's gender awareness. As the young women's awareness and understanding grew, their sense of responsibility towards their own voices and selves was enhanced. Most of them challenged their own previously silenced voices and experimented with their capacity to speak up about what made them unhappy.

Their thoughts appeared more organized and their expressions became more concise and convincing. During the second stage they learnt that their resilience increased when they worked together and sought support from each other. As Ghada pointed out: 'In a world like ours, we need more than one Scheherazade to address change. Together we do it more effectively.'

Their growing understanding also increased their sense of responsibility towards addressing gender abuse and its ramifications in their wider environments. It was this that gave them the idea to do the radio talk shows. Realizing that they could make a difference in other women's lives in turn enhanced their self-confidence and appreciation of themselves and their newfound voices. The study indeed revealed that the process of becoming gender aware enhances self-confidence and awakens responsibility for self and others.

The young women learnt that to become a Scheherazade and effect change is not only about learning to enhance one's voice but also about making a deliberate choice. It was the choice to become gender aware that set their process of self-empowerment in motion, and all along this research journey they had to make the choice to actively participate and overcome their limitations. Each of these young women will have to continue making the choices that allow them to be Scheherazades in their own ways and to bring about positive changes for themselves and others.

Acknowledgements

Thanks to the assistant investigator, Raphaella Fischer, for her valuable contribution in conducting, sharing and reflecting with me in the two stages of the research, and mainly for her valuable participation in producing the GRACE Palestine short film. To the research student participants – Amani Zubei, Dalia Deereya, Daisy Giacaman, Fida Attalla, Ghada Hadwa, Haya Toubai, Inaam Sheikah, Lina Abed Rabo, Maram Iseid, Marian Saadeh, Mary Abu Ghattas, Nadeen Baboun, Nadine Antar, Nameer Kiresh, Ramma Halaika, Rand Jaouni, Rawan Gedeon, Razan Zeidan, Suzie El Khateeb, Watan Zubeidi and Wisam Sub Laban – I extend my ultimate respect and love for their commitment, their readiness and their belief in their own voices. They are the ones who gave GRACE Palestine research an entity and existence.

References

Blau, I. and A. Caspri (2010) 'Studying invisibly: media naturalness and learning', in N. Kock (ed.), *Evolutionary Psychology and Information Systems Research*, New York: Springer, pp. 193–216.

Buskens, I. and A. Webb (2009) *African Women and ICTs: Investigating Technology, Gender and Empowerment*, London: Zed Books.

Chaban, S. (2011) 'Promoting gender-sensitive justice and legal reform in the Palestinian territories: perspectives of Palestinian service providers', *Journal of International Women's Studies*, 12(3), http://vc.bridgew.edu/cgi/viewcontent.cgi?article=1118&context=jiws, accessed 20 May 2014.

Halewood, N. and C. Kenny (2007) 'Young people and ICTs in developing countries', www.cto.int/wp-content/themes/solid/_layout/dc/k-r/youngsub.pdf, accessed 20 May 2014.

McKenna, K. Y. A., G. Seidman, A. Buffardi and A. S. Green (2007) 'Ameliorating social anxiety through online interaction', manuscript under review, Ben-Gurion University, Israel.

Selby, J. (2006) 'Edward W. Said: truth, justice, and nationalism', *Interventions*, 8(1): 40–55.

Shalhoub-Kevorkian, N. (2003) 'Liberating voices: the political implications of Palestinian mothers narrating their loss', *Women's Studies International Forum*, 26(5): 391–407.

— (2010) 'Palestinian women and the politics of invisibility: towards a feminist methodology', *Peace Prints: South Asian Journal of Peacebuilding*, 3(1), www.wiscomp.org/pp-v3/pdfs/nadera.pdf, accessed 20 May 2014.

World Youth Report (2003) 'Youth and information and communication technologies (ICT)', www.un.org/esa/socdev/unyin/documents/ch12, accessed 20 May 2014.

14 | Jordanian bloggers: a journey of speaking back to the politics of silence, shame and fear

RULA QUAWAS

Legal obstacles combined with and hedged by multiple challenges – such as poverty, illiteracy, unemployment, limited access to land, social discrimination and traditional societal constraints, a moral economy where men protect and women are protected, sexual abuse and other forms of domestic violence – prevent many Arab women not only from fully participating in the economy and political arena but also from achieving economic independence. It becomes very clear that the interlocking challenges that Arab women face on a daily basis embed or configure them as second-class citizens, with particular implications for their disempowerment and oppression. However, since the advent of the Internet, and within a blogocentric framework and from a blogocentric perspective, some Arab women have been forging virtual relationships in their countries and across continents, creating national as well as transnational communities in which information can be pooled, problems aired and coalitions built to define and seek a world in which we can all flourish and coexist. For surely blogs are places of viewing, listening and observing: they are modern equivalents of the early Arab twentieth-century salon. Whether they are living rooms for receiving intellectual guests or just a room of one's own, these modern 'salons' are an always unfinished, always provisional space.

Among other things, Arab women have access to the resources of the information and communication technologies (ICTs), and for the most part they use these tools to wield influence over their lives and communicate meaningfully with other people all over the globe. ICTs play a pivotal role in organizing the images and discourse through which people make sense of the world, and they provide for most Arab women – who live in a freedom-deficit world – an unfettered space to circumvent the numerous restrictions and acts of censorship imposed by the culture of shame, silence and fear, by the culture of religion, by society and, more often than not, by the hegemonic political system. Through networked or meshworked technology that blurs the geographic, national, religious and ideological boundaries that used to be so abrasively clear-cut, and through sustained discursive contestation, some Arab women are increasingly beginning to engage in an exercise of re-visioning. This takes them beyond the patriarchal thinking through which women have been trained to see and allows them to speak back to the patriarchal order and the forces that would try to silence them, and to reconstruct their identity by exploring and representing their subjectivity.

Since cyber-technology allows a greater flow of information of all types and across social classes, it circumvents Arab women's isolation and offers them direct access to affordable information that they need, without them having to rely on someone from outside to bring the information to them. Today ICTs – which are used by approximately 1.5 billion people – are by no means a magic wand but can be regarded as one of the most effective tools in the hands of Arab women. For them ICTs are transformative and emancipatory tools that offer alternative representations and a counter-hegemonic discourse. These tools enable a medley of Arab women to reach beyond and behind the narratives of prejudice, ignorance and stereotypical representations of women, and to foster an interactive dialogue that is neither oppressive nor exclusionary. This critical weblog dialogue celebrates a world of absent presence and of plural cultures and peoples located at the periphery. Since the concept of gender is now understood as a performance or social achievement that is constructed in interaction (Butler 1999), we can see the construction of gender identities as shaped together with the technology (politics of technoscience) in the making.

Some Arab women use the blogosphere at full throttle to report, analyze, contest and explain in their own performative and effective words their plight and the promise of a better future. Their revelations of their personal lives and thoughts create a new experience and are in complete contradiction to the famous Arab cultural duality of *zaher* (appearance, or outer self) and *baten* (inner self), where people present an appearance that in fact functions as a veil to cover and protect their inner self. These new modes of talking about the self are especially interesting in a country like Jordan, where women have always had a culture of self-effacement in public, and where the use of 'I' is still difficult and is often replaced by 'we'. Certainly Jordanian women's demystification of their private life, in a culture such as this, can have and is having a significant impact on the self and on other social interactions.

The Arabic blogosphere, which is part and parcel of the global blogosphere, is experiencing a steady growth that is being driven, in part, by a rising desire – especially among young people – to engage in public debate across a range of political, social and cultural issues. Marc Lynch

(2007: 2), an expert on Arab media, contends that Arab bloggers have had a 'discernible impact' in a wide range of Arab countries, including their role in the 'Kefaya movement in Egypt, political protests in Bahrain, the turbulent post-Al Hariri period in Lebanon, anti-corruption campaigns in Libya and the 2006 Kuwaiti elections'. In its own way the blogosphere creates a culture of polyvalent voices, of democracy and of speech. It creates what I would like to call a 'blogtiza', which is similar to the vision of the *mestiza* (a person who expresses a multitude of cultures and operates in a pluralistic mode transferring cultural and spiritual values from one group to another): a 'blogtiza' draws attention to the emergent role of women's bargaining and negotiating, their subversion and resistance as well as their more intangible, cognitive processes of reflection and analysis, pointing towards a new consciousness from which deeper political and cultural transformations are thought to follow. A blogtiza is seen as a new entity that challenges and subverts hegemonic identities in the sense that it has the potential to see from various perspectives and to understand from various points of view. Its between and betwixt position creates a digital space where a nomadic subjectivity or a new identity position travels virtually and engages in new cultural ways of beingness and becomingness. This identification affirms the inextricable bond and allegiances between women and new information technologies.

By using ICTs sensitively and appropriately, young people in the Arab countries subvert the rationale of the hegemonic discourse and relocate an alternative site of political and cultural negotiation, creating a vibrant space of critical discourse that allows for a vigorous marketplace of ideas and opinions. The recent revolutions in Tunisia, Egypt, Libya and Syria testify to the paramount role of ICTs in creating new ways and means for people to organize, network, campaign and bring about social actions that may not be in the interests of governments and corporations.

This research stands as a comprehensive study of some Jordanian women bloggers who wrote blogs in the English language between the years 2009 and 2012. Through a hermeneutic-interpretive reading, grounded in an analytical interpretation of the ongoing production of women's self-representation in blogs as it intersects with hegemonic representations of women, and given the trends of feminist theory and their impact on women's empowerment, I investigate and analyze a specific collection of women-generated home-grown knowledge that is resting actively and vibrantly, rather than inertly, in the Jordanian blogosphere and that is shared with a real global audience through a shared digital platform. Also, since qualitative interviewing is a philosophy, a conversation with a purpose and an approach to learning, as Rubin and Rubin argue (1995),

I have used the free-attitude interview (Buskens 2005) with some women bloggers who have the most links to their sites. I consider the interviews as 'sites of knowledge construction' (Mason 2002: 227) where both interviewer and respondent engage in 'meaning-making work' (Holstein and Gubrium, 1995: 2). I have also conducted some in-depth interviews with professional women working in what is commonly referred to as the 'traditional media' in order to obtain their perspectives on blogs and on the relationships between their newspapers and the Jordanian blogosphere.

The study is a mix of texts and contexts, interwoven by reading intratextually but also with regard to the social and cultural contexts of their inception. Such analytic and interpretive readings have not resulted from reading the blogs in a piecemeal and decontextualized way but from reading them as a whole, a totality. The findings teach us that we are unable to change anything unless we begin by changing what is in our hearts, holding both men and women to the same standards of behaviour and confirming social agency and not sexualizing it. In writing this study, I want to offer a reading of blogs written by Jordanian women, a reading that confirms that Arab women can struggle, using their written voices, for equality from within the framework of Arab societies and that they can begin to reclaim their interpretive rights. Freedom does exist and it has helped to constitute a broadly shared discourse of meanings that contests inequality and patriarchy.

In Jordan, blogs have come to comprise a genre of online discourse that breaks gatekeeper monopolies on public discourse. Jordanian women bloggers use blogs as a robust platform of moderate (if not radical) feminism that places them in heterosocial space to challenge prevailing political and religious orthodoxies and allowable opinions and to speak up about their experiences. In this way they change the meaning of their beings radically, from a confined object to a free subject, a free agent who can act and make free choices. Using their real names or pseudonyms and writing in English or a mixture of English and Arabic (using '3arabeezi' or 'Arabish' words), some Jordanian bloggers, who are familiar with codes and customs and with the mental artefacts of society and conceptions of the world, author their own Internet narratives and begin to combat the inclinations that lead to an authoritarian mindset. They stop being inhibited by convention and propriety, by their internalized, deep-seated fears of being and saying themselves and by the snares of self-censorship. As they have illustrated in interviews, they create their own words that allow them to become aware of reality in order to fight for their own emancipation. This in itself is a quality of mind that is essential to a democratic transformation of the Middle East.

Although most Arab women are absent or even exiled from themselves and live in muted bodies and in snares of silence, euphemisms and circumlocutions, they are not voids that wait for sustenance, fulfilment or plentitude from men, who have left them only absences, defects and negatives to name who they are. So pleasing and phallophiliac have women become in Arab countries that they have forgotten the feel of their own skin and the multiplicity of their tongues. Naming them cultural custodians or preservers and the emblem of the honour of their communities, Arab men invest women with symbolic value that deprives them of their autonomous will and polyvalent voices. Mahmood states that, in order for an individual to be free, 'her actions must be the consequence of her "own will" rather than of custom, tradition, or social coercion' (Mahmood 2005: 11). Freedom, in this formulation, is about a woman's ability to autonomously 'choose' and to realize 'an autonomous will', one that is 'unencumbered by the weight of custom, transcendental will, and tradition' (Mahmood 2005: 11). One cannot help but ask how Arab women can derive autonomy and free will from an ascribed identity that demands their obedience and silence. The answer is that, as Miriam Abu Adas eloquently points out in a personal interview conducted on 8 July 2010, a woman does not create herself in silence but through words, actions and reflections. She adds that when speaking we do not necessarily know what we are going to say until we say it; when writing, we are often surprised by what we discover in our own minds.

Interestingly enough, some Arab women are changing the debate about women and using the blogosphere as their platform for a new way of interpreting human experience and for insurgent thought. In their blogs they not only reject the biological yoke of femininity and refuse to be assimilated into the iconography of Arab womanhood but they also reimagine a world quite different from the patriarchy in which women are deemed second-class citizens, and demand to belong to no one but themselves. They recognize and resist their social and cultural programming by reading against the grain and against sexist ideologies.

The best and most popular blogs, which have had a visible presence and which provide discussion forums for public and private issues and for oppositional politics, are Andfaraway.net, Madas.jordanplanet.org, Jordanianobservations.wordpress.com, Naydynmoody.blogspot.com and Queerink.tumblr.com. A closer look at these blogs shows that the bloggers develop powerful and political voices, analyze national and international issues and air public and private concerns in their blogs. Even though these blogs are individual-centred and express the aspirations, thoughts and sentiments of individual bloggers, they have become part of a wider community through the addition and the significance of blog rolls and links. They have come to create circles that open up spaces for dialogue between themselves and their readers: circles that accept the rights and freedoms of individuals and respect pluralism and freedom of expression and speech.

Among other things the Arab blogosphere produces critique, dialogue and friendship and serves as a proving ground for reconceptualizations of Arab womanhood. The conventional or cultural script of 'true woman-hood' as inscribed and texted by Arab culture is dismantled by some Jordanian bloggers who have made conscious choices to defy the status quo and redefine the social order. Writing a blog, as stated by all of the bloggers I have interviewed, is a means to create a space for self-making or self-invention and a springboard for subversive thought – precursors to transformation of social and cultural structures. Writing blogs is the anti-logos weapon that gives Arab women more of a voice in society as well as more autonomy, authority, openness, visibility and global outreach and dialogue among peoples.

Specifically, some Jordanian women bloggers exercise their agency to own a blog, name it, design it, write up blogs, respond to postings, use their original names or not use them and choose topics that touch their lives as women in the making. Their writings, as they have clearly stated, are centred in the truth of who they are and characterized by responsibil-ity and accountability; they do not embody a drama of victimization but of empowerment. The Jordanian women bloggers put great value on who they are and wear their crowns accordingly. They are, after all, the daugh-ters of Sheba.

The blogs depict the heterogeneity and diversity of Jordanian women in a way that shatters the stereotypical and homogeneous images that depict them as helpless and passive victims of a relentless Arab and Muslim community. By writing their blogs some Jordanian women trans-form themselves from victims into agents of resistance, just by telling or 're-storying' their stories and protesting the vast injustice done to them. In doing so they turn the tide of stereotyping and misunderstanding and perform an act of liberation.

Clearly, writing can be seen as an act of resistance, an emancipation to free the 'I' of the woman, long considered in Arab societies as nonexistent or impaired. To write is to define one's self distinctively, and this is why examining blogs entails questions around selfhood, subjectivity, iden-tity, agency and voice. Such terms are connected with the acquisition of the 'I', especially when expressed and affirmed through the act of writ-ing. Besides, women who write their stories and perspectives reshape the national memory of women by pushing their experiences from the periphery to the centre, and recreate their lives by themselves.

Jordanian women bloggers are blogdacious, for they know exactly what it means to write and to be a free agent capable of making her own world through the action of writing. Indisputably the writing of blogs is an act of liberty and of agency. Over time women have been taught to think as men and to identify with a masculine experience and perspective, which is presented as the human one, and to accept as normal and legitimate a male system of values, one of whose central principles is misogyny. As Fetterley (1978: xx) reminds us, 'the cultural reality is not the emasculation of men by women but the *immasculation* of women by men'. The experience of *immasculation*, which in its own way reproduces androcentrism, teaches women how to think like men and apprentices them in self-loathing and self-doubt. Since women, according to Daly (1973: 8) are not free to use their power to name themselves, the world and God, they have to reclaim their right to name and to go beyond the phallogocentric value system imposed by patriarchy. In other words, they have to discover and recover their voices and cancel out others who speak about them, to them and at them but never for them.

By writing their blogs, some Jordanian women become resisting rather than assenting readers, and exorcize the male mind that is implanted in them. The consequence of this exorcism is the capacity for what Rich (1972: 18) describes as 're-vision': 'the act of looking back, of seeing with fresh eyes, of entering an old text from a new critical direction'. The consequence of this re-vision is that women are no longer bound to men's reality but become interlocutors on both sides of the cultural divide and the architects of their own reality, thus changing the world they live in from a monologue to an active dialogue, and substituting a culture of marginalization with a culture of equality and equity. Culture, for these women, is a viable way of speaking back rather than double-speaking, of subverting the status quo and of destabilizing predominant ideologies. Culture becomes a way to comprehend how they live their lives – 'a structure of feelings', in the words of Williams (1961: 65). Their voices thus become an expression of their lived experiences that insist on their agentic notion of being free human beings not bound by a set of habits or traditions. They release their shame, free themselves of it and put it back where it belongs; they talk (and write) back to those who seek to silence them and to marginalize their existence.

Jordanian women bloggers contribute to the development of their country, bearing in mind that development – as Sen (1999) notes – is more concerned with enhancing the lives we lead and the freedoms we enjoy than with the growth of gross national product, industrialization or technological advance. If nothing else, blogs are a healthy antidote to patriarchy, which dismisses women writers simply for the crime of being female and confuses pen and penis (the model of the pen-penis writing as illustrated by Gilbert and Gubar (1977)). Cixous (1976: 878), a French advocate of *écriture féminine*, exhorts all women to 'write woman', to write from the body and thus take 'up the challenge of speech which has been governed by the phallus'. Jordanian women bloggers take up this challenge of speech and have begun to contribute to the feminist discourse by debunking some self-denying myths that are perpetuated about Arab women, myths that bespeak submissiveness, domesticity, piety, purity, meekness and silence. The trajectory of Arab women changing and making change is becoming evident and clear.

Through the Arab blogosphere Jordanian women produce themselves as speaking subjects, and their self-representation most often proceeds by moving against normative constructions of Arab women that are continually produced by hegemonic discourses and social practices and towards new forms of representation that disrupt these normative constructions. The process of writing blogs and of self-constructing and self-representation creates an empowered woman, one who occupies a speaking subject position of authority within a network of strands that may be termed politics, ideology, economics, history, sexuality and so on. The very act of writing, for women who have no rights, no identity and no existence, is basically an assertion of individuality and autonomy and often an act of defiance. It is, in essence, an act of being, creating and existence.

For instance, one Jordanian blogger, Farah, feels very strongly about the issue of crimes of honour, dedicating multiple posts solely to these crimes. She blogs about the legalities behind honour crimes and also links to news stories about current happenings, trying to show the illogicality and atrocity of these crimes. As she says: 'it is like honour crimes have become integrated into the country's tradition and customs'. Another blogger, writing under the pen name Madas, objects to the fact that a woman, no matter how modestly she is dressed, cannot walk on the streets in Amman without being subject to catcalling or other inappropriate behaviour from men. She mentions an incident where a man in a car acted like she was a prostitute and followed her all the way to her destination.

Yet another blogger speaks of how she has been exiled from her own self, to the extent that she has forgotten the feel of her own skin. Through writing her blog she challenges the social order's prescriptive definition of women's heterosexual behaviour and comes to grips with her homosexuality. She refuses to go on living in the cracks of deafening silence and demands to belong to no one but herself. She has become the female hero of her story, not the sacrifice. Her pages are no longer blank, written in invisible digital ink; they are present, visible and centred in the truth of who she is.

Ostensibly the voices of some Jordanian women bloggers operate against the discourse systems that work to negate any female subjectivity. By writing their blogs, Jordanian women come to transform themselves from victims into empowered agents of resistance. They are not angelic upholders of or collaborators with the hegemony of male power and ideology. They are self-possessed women who are capable of growing and of performing a hermeneutic sleight of hand, women who ask: 'Who, as a woman, am I?' They are new women living in a new world, new women whose strong voices engage in thinking, deliberating, questioning and negotiating. They are re-emerging from the abyss of invisibility and are providing models for positive change. By understanding the connection between the silence of submissiveness and the voice of self-representation, they assert their spirit and self and become the victor and not a victim in life's struggle.

The Jordanian women bloggers have found an intellectual territory in the blogosphere, a frontier where they can contest traditional meanings and transgress some personal boundaries. On the whole, the Arab blogosphere weaves a collective thread that enfolds the warp and woof of women's embodied rather than embedded self-representation: their agentic voices, their subjectivity and their empowerment. Jordanian women's voices, which have been hijacked, appropriated or 'othered' by the Arabo-Islamic culture for many generations, are unleashing themselves from the mire of aphasia and voicing their dreams of creating and initiating a discourse that is no longer reported or spoken for. The blogosphere is the catalyst that reverses or subverts the hegemonic male discourse and grants speech to women's voices, which were previously consigned to silence.

Through blogs Jordanian women come to unlearn not to speak, and effect a drastic change in their anecdotal status in the sense that they speak not at the instigation of man but at the instigation of their right to own their authentic voices and speak back to the patriarchal system. In this vein the bloggers turn from observed and passive objects into active, speaking subjects and look through a different, self-reflective lens that mirrors their re-visions, reflections and recreations. Using the blogosphere as a medium or tool, they deal with differences of opinion and scathing dissent, and begin to self-represent themselves; to think, deliberate, question and negotiate the traditional ways of defining Arab women as subordinate and silent; and to create a space for self-speaking. They assert their powerful presence to speak not the language of men or the silence of women, and bear witness to their selved lives and speak as women, or in place of the silent woman, for the woman, in the name of the woman. They are learning what the heart is and what it feels to enshrine whole-heartedness, and forge in the smithy of their souls the uncreated conscience of their race and unscripted national memory of women.

The very idea of a woman's voice as *awra*, or vice and temptation, with its moral essence (that which is shameful, defective and inadequate), is clearly transmuted through and by the blogosphere into an eloquent womb-like metaphor of creation that births women's self-authorship and self-affirmation and nurtures a culture of speaking back. By writing their blogs, Jordanian women claim for themselves the primacy of birthing, defining themselves as midwives in possession of the creation of speech, a speech of presence, fullness and richness of action. They are produc-ing alternative discourses and images about womanhood, citizenship and political participation in their societies. They are creating alternative discursive spaces where it is possible to redefine patriarchal gender roles while questioning the sociocultural, economic, political and legal insti-tutions constraining them. By engaging in an ongoing robust dialogue, they undo hegemonic recorded history and also increase the volume of women's voices, initiatives and activities at the local and international/ national levels without relying exclusively on traditional media. Most importantly, they encourage women to think about new ways to estab-lish professional relations, forge alliances and broaden the scope of their interventions.

The blogs of Jordanian women point towards women's relentless efforts to engender the public sphere (a commonly used paradigm for understanding the impact of ICTs on the political spaces of the Arab world) and to promote a culture of equality celebrating partnership instead of hierarchical gender relations. The bloggers' voices are formed in the deep centre or core, the fertile realm of dreams, the unconscious and the womb, and grow from the space of existential affirmations and self-love. Their emerging, engaging voices manifest the true desire to become purged once and for all of the psychology of oppression and the dark spaces of fear, shame, silence, alienation and inequality of power.

Through their eloquent public-speaking voices they come to reinforce their authority as thinking, authoring and author-itative women who stimulate and inspire women readers to develop their minds and who help transform the collective voice of Arab womanhood. Their blogs mark the intellectual independence of women and educate women's powers of self-expression. More than ever, Jordanian women are not only affirming their speaking positions through blogs and demonstrating to the whole world their rights to justice, dignity and a way of living empathetically across differences but are also creating a new way of speaking and uncovering in their own blogs a sense of what we would now call agency – intelligent political resistance to the codes and scripts of their culture. They are creating a far-reaching and a far-ranging emerging discourse on women's issues and on their development within and beyond the Arab world. Their blogs show Jordanian women to be acting as guides, interpreters, critics or curators of a mosaic narrative defined by its expressiveness and its dynamism and to be stimulating discussions on changing mindsets and, one hopes, pushing for other changes in attitudes towards gender and on changing laws.

References

Buskens, I. (2005) *Free Attitude Interview Manual*, http://issuu.com/gracenetwork/docs/fai__final, accessed 20 May 2014.

Butler, J. (1999) *Gender Trouble: Feminism and the Subversion of Identity*, London: Routledge.

Cixous, H. (1976) 'The laugh of the Medusa', trans. K. Cohen and P. Cohen, *Signs* 1(4): 875–93.

Daly, M. (1973) *Beyond God the Father*, Boston, MA: Beacon Press.

Fetterley, J. (1978) *The Resisting Reader: A Feminist Approach to American Fiction*, Bloomington, IN: Indiana University Press.

Gilbert, S. and S. Gubar (1977) *The Madwoman in the Attic: The Woman Writer and the Nineteenth-Century Literary Imagination*, New Haven, CT: Yale University Press.

Holstein, J. and J. Gubrium (1995) *The Active Interview*, Thousand Oaks, CA: Sage.

Lynch, M. (2007) 'Blogging the new Arab public', *Arab Media and Society* 1(2) www.arabmediasociety.com/?article=10, accessed 20 May 2014.

Mahmood, S. (2005) *Politics of Piety: The Islamic Revival and the Feminist Subject*, Princeton, NJ: Princeton University Press.

Mason, J. (2002) 'Qualitative interviewing: asking, listening, and interpreting', in T. May (ed.), *Qualitative Research in Action*, London: Sage, pp. 225–41.

Rich, A. (1972) 'When we dead awaken: writing as revision', *College English*, 34(1): 18–30.

Rubin, H. and I. Rubin (1995) *Qualitative Interviewing: The Art of Hearing Data*, Thousand Oaks, CA: Sage.

Sen, A. (1999) *Development as Freedom*, New York: Anchor Books.

Williams, R. (1961) *The Long Revolution*, Ontario: Broadview Press.

THREE | **ICT-enhanced relating and becoming: personal and social transformation**

15 | Sex, respect and freedom from shame: Zambian women create space for social change through social networking

KISS BRIAN ABRAHAM

Introduction

In Zambia, tradition guides women's conduct and expression of sexuality because of the shame that women can bring to family and society. A well-known Bemba (native tribe of Zambia) saying underpins this: 'A husband's infidelity does not ruin a marriage.' A woman's sexuality is to be solely expressed in matrimony for the pleasure of her husband and she is not sovereign in and over her own body. It is therefore considered inappropriate for women to meet male strangers and engage in conversation without the permission of partners or parents, while it is expected that a man sexually will explore as many women as he chooses.

At women-only marriage-preparation events, women are instructed on how to sexually please husbands, take care of the home and be submissive wives. Men are not allowed to attend these nor are they expected to follow similar stringent rules before marriage. It is clear that, in the cultural and religious curriculum that has the roles set for each gender, women are traditionally considered more as a means of reproduction than as sovereign beings, with enjoyment of their own sexuality removed from their reproductivity (Wolf 2012).

In addition to insistence on the separation of the sexes, aggression towards women is expressed across all classes of society (Gender in Development Division 2008). The Zambian Minister of Defence, himself reported for beating his wife several times (Zambian Watchdog 2012), is on record as saying that beating a wife is a sign of love in his 'culture' (Nkonde 2013).

Female sexuality is particularly targeted for judgement and aggression. Mobs of male assailants citing Christian and cultural principles have been attacking women for their choice of dress on the city streets (Telegraph 2002; Zed Chronicle 2011). After the attacks, women are blamed for having brought the violence upon themselves because they chose to dress 'immorally'. Such attacks by male street hawkers on women have become endemic, the reason given being that these women wear 'sexually provocative' clothing (Zambian Watchdog 2013). Even when these women are consciously expressing the fact that they are sexual beings through the way they dress, there is seen to be no justification for this; women's intent does not really come into the equation: the fact that men feel sexually provoked by women's bodies is used as a rationalization for 'stripping' women and shaming them publicly (Post Online 2012a).

Women are aware of the potential for violence when they are perceived to be expressing their sexual selves, as this is well documented in the media (FEMNET 2012).[1] Despite this, some women are defiant and choose to represent themselves as they wish without shame, thus challenging the deeply misogynistic underbelly of Zambian society.

Research focus

In parallel to women 'taking back the streets', a similar phenomenon is happening in virtual space. Zambian women have initiated social networks where women and men can connect with each other in unrestricted ways. In these spaces women express themselves on the issue of sexuality without fear or shame. These Internet conversations between women and men about sex have led to relationships and partnerships where issues of common interest are explored. In this way barriers that were set by age-old traditions are traversed and female–male relationships that were developed in the freedom of virtual space have been imported into physical space in a seeming deconstruction of norms.

This chapter examines some of these events and tries to explain them as part of the process of gender transformation in Zambian society, in the context of the promise of freedom that information and communication technology (ICT) seems to offer. Between 2009 and 2012, I explored several Internet dialogues initiated by Zambian women and the ways in which they challenged patriarchal culture and created space for women and men to experiment with alternative gender behaviour.

Research methodology

Six respondents and five closed Internet social-networking discussions were selected. These Internet social-networking websites were managed by women in Lusaka to discuss sexual taboos. Membership of each group averaged five hundred people of both sexes, of various ages and from diverse geographical origins. I subscribed to social-networking sites, joined social-network discussion groups and held several online conversations with male and female group members of mixed ages on their use and experience of social networks. I participated in physical meetings organized by group members with the consent of group administrators.

I also conducted qualitative in-depth interviews with five leaders of these social-network groups and about ten group members.

Research findings

Religion and culture keep the sexes divided and women submissive and inferior

Religion and culture are the two main yardsticks by which morality is measured in Zambia. In all spheres of life, including the Internet, women are expected to behave according to the requirements of these two belief systems in order to avoid public ridicule. Zambia was controversially 'declared' a Christian nation by late President Frederick Chiluba on 29 December 1991 as soon as he assumed office (Phiri 2003; Post Online 2012c). Steps have been taken to enshrine this (Chanda 2010) within the national constitution in the draft of 2011 – still in draft in 2014 (Lusaka Times 2014) – ignoring protests by sections of the public and civil society, including the Catholic Church, which promote the idea that Zambia is and should be a secular state (Kalito 2012).[2] The current constitution recognizes the authority of traditional courts and their customary laws in what is a dual legal system (statutory and customary law) (Ndulo 2011).

Catherine Shawa, an *alangizi* (female traditional marriage counsellor), had the following to say about the conduct of women and their use of cell phones:

A newly married woman should change her mobile phone number to avoid being called by men who know her number so that she can start a new life with her new husband and make it a point to know as few men as possible – this way she will maintain the marriage without conflict.

The undertones of potential violence are detected in guidance embedded in the curriculum of traditional marriage lessons. It is noteworthy that use of ICTs and the practice of social networking are major themes. With regard to women's conduct in the presence of men, Shawa prescribes the following: 'During marriage negotiations, women will sit on the floor and avoid eye contact with the men who are to sit in an elevated posture so as to show submission of the women to men.'

Joe Chilaizya, Deputy Ambassador to China, shares his interpretations of culture:

Land allocation right now still does not favour women. We are suffering because of culture. It is traditions that say a woman cannot eat an egg. All those little rules were meant to let men have undue advantage over women. In an egg there is so much nutrition a woman needs to use. And you are denying her that. That is stupidity.

Separation and division of the sexes is considered essential and women are kept submissive and inferior with rationalizations provided by religion, culture and morality.

Freedom of association, sex and social networks

Radical discussions are taking place in these social networks. Members participate unencumbered by the shaming that would come with the label of 'inappropriate/unacceptable behaviour', against a backdrop of the strictest moral codes of conduct a traditional society such as Zambia can muster. While these groups were initiated by women motivated by their need for free self-expression, the groups also attract male participants. Some of these men want to experience such an alternative unrestricted social space for themselves, but some want to intervene in what is happening and shut down the 'deviant' behaviour of women in these groups.

During these social-network group discussions, traditional norms that enforce subordination of women are critiqued. Linda, a female call centre manager, shares her experiences with Facebook and her creation of a Facebook group:

> At my job I am confined to the office desk and have to deal with few people at a time, but that hasn't hindered me because I discovered that with Internet social networking I could still reach out to so many more people than I would even reach in person. I have reached out to thousands of people, most of whom I have never met. I created this group to discuss sex because it is a taboo issue and many people lack the confidence to discuss these issues in public.

Social-network discussion groups are tackling sensitive sexual topics. Membership of these groups is by invitation only and participants are expected to subscribe to certain behavioural rules. Linda's group is called 'Real Adults Talk with Waleka'. She shares how group members who first met in cyberspace are meeting physically and undertaking social activities in their own communities:

> The response was overwhelming when I created this group. Friends started adding their friends who started adding their friends, and then we started having get-togethers, meeting physically where we would openly talk and get to know each other. We have group members from outside Lusaka Province in the Copperbelt, in the United States of America, in Australia and all over. In Copperbelt Province members

have even started doing community service projects where they live – people of diverse backgrounds, social standing and mixed gender and age.

An excerpt from the rules of conduct for this group reads in part as follows:

> Welcome to Real Adults, a forum for discussing topics that focuses [sic] on sex … sex has always been a delicate issue, a taboo topic in most societies but here we say it as it is but are very mindful of how we express ourselves to not injure the next person's feelings … let us all respect each other's opinions. The use of foul and insulting language is strictly forbidden … posting of pornographic material is also not allowed in here … in here, we talk about sex in a mature way.

A male group member reflected that in the Real Adults Talk with Waleka Facebook group men and women debated sexual taboos without limitations:

> The group is a forum for people to talk about sex, to meet people of their kind and just to get males to understand the female perspective on sex and females likewise do the same with males. We talk about dry sex,[3] sexual positions and how to treat our partners.

There is no limit to the number of men a woman can have as friends in her Facebook account (Kitwe Times 2012). Using the Internet as an alternative living space in parallel with their physical lives is an option for some women who spend their time in seclusion at home or at work. A respondent shared her fear of her spouse getting to know the company she keeps via her Facebook account: 'I cannot share my account log-in details with my husband as he will just get annoyed when he sees some of the conversations; I keep my personal life away from my Internet life.'

Threats to freedom of expression on the Internet

Linda Waleka Manda's first Facebook page was censored by Facebook:

> I started a page in 2010 and I would openly talk about sex, but then certain people found it offensive for a woman openly discussing sexual issues in public on the Internet, so they reported me to Facebook and my first account was closed. I think the whole discussion that I had, was a discussion on oral sex.

Linda has had several of her pages reported to Facebook by people who do not approve of the content she posts and she has resorted to creating secret groups inviting only people she trusts to avoid being reported and censored. Group rules are set and must be adhered to in order to stay a member. The rule system resulted in a process of 'self-selection' whereby only people adhering to the same values would participate in the privileged conversations of this group. It became a community with its own culture.

There have nonetheless been cases where women have been attacked by social network 'friends', resulting in women retreating from Internet social networks and/or changing their names. In some cases virtual fights have led to physical fights and even violence. Another way of threatening the women was to get police involved. As a group moderator explained:

> A male group member was soliciting for sex from female members and we deleted him ... We have had to eject several people who broke the rules ... but he went and reported us to the police so we deleted the group and re-uploaded it, excluding him. He then went and reported me to my boss, claiming that I was using my office computer to manage a porn site. He also went and threatened to beat another member of the group and this intimidation went on till the human resource officer at head office heard about it. Luckily, our human resource officer knew this guy and had heard that he had done this to other women elsewhere before, to an extent where he even used blackmail to intimidate that victim.

Royce Bwalya Mwape, a student at the National Institute for Public Administration, had her Facebook identity taken over by unknown assailants:

> I received a friend request from someone I do not know but since they had the same Facebook friends as I, I thought it might be safe to make them my friend as my other friends might know them. This person then changed their name to mine (Royce Bwalya Mwape) and started sending friend requests to all my friends. My 'friends' accepted the requests from this person, thinking it was me. After this person had assumed enough of my friends as their friends, they started posting pornographic pictures on their profile in their Facebook account as an identity picture claiming it was me. Everyone thought it was me in the pictures and the Police even instituted an investigation so they could arrest whoever was posting the naked pictures. My name was on radio, on the streets, everywhere with people claiming that 'Royce Bwalya

Mwape' is the girl who is posting naked pictures of herself. In the end, I had to close my Facebook account completely and change my name to Royce Nabwalya Mwape on Facebook.

Royce believes that this attack might have been carried out by a man whose sexual advances she had refused. The attempt to destroy her identity almost succeeded, with radio hosts and social-network users reporting police interest in arresting Royce for lewd behaviour (her alleged behaviour would be considered a crime under Zambian law) (Globe 2012; Post Online 2012b). Royce's friends created several Facebook pages to counter the smear campaign, but in response there were just as many Facebook pages created claiming that Royce had posted the pictures. Deleting her Facebook account and changing her name for fear of further victimization and attacks created feelings of self-alienation in Royce and yet these efforts did not suffice to safeguard her from the onslaught in physical space. Royce eventually had to change her name and became 'Royce Mwape', dropping the 'Bwalya' altogether.

Discussion

Anonymity and freedom of expression

Framing and categorizing people according to gender, sexual orientation and/or other aspects of personal identity take on a new meaning in cyberspace, where people can decide how they will present themselves and which identity they prefer to be known by, because there is the option of anonymity as people approach and engage with each other: one can never be sure who and what the other person is like. This facilitates a focus on the content that is shared and not in the first instance on the person who is sharing. Since typical gender prejudices are therefore not immediately evoked as they would be in physical space encounters, gender relations are 'freed up' to some extent.

Freedom, reflexivity and self-awareness

When people join social-network groups, they join on the basis of what interests them at a personal level and not because of their inherited cultural identity. This alignment with personal and individual interests makes it possible for user-defined cultures to emerge. When joining a specific Internet social-network group, users typically question the group's guidelines before they join. In asking themselves what they would gain from joining a group, they act in stark contrast to 'reallife' social situations in which their inherited gender roles take precedence and where they follow the cultural rules of association in an unreflecting and unexamined way. Furthermore, the traditional sexist practices have lost potency as the rules within these groups are deliberately designed to prevent such sexism and hegemony from happening. When prejudice takes place, critiquing of it exposes such sexist behaviour as not only undesirable but also as a choice, communicating that it is possible to behave differently from the socially acceptable gender rules that are prevalent in and rule behaviour in physical space.

Female sexual agency

In the sex-talk groups, women initiated dialogues on their sexual preferences and described what pleased them, in a marked departure from the passive sexuality expected of them in the Zambian interpretation of the female role in heterosexual matrimony. Women are not expected to initiate sex in explicit ways, despite the fact that they too aspire to a healthy enjoyment of sex. The social networks provide a self-elected membership of a platform that eliminates the shame and judgement that would be present if women acted with sexual independence in their own homes.

When women question and critique cultural and religious norms by manifesting themselves as sexual beings in social-network spaces, attacks from fellow social-network users (and men in particular) sometimes occur. These attacks mirror the physical attacks women sustain on the street when the way they dress evokes sexual connotations. This backlash of threat and violence seems intended to confine women to their traditional place and to keep female sexuality under male control. It is as if the men consider any confrontation with female sexual agency that does not happen on their terms as either an 'open' invitation or as morally repulsive. Is this because men cannot control their sexuality and find it convenient to blame women when they feel aroused? Is it because the concept of 'women as sex objects' is culturally accepted but 'women as sexual agents' is not? And is religion evoked to strengthen male supremacy by making women feel immoral if they employ sexual agency or are seen as doing so?

Conclusion

It is imperative to undertake further research into how social-networking spaces can contribute to women's empowerment, challenging and possibly transforming misogyny. Women have the inherent right to discover their own destinies outside inherited cultural and religious norms, and social-networking spaces have an important role to play in this respect.

Misogyny is deeply embedded in Zambian traditions, and religion provides the perfect rationalization for it. In *Is Multiculturalism Bad for Women?*, Okin (1999: 13–15) states that culture and traditions are so closely linked with control of women that they are virtually equated; she discusses the possibility that religion's sole aim could actually be the control of women by men.[4] Religious doctrine is indeed used in Zambia to rationalize violence against women on the streets as well as on the Internet. While women have found, to an extent, a safe haven in Internet space where they have even created a sort of social revolution in terms of sexual freedom, this does not solve the issue of misogyny in the 'streets' and homes of physical space. This mindset encroaches into cyberspace, as is evident in the attacks on the women's talk groups, the closing of Facebook pages and police involvement. Nor is Internet space a substitute for physical space: women have bodies and need to move around.

For ICT to be able to fulfil its promise of freedom in providing spaces and opportunities to critique existing degrading and disempowering social relations and experiment with new, more empowering and nurturing ones, and bring those models into physical social space, Zambia as a society has to face misogyny and transform it.

The way in which Internet spaces are functioning as commercial entities in a neoliberal market economy also has to be rethought. When social-networking spaces play to the tune of the most powerful groups and/or the groups that hold the most purchasing power, it has to be realized that in sexist and capitalist societies these groups will inevitably be made up of men (Dohnet 2013; Womack 2013). As it has become obvious that there are men who use the Internet to pursue misogynist agendas (Daily Mail 2013), it can be claimed that, in following a 'free market' ideology, spaces such as Facebook reinforce conservative and sexist mindsets. The increase in misogyny on social-networking spaces has not gone unnoticed: on 21 May 2013 an open letter to Facebook written by a coalition of women's organizations (Women, Action, & the Media 2013) called for Facebook to train moderators to recognize and remove gender-based hate speech, among other forms.[5]

At the same time, as this study revealed, Facebook closed pages that were not offensive but that had evoked the ire or complaint of a powerful individual or group. People self-organizing on the Internet on the basis of affinity instead of cultural identity has led to social change in many places, including in Zambia.[6] In creating social-networking spaces where sexual and gender identities can be expressed, Zambian women have done something revolutionary for Zambian society: engaging with each other on the basis of shared interests instead of traditional identity is an act of critiquing the traditional status quo and opens pathways for others to follow. It is therefore of crucial importance to make sure that attempts to manage these spaces as 'markets' dominated and controlled by commercial interests do not obstruct the use of Internet spaces for free and individual expression, exploration and association.

Recommendations

Implement a new people-driven constitution in Zambia

There is a need for the implementation of a Zambian constitution that is gender sensitive and contains explicit provisions for the empowerment of women and other marginalized groups in Zambia. This will ensure that women's economic, cultural and social rights are provided for and guaranteed in the constitution with ultimate removal of various discriminatory clauses especially present within Article 23 of the constitution. This should lead to the domestication of the Southern Africa Development Community Protocol on Gender and the United Nations Committee on the Elimination of Discrimination against Women[7] protocols to guarantee the rights of women and engender the language within the constitution. The current constitution is mostly silent on discrimination against women and in some cases superimposes the authority of customary law over matters of economic rights to the disadvantage of women. A constitution that makes gender awareness clear will also ultimately make discrimination against women justiceable.

Safeguarding of women's welfare in cyberspace

Social-networking sites and other Internet platforms need to take a clear public stance against the dangerous tolerance of misogyny through hate speech, promoting vices such as rape and domestic violence. Social-networking sites must review and update guidelines that their user-operations teams use to identify hate speech and implement in-house training to reflect those new standards. Women's welfare should be given prominence in deciding what posts or Facebook pages are offensive or not, even when this would affect the bottom line.

Basic literacy

At the most basic level, there is need to prioritize the promotion of functional literacy programmes for women as illiteracy is a major barrier to the empowerment of women and their effective use of ICTs for development.

Notes

1 To respond to this violence in southern Africa, FEMNET in Malawi has sounded an urgent call to action via the 'Strip-me-not' campaign (FEMNET 2012). This phenomenon seems not to be confined to southern Africa. In Canada a movement to counter the blaming of female victims of sex-related crimes has emerged in public-protest events termed 'Slut walks'.

2 Zambia has always been a secular state with tolerance of religions other than Christianity and recognition of seventy-two local tribes from across the country.

3 Women are pressured to use herbs to reduce vaginal moisture so that their male sexual partners can enjoy sex more as they will 'feel tighter'. 'Dry sex' has been found to cause cervical cancer, among other ailments.

4 Okin (1999) singles out the patriarchal religions of Judaism, Islam and Christianity with their particular characterizations of women as overly emotional, untrustworthy, evil or sexually dangerous, making their rights over their own children questionable. To underpin this she cites how the book of Genesis in the Bible presents the 'woman' as the reason for the fall of mankind from God's favour and how Abraham, also in the book of Genesis, attempts to sacrifice his only son (Isaac) on God's instruction without consulting Sara, mother to the boy.

5 Women, Action, & the Media, the Everyday Sexism Project and author–activist Soraya Chemaly launched the campaign. Participants sent over sixty thousand tweets and five thousand emails. In an unprecedented response, Facebook committed to changing its user guidelines and the way it moderates photos and posts that celebrate rape and violence against women. It will be interesting to see how this commitment evolves over time.

6 As became evident during the 2011 elections in Zambia, a wave of political debates and expression representing discontent with the twenty-year rule of the Movement for Multi-party Democracy took place on Internet social networks, showing how this new technology can play a leading role in people clustering together around common-interest issues to influence major political milestones in real-life situations.

7 CEDAW (the Committee on the Elimination of All Forms of Discrimination against Women) is a landmark international agreement that affirms principles of fundamental human rights and equality for women around the world. CEDAW is a practical blueprint for each country to achieve progress for women and girls (see www.womenstreaty.org/index. php/about-cedaw).

References

Chanda, E. (2010) 'NCC resolves to maintain "Christian nation" declaration', *The Post Online*, 23 April, www.postzambia.com/post-read_article.php?articleId=8440, accessed 28 January 2013.

Daily Mail (2013) '"Misogynistic" pickup artist raises $17,000 on Kickstarter for dating guide on how to sleep with a woman even if "she's resisting going home with you"', *Mail Online*, 19 June, www.dailymail. co.uk/femail/article-2344635/Misogynistic-pickup-artist-raises-17-000-Kickstarter-dating-guide-sleep-woman-shes-resisting-going-home-you.html, accessed 1 July 2013.

Dohnet, J. (2013) 'US social ad revenue to hit $11 billion by 2017', *Clickz*, 11 April, www.clickz.com/clickz/news/2261023/us-social-ad-revenue-to-hit-usd11-billion-by-2017, accessed 20 May 2014.

FEMNET (2012) 'Malawi: Strip-Me-Not campaign', 29 January, www.siawi.org/article3011.html, accessed 16 April 2012.

Gender in Development Division, Republic of Zambia (2008) 'National action plan on gender-based violence (NAP-GBV) 2008–2013', Lusaka: Cabinet Office, Republic of Zambia, http://countryoffice.unfpa.org/zambia/drive/GBV-NAP_2008-2013_FINAL.pdf, accessed 20 May 2014.

Globe (2012) 'Magistrate Mwiinga fines Iris Kaingu', *The Globe*, 25 October, http://theglobenewspaper.blogspot.com/2012/10/magistrate-mwiinga-fines-iris-kaingu.html, accessed 1 July 2013.

Kalito, K. C. (2012) 'Proclamation of Zambia as a "Christian nation" is a non-event, says Mpundu', *The Post Online*, 2 April, www.postzambia.com/post-read_article.php?articleId=26448, accessed 4 July 2013.

Kitwe Times (2012) 'Facebook: new Zambian marriage breaker in town?', 16 April, http://kitwetimes.com/?p=917, accessed 16 April 2012.

Lusaka Times (10 January 2014) 'Church dismisses constitution hijack claims by President Sata', *Lusaka Times*, 10 January, www.lusakatimes.com/2014/01/10/church-dismisses-constitution-hijack-claims-president-sata, accessed 5 June 2014.

Ndulo, M. (2011) 'African customary law, customs, and women's rights', Cornell Law Faculty Publications 187, http://scholarship.law.cornell.edu/facpub/187, accessed 3 June 2014.

Nkonde, F. (2013) 'Beating a wife is a sign of love – GBM', *The Post Online*, 23 May, www.postzambia.com/post-read_article.php?articleId=33103, accessed 10 June 2013.

Okin, S. M. (1999) *Is Multiculturalism Bad for Women?*, Princeton, NJ: Princeton University Press.

Phiri, I. A. (2003) 'President Frederick J. T. Chiluba of Zambia: the Christian nation and democracy', *Journal of Religion in Africa*, 33(Fasc. 4): 401–28.

Post Online (2012a) 'Choma call boys strip woman', *The Post Online*, 30 May, www.postzambia.com/post-read_article.php?articleId=27569, accessed 3 June 2014.

— (2012b) 'Iris Kaingu gets K10.8 million fine in pornography case', *The Post Online*, 25 October, www.postzambia.com/post-read_article.php?articleId=29411, accessed 28 January 2013.

— (2012c) 'Proclamation of Zambia as a "Christian nation"', *The Post Online*, 2 April, www.postzambia.com/post-read_article.php?articleId=26452, accessed 28 January 2013.

Telegraph (2002) 'Zambian women stripped for wearing mini-skirts', *The Telegraph*, 15 January, www.telegraph.co.uk/news/1381558/Zambian-women-stripped-for-wearing-mini-skirts.html, accessed 16 April 2012.

Wolf, N. (2012) *Vagina: A Cultural History*, London: Hachette.

Womack, B. (2013) 'Facebook seen reporting sales jump as mobile-ad options expand', *Bloomberg*, 1 May, www.bloomberg.com/news/2013-05-01/facebook-seen-reporting-sales-jump-as-mobile-ad-options-expand.html, accessed 1 June 2013.

Women, Action, & the Media (2013) 'Open letter to Facebook', 21 May, www.womenactionmedia.org/facebookaction/open-letter-to-facebook, accessed 7 July 2013.

Zambian Eye (2011) 'Women comply to call boys' dress code', *Zed Chronicle*, 21 November, http://zedchronicle.com/?p=4962, accessed 3 June 2014.

Zambian Watchdog (2012) 'Flashback: GBM batters wife, says he beats her because he loves her', *Zambian Watchdog*, 16 April, www.zambianwatchdog.com/flashback-gbm-batters-wife-says-he-beats-her-because-he-loves-her, accessed 16 April 2012.

— (2013) 'UCZ bishop regrets prevalence of sagging jeans and mini-skirts', *Zambian Watchdog*, 20 May, www.zambianwatchdog.com/ucz-bishop-regrets-prevalence-of-sagging-jeans-and-mini-skirts/comment-page-1, accessed 16 April 2012.

16 | Ancient culture and new technology: ICT and a future free from FGM/C for girls in Sudan

EINAS MAHDI AHMED MAHDI AND INEKE
BUSKENS[1]

Introduction

The action research project on which this chapter is based aimed to open up debates around the acceptance of a national law in Sudan that would criminalize female genital mutilation/cutting (FGM/C)[2] and to investigate whether and how information and communication technology (ICT) could contribute to this endeavour. FGM/C[3] is understood as violating women's human rights and the rights of children (World Health Organization, UNICEF and UNFPA 1997) and on 20 December 2012 the United Nations General Assembly passed a resolution banning the practice (UN Women 2012).

FGM/C is not only an issue for Sudan; it is also a global issue. Since the 1970s FGM/C has presented scientists, policy-makers and the general public with the dilemma of how to choose between respect for cultural diversity on the one hand and a universal humanist and moral imperative on the other. Fran Hosken's *Women's International Network News* was for a while the only way the West could make sense of a phenomenon that had health-care personnel who cared for Sudanese women in European hospitals (for instance) stunned and bewildered.[4] Such occurrences fed into the wider public dialogue as more and more women from practising countries came to live in the West, sometimes to look for refuge but sometimes just to live and work. Every year twenty thousand young women seek asylum in the European Union for reasons related to FGM/C (United Nations High Commissioner for Refugees 2013).

With ICT forming and informing our global knowledge society, FGM/C has become a cause for anybody who is digitally literate and wants to take the issue on. Browsing the Internet makes clear how this almost unfettered openness is feeding a sensationalized image of what Sudan and Sudanese women are about. The anti-FGM/C outrage is indeed understandable from an outside perspective, but not all that effective from an inside perspective. As early as 1980, Nawal El Saadawi, the Egyptian physician who was one of the pioneers advocating for the abolishment of the practice, requested outsiders to find a respectful and useful channel for their outrage (El Sadaawi 1980; Gruenbaum 2005b).

The discourses around the practice conflict on many levels within as well as outside Sudan: international development and global health practitioners, grounded in a Western understanding of universal values, speak the language of individual human rights, while researchers grounded in cultural anthropology and culture studies tend to think in terms of cultural self-determination and cultural rights. Many anti-FGM/C activists from the non-Western world have adopted human-rights discourse, which is indeed not the way one would speak about the practice and its meaning in the communities where FGM/C is practised (Abusharaf 1995, 2000, 2001; Shweder 2000: 117).

Both perspectives, however, are wrought with conceptual and ethical dilemmas: communities are not homogenous entities, constituted as they are of unequal power relations with dissent always present even when it is often dismissed, especially when women and girl children are concerned; cultures are always changing and in flux, hence giving them an ahistorical time frame is a misrepresentation of reality; deciding which voice to give pre-eminence to is therefore always a judgement in the moment and hence a fallible human decision. It is thus not surprising that the practice of FGM/C, which limits girl children's capabilities severely in the light of understandings of freedom (Sen 1999) and human development (Nussbaum 2000, 2003), brings the Western ethic of the individual being able to claim rights from a community to a confrontation with the African ethic of the individual's duties and responsibilities towards the community.

This text is grounded in a collaboration between a Sudanese insider and a Dutch outsider. The authors underwrite Moore's (2007: 327) perspective:

What of those women who oppose female genital operations but are not white, Westerners, or feminists? ... In all the cultures and contexts of the world where female genital operations are practised there are women and men who are opponents of these practices, but this does not mean that they are necessarily allying themselves with Western liberal traditions and ideas of human rights, or giving up on cultural and religious values ... Their agency is not the result of having given up on false consciousness, but of setting forth new goals and aspirations in the context of changed ideas and circumstances.

With this text (in electronic and hardcopy format) the authors hope to participate in the conversations around the practice both offline and online, from a perspective that is grounded in mutual learning between insiders (practising) and outsiders (not practising) from Sudan and beyond and in this way contribute to the eradication of the practice in a way that is respectful and appreciative of the dignity of Sudan and its peoples.

FGM/C in Sudan

FGM/C is deeply entrenched in Sudanese society and is woven into the personal identity and fabric of female dignity, spirituality, sexuality and reproductive power. Nahid Toubia, a Sudanese surgeon who became one of the pioneering researchers and care-givers in this field (Toubia 1994; Izett and Toubia 1998), explained in an interview with the BBC World Service (Toubia 2002):[5]

> By allowing your genitals to be removed [it is perceived that] you are
> heightened to another level of pure motherhood – a motherhood not
> tainted by sexuality and that is why the woman gives it away to become
> the matron, respected by everyone. By taking on this practice, which
> is a woman's domain, it actually empowers them. It is much more
> difficult to convince the women to give it up, than to convince the men.

Although FGM/C is pre-Islamic, resonance with the Islamic modesty code of family honour, female purity, virginity, chastity, fidelity and seclusion has woven this practice, its ideology and its discourse tightly into the sociocultural fabric of Sudanese society. Yet opposition to the practice can be traced to 1821, when El Sheikh Hasan Hassona advocated the concept that people (men and women) can be circumcised symbolically without actual physical surgery (Abusharaf 2001: 118). This approach towards eradication of the physical aspect of the practice while retaining the symbolical meaning is echoed in the discourse of Abdel Magied and Omran (1999), who suggest that: 'The uncircumcised female is the ideal state of circumcision.'

Infibulation (type III, also called 'Pharaonic circumcision') is the form of FGM/C that is most prevalent in Sudan (in Egypt it is termed 'Sudanic circumcision'). Infibulation leads to many health complications of an immediate as well as a delayed nature.[6] Female Genital Mutilation is linked to increased anxiety levels and post-traumatic stress disorder (Behrendt and Moritz 2005; Kizilhan 2011).[7]

Statistics on the prevalence rates of FGM/C in Sudan have indicated a decrease in the practice from 96 per cent to 88 per cent from 1979 onwards (Federal Ministry of Health 1999), and studies indicate that women's intentions to circumcise their daughters have decreased (Ahmed et al.

2009), but the latest UNICEF report indicates that no decrease in prevalence has been observed over the past 25 years (UNICEF 2013: 114, 115, 174). British colonial efforts to eradicate it may have worked adversely (Boddy 2008). Western outrage at the practice may still contribute to affirming the custom in the spirit of resistance to Western dominance (Gruenbaum 2005b).

Although the national FGM/C law was drafted in 2007, to date it has not been considered by the government. Because Sudan is an Islamic state, religion plays a key role in the orientation of the state. When the Religious Scholars Committee, Sudan's main clerical authority, publicly advocated and issued a *fatwa* factually endorsing FGM/C in 2009, this *fatwa* became applicable to all Muslims including their political institutions.

Sudan's civil society is undertaking significant efforts to inform the general population about the medical and human-rights implications of FGM/C. The most prominent anti-FGM/C initiative at the moment is the Saleema campaign, which is supported and executed by local non-governmental organizations and UNICEF (2010). *Saleema* is an Arabic word meaning 'whole', 'unblemished', 'as created by God'. *Ya ghalfa* and *ya nigsa* are the words used to bully girls who are not cut, and this peer pressure often brings them to ask their mothers to 'make them also special' and end the bullying torment. The essence of the Saleema campaign is thus about giving people another language in which to think and speak about girls' bodies in relation to FGM/C.

Many theories have been brought to bear on FGM/C, in terms of its history (Mackie 1996, 2000; Lejeune and Mackie 2008), the meaning of its practices (Gruenbaum 2005a; Berggren et al. 2006; Boddy 2007), its discourses (El Sadaawi 1980; Abusharaf 1995, 2000; Gruenbaum 2005a; Wade 2012) and the possibility of its eradication (UNICEF Innocenti Insight 2010; Berg and Denison 2013; UNICEF 2013). At the onset of this research, however, we worked from the understanding that for processes of social change to happen the people in question have to be in charge of the knowledge quests themselves. They have to want to understand how they maintain the practice they want to change with their own thoughts and emotions, their own doing and being. In this way, they will be able to formulate, test and implement their own theories of change.

Methodology

The research took place in the period 2009–12, partly in Khartoum (the capital city) and partly in Kordofan State. At the start of the project Einas Mahdi Ahmed Mahdi, the principal researcher, met in Khartoum with the various non-governmental organizations and individuals who are committed to the eradication of FGM/C. As the next step a group discussion was held with religious and political leaders to discuss the law and what needed to be done in order to get it accepted. Subsequently forty in-depth interviews with educated men and women were conducted (in which Tyseer Omeer's contribution was indispensable). The interview sample was diverse, varying from university lecturers and high-school teachers to lawyers and doctors, and including both old and young people with equal representation of women and men. After the initial structured questions, the interviews were open-ended and centred on the experience of FGM/C (for the women), the reasons for it, the consequences of it and the potential for it to change.

Those who were interviewed were in the following age ranges: 32 per cent 16–25 years; 15 per cent 26–35 years; 21 per cent 36–45 years; 20 per cent 46–55 years; 12 per cent 56–65 years. In terms of marital status, 47.5 per cent were married, 47.5 per cent were unmarried, 2.5 per cent were widowed and 2.5 per cent were divorced. In terms of education, 25 per cent had secondary schooling, 32.5 per cent were graduates and 42.5 per cent were post-graduates.

Of the women, 85 per cent were circumcised; the uncircumcised women were in the age category 16–25 years. The decision to have daughters circumcised was made by the mother in 40 per cent of cases, the grandmother in 46.7 per cent, 'following custom' in 12 per cent and the father in 1.3 per cent of the cases. It was paid for by the mother in 42.8 per cent of cases, grandmother in 52 per cent, father in 4.2 per cent and others (aunts) in 1 per cent of the cases.

First-phase findings

The custom that is bigger than the law

Some respondents believed that FGM/C was a crime and that the law should punish everybody involved. Others considered it a problematic issue but definitely not a crime; they felt that this was an old custom, older than any law, and that the law should respect it. 'This custom is bigger than the law', was a recurrent theme in both the interviews and the focus-group discussion.

The majority of men are against it

When the male respondents were asked, 'Would you consider female circumcision for your daughters?', 16.7 per cent answered yes and 83.3 per cent answered no. This high percentage of men who were dismissive of the practice can be linked to their education level (most of the males were graduates and post-graduates) and the fact that they were aware of the health complications of FGM/C. It could also be because they, as Toubia (1994) suggested, do not have a vested 'identity' interest in keeping it in place.

'I could not convince my mother and/or mother-in-law'

The lawyers and legal advisers who supported the issuing of the law failed to convince their own older female relatives to get rid of this practice. One of the legal advisers who participated in issuing the Child Law of 2010 shared the following:

> Despite my own personal belief, I failed to convince my mother and mother-in-law to leave my daughter uncircumcised. I made a plan with the reliable and reputable midwife to deceive them and convince the old mothers that I did circumcise my daughter and thus I protected my marriage and family.

Other men were not so fortunate and had to let circumcision happen.

Men, women and sex

A few women considered FGM/C as a necessity to keep a man, because it was understood that a tight vagina would give men pleasure. FGM/C was just what needed to be done to keep a man interested, so that he would not get a second wife. None of the men shared this perspective; for them, it was just something that women did.

The role of midwives

Quite a few women thought that FGM/C was perpetuated because it gave midwives an income. Men expressed the opinion that because the government was not paying midwives (enough) they needed to continue to do infibulation, which would also make it likely that re-infibulation would need to be done later. The respondents were also aware that the communities would protect rather than report the traditional birth attendants and midwives who did the procedures (even in cases where the girl died), even though what they did was practically illegal.

Betrayal of trust and intimacy

As the operation is typically initiated and presided over by grandmothers when girls are very young, the theme of betrayal and lost intimacy was an important issue for quite a few of the women. Since women's and men's worlds are in a sense autonomous spheres, and girls and women grow up to rely on and find their identity within women's worlds, the betrayal of trust and loss of intimacy that the procedure came to signify for many women would indeed be a life-changing experience. Many girls ended up 'hating all the relatives who were involved in committing this crime'. One of the respondents was very vehement:

> I have hated my grandmother throughout my life and I still remember
> my granddad's words to my mother, which are still throbbing in
> my ears: 'I am not going to forgive you unless you circumcise your
> daughter.' Moreover, I am going to kill that midwife if I have a chance.

Working with the youth

Various participants expressed the hope that youth involvement, especially in the rural areas, would see the rise of a new awareness and the end of the role of the grandmothers. One of the respondents, a doctor who had been working to raise community awareness around FGM/C for more than thirty years, said that the responsiveness of the communities was very weak, particularly among villagers and Bedouins. He could not see that changing without directly involving the youth. This perspective on the role of youth formed and informed the study by Mottin-Sylla and Palmieri (2011).

Appreciating the sharing, needing more information

Many women appreciated the opportunity to share their personal experiences during the in-depth interviews. Their emotions and memories revealed that the experience had left deep wounds, and talking about it and being heard and acknowledged appeared important. Many respondents indicated that they needed more information about the practice itself and why up to now no law against it had been accepted in Sudan.

First-phase findings

It became clear that the next step for this project in search of an effective strategy towards a 'future free from FGM/C for girls in Sudan' could not be simply promoting acceptance of the law. The recurring theme of the need to respect cultural tradition emphasized that FGM/C has to be understood as a ritual that affirms relationality and commonality, binding individuals to each other and their communities. As Abusharaf (2001: 136) argues, 'within communities that adhere to circumcision, this tradition is perceived as a cultural right, not as a breach of rights'. Instead of using ICT to support the acceptance of the law, the research focus thus shifted towards the use of ICT to explore how individuals and communities could use ICT to discuss their experiences and perspectives in relationship with each other.

Concluding the first phase, the principal investigator shared both her personal experience and that of her respondents on a radio programme broadcast in Kordofan State. Although an elderly relative reprimanded her because sharing this in public was seen as bringing shame on the family, it was essential that she did this. The project was about opening up debates and she needed to adhere to the project's purpose, even when that meant that she had to challenge the code of silence around FGM/C that keeps it a 'women-only' and hence secluded issue. This radio show opened the second, intervention phase, which included a radio talk show, a website and an interactive radio programme for the rural areas.

Second phase: interventions and findings

A radio show hosting a religious debate between a moderate and a fundamentalist religious leader

The radio programme hosted a religious debate between fundamentalist and moderate viewpoints and was facilitated by a professional talk show host. Listeners called in, asked questions and debated issues. This religious debate enabled educated women to think issues through for themselves, especially when the moderate religious leader focused the listeners' attention on the fact that the Qur'an mentions many things concerning women, such as marriage, divorce, inheritance and testimony. The Qur'an further gives very detailed instructions about pregnancy, suckling, weaning and menstruation, and, while many verses point to decency in dress and other aspects of modesty concerning women's lives and choices, there is not a single verse mentioning female circumcision. Furthermore, when women called in to ask the moderate religious leader about the Hadiths, the four prophetic sayings that are claimed to call for female circumcision, he assured them that they are weak sayings.[8] There is no basis for the type I variant of FGM/C, which is called *sunna* in Sudan, traced back to prophetic Sunna in Islam. There is also no evidence that the prophet Mohamed mutilated his daughters.

The women seemed to be quite satisfied with this moderate opinion, which traced circumcision to old traditions and beliefs and not to Islam, as the fundamentalist speaker claimed. The debate revealed the weakness of the fundamentalist argument, especially when this speaker discussed how foreign interference in Muslim society aims to stimulate depravity in society and when he preached that uncircumcised girls were more lustful than men and would not be controllable.

The debate also showed that women appreciated the serious discussion of the issue. From the interjections it appeared that those who had suffered health problems during childbirth and psychological problems before and after marriage were especially keen to speak. They expressed their deep concern that this practice should be ended and spoke of the necessity of making a law to prohibit and criminalize it.

It became clear that a large number of women were aware of their rights concerning life, body safety and dignity of living, and that they were ready to fight for these by explaining the danger of female circumcision, which they framed as a 'deformation operation of the female sexual organ' that can lead to harmful results (both physical and psychological) and may destroy the female's sexual life.

A website

The project website provided health and human-rights information and was used especially by young people. Awareness was raised about the hazards of FGM/C, especially in the rural areas where hospitals are few and infrastructure (in terms of roads and communication) is not good. This prompted the youth to initiate spontaneous campaigns in their communities.

An interactive radio show for rural areas

During this interactive radio talk show, women who were against circumcision phoned in and reported how they had suffered during delivery and how they had nearly lost their children because they lived in remote areas with no health unit nearby and had had to travel a long way. There were stories of suffering and caesarean operations. One of the grandmothers mentioned that one of her relatives in Darfur was still suffering from a urinary fistula. This had prompted her and her family not to conduct the practice on their children in the future.

There were, however, also women who were in support of circumcision, claiming that female genitals are very ugly and therefore need to be removed for women to look beautiful. Others thought that when the woman's sexual organ is tightened up, it is more enjoyable and exciting for the partner, and that the woman will then get all sorts of rewards from her husband in return. Some women mentioned that in some communities uncircumcised girls would not have the chance to get married. Stories were shared of girls being sent back when the husband upon marriage discovered that they were not circumcised; once returned to their families, they would not have any chance to get married again. After a lot of discussions, some of these mothers and grandmothers declared that they were not going to mutilate their daughters. Although these were small groups, they seemed to be good seeds to start with. While it will take time and patience, this will be the first step towards change.

Discussion

Ambivalence and dissonance

The forces that fight against FGM/C in Sudan and the forces that want to retain it as part of an authentic Sudanese religious-cultural identity are both very strong. While these two stances are represented by certain groups, organizations and individuals, these conflicting sentiments also reside in individual human beings. Being ambivalent about a cultural practice is normal. However, ambivalence in combination with a culturally sanctioned silence and pervasive lack of communication will favour tradition, especially when there are stakeholders that have a firm interest in maintaining the status quo. The research project, with its design grounded in communication and reflection, brought this intrapersonal and interpersonal ambivalence into the open and dissonance and discrepancy therefore ran as red threads through the findings of this second phase.

For a start, the discrepancy between the prevalence of the custom and the support for it among Sudanese women is striking. The fact that women appreciate the many negative physical effects and yet choose to continue the practice resonates with Abusharaf's (2001) narratives and the findings represented in the 2013 UNICEF report (p. 115).

Furthermore, the lack of shared understanding between wives and husbands about such a crucial dimension of their relationship is remarkable. Berggren et al. (2006: 34) argue that the misunderstandings between husbands and wives about what each thinks about FGM/C could actually perpetuate FGM/C through the generations: wives may not know that their husbands actually do not like their infibulated state, but, noticing that they do appreciate the reinfibulation after delivery – which, as the husbands explain, may be necessary because of the damage done by the initial infibulation process – the wives in turn may interpret their husbands' wish as an expression of their preference for a tight vagina. This then would spur them into getting their daughters infibulated as well.

There is lack of communication between young girls and their mothers and grandmothers. The decisions around FGM/C are mostly made by women for whom the pain of the initial infibulation, sexual intercourse and delivery is no longer a current reality. In this 'maternalistic' space, the voice of the girl children 'to whom it is done' is missing from the discourses. Their voice is culturally silenced. The fact that the practice is done against their consent is the core of Nussbaum's (1999) argument against it.

Furthermore, female sexuality and what it means to women, men and society at large, which is the topic that should be at the heart of the debates around FGM/C, is shrouded in silence too. In Chapter 19 Nour Ibrahim describes how mothers refrain from giving their daughters sex education for fear that this may incite their sexual curiosity and hence endanger their virginity, virtue and marriageability. It is, however, this silence that actually leaves young women wholly unprepared to handle themselves as sexual beings in a new, more connected world, and even set them up to create the realities their mothers were so afraid of.

There is also the dissonance between the various religious interpretations of FGM/C as a practice for proper Muslim women. There is a discrepancy between what is written in the Qur'an about FGM/C and what fundamentalist teachers claim is there.

Finally, the languages that our respondents used varied widely: from those of care and connectedness, of community and belonging and of a betrayal of this intimate bond of trust to discourses, of rights, crime and punishment and of unforgiveable harm. This discrepancy resonates with the varying academic and advocacy perspectives on FGM/C that frame the practice on the one hand as a cultural ritual that binds individuals within and to communities and on the other as a form of harm inflicted on girl children who are not given a voice.

Working with dissonance as an opportunity for reflection, communication and critical agency

The above-mentioned areas of dissonance are opportunities for reflection and communication because they are the cracks in the sociocultural grid that has woven people, practices and discourses so tightly together into one fabric of personal and social cultural identity. In the second phase, these cracks were used by people who would normally never discuss these issues with each other, to engage each other directly and share openly: women spoke up about what FGM/C meant for them as young girl children and what it still means for them now, as mature women. In questioning traditional norms and values, women were developing their capacity for critical agency (Sen 2001). Religious leaders publicly discussed their conflicting interpretations on television. Women and men listened to each other speak over the radio and mothers and daughters listened to each other speak.

ICT-based and ICT-enhanced action research can accommodate individual needs and possibilities

Whether it was an old ICT such as broadcast radio or a new one such as a website or interactive radio, ICT appeared to be perfectly suited to allowing people not only to obtain the information they needed but also to understand each other's perspectives. Because different people brought different hopes and fears to the issue, they had different needs for openness versus safety and privacy and thus their communication needs were also different. It seemed that, especially in the case of a delicate topic such as FGM/C, being able to remain partly hidden and yet capable of full participation was very conducive to open and truthful sharing. Furthermore, the ability to respond at a time when one was ready to respond made ICT very suitable as a research tool for connection grounded in and enriched by reflection.

The various ICT tools and platforms were used in this project in such a way that the many convictions and lived experiences that were seeking recognition could be heard and acknowledged. As ICTs facilitate personal sharing with the communicating parties defining what they disclose of themselves and the time they need for their response, they are the ideal tools for the self-reflective discourses that needed to happen. Our project has shown that an ICT-based action research project is feasible in the context of the debates around FGM/C in Sudan as it can be adapted to the many and very diverse social contexts. The group that was not included in this study in an explicit fashion, although it was not explicitly excluded, were the midwives. A further evolution of this approach could find ways to include them in these conversations (Berggren et al. 2004).

Conclusions

On 19 August 2013, in response to a particularly massive Saleema campaign, anti-FGM/C activists and other bloggers complained that the Saleema campaign was not clear in its message: FGM/C was not even mentioned, they claimed, because the organizers were afraid to challenge the fundamentalist religious leaders (Abbas 2013). But what if this lack of frankness on the side of the organizers was prompted not by fear of fundamentalist reprisals but by care and connectedness? What if the hesitancy to make the bold claim that uncut women are *saleema*, whole and unblemished as God made them, was prompted by the organizers' ambivalence about the concept of *saleema* itself? If Saleema is claiming that uncut women are *saleema*, where does that leave 90 per cent of all Sudanese women that are cut? Furthermore, the conceptual message of the Saleema campaign, although it resonates with the religious understanding of the body as created by God, dismisses the acknowledgement of the virtue of the practice and, by focusing on what the surgery takes away, it is dismissive of what it gives.

FGM/C is a complex issue. It is a lived experience for almost every man, woman and child in Sudan. The practices of doing what a woman does form and inform being what a woman is on many deep and probably unexamined levels. FGM/C appears to be so 'natural' for most women that many of them will continue the practice even when they do not like it. Since the operations are done on children who are not given a say in the matter, the custom can be recreated for future generations unchallenged in a perpetual cycle. Furthermore, Western outrage and condemnation from British colonial times up to the present may have entrenched the practice.

All this, however, cannot explain why in more than a hundred years of eradication efforts from insiders and outsiders, from within Sudan and beyond, the practice is still so prevalent. FGM/C is spoken of as bigger than any law and it is indeed more ancient than the nation state. In order to realize a future for girls in Sudan free from FGM/C, what is embodied and embedded in the practice, which is so valuable and precious for Sudanese society in general and women in particular, has therefore to be given a voice. Perhaps the approach of acknowledging the virtue of the practice and understanding its meaning can suggest ways in which it can be transformed so as to retain its value for the communities while letting go of the harmful physical effect for the individual girl children.

While there would thus definitely be a place for broad-based conceptual campaigns that affect thinking about women's bodies and FGM/C, such as the Saleema campaign endeavours to do, co-creating opportunities for sharing of knowledge, perspectives and experiences at places where the cracks in the grid can be opened a bit more would be a feasible and fruitful method for both research and intervention efforts and should be explored further.

Recommendations

Radio broadcasting can cover large areas and invite rural communities to participate and share their experiences. Young people can be taught how to programme and facilitate websites and Facebook pages. Television and radio programmes can provide forums for dialogue between opposing standpoints of political and religious leaders. Through sharing information about health and sexuality and exploring how religious life and community life would be without FGM/C, ICT can be used to explore modes of community communication and reflection for an inclusive form of sociocultural renewal.

The principal researcher (first author) functioned like a native anthropologist and, as such, transcended in and through her research the insider–outsider polarity. It was her capacity for self-awareness, critical reflection and compassion for self and others that enabled her to call attention to the cracks in the grid, turn them into opportunities for communication and stay connected with her conversation partners regardless of whether there was resonance or not. This capacity and the ways in which it can be nurtured and developed warrant further exploration.

Regarding the dilemma in FGM/C discourse, infusing the language of human rights with the concept of right to culture (Hernlund and Shell-Duncan 2007) has definite merit in the endeavour to transcend the polarity between Western thinking in terms of individual rights and African thinking in terms of community rights. It may, however, be timely to consider creating a conceptual framework that would create the space for the emergence of a dialogue that is truly global in nature. As Mackie (2000: 280) and many others have emphasized, parents continue this practice out of love for their children. Several approaches can be explored in this direction, including Ubuntu, considered to be an African form of humanism, grounded in the understanding of 'I am because we are'; Gilligan's (1993) understanding of connection rather than rights being the ground of moral development; Tronto's (1994) ethic of care grounding economic relationships instead of the individualistic striving towards betterment and profit; and the Stone Center's scholars' exploration of a 'self in connection' rather than an atomistic, individualized self (Jordan et al. 1991).

Outsiders can make valuable contributions to the debates around FGM/C in Sudan when they realize that this cultural practice, with the emotional outrage it evokes, functions like a mirror reflecting the self: in one's judgements one becomes known to oneself. But holding on to one's judgements turns one into an outsider. Accepting non-judgemental compassion as a research attitude will transform boundaries between insiders and outsiders into avenues for sharing knowledge, experiences and perspectives that grant everyone recognition and inspire everyone to find a voice. This will create the space for what Moore (2007: 326) calls a 'comparative anthropological project' and will enable researchers and advocates from inside and outside Sudan to craft the respectful and useful channel for their outrage that El Sadaawi (1980) asked for so long ago.

Notes

1 Tyseer Omeer, who was initially partnering Einas on this project, had to leave because she took up a PhD scholarship overseas.

2 In this text we use the term 'FGM/C' when we speak from an international policy and research viewpoint, 'infibulation' when we speak of Sudanese data and context, and 'circumcision' when Sudanese respondents speak about the procedure. 'Female genital cutting' is perceived as a less stark and less Western ethnocentrically coloured term than 'female genital mutilation', the term Fran Hosken coined in

1979 and that started to be used by Western feminists. The term 'female genital mutilation' was, however, endorsed by the Inter-African Committee on Traditional Practices Affecting the Health of Women and Children during its regional meeting in 1989 (unpublished report) (Izett and Toubia 1998). For an overview of the various types and their implications see World Health Organization (2014).

3 The efforts to eradicate the practice in Sudan have a long history but both laws and religious messages have been ambiguous (Herieka and Dhar 2003), although the Ministry of Health has issued various policy documents that support the abolition of the practice (Ministry of Health 2002). Sudan was the first country to accept a law against FGM/C, in 1946, when it was still under British colonial rule. This history was, however, fraught with tension (Boddy 2008). After independence and especially when Sharia law was adopted in 1983, the law against FGM/C was dropped. Article 13 of the law, which prohibits all forms of FGM/C, was removed by the Council of Ministers from the Child Act of 2009. This decision followed a *fatwa* of the Islamic Jurisprudence Council, which called for a distinction to be made between the various forms of FGM/C and not to ban type I, which is known in Sudan as *sunna*.

4 The second author's involvement with FGM/C dates back to a moment in 1977 when a cultural anthropologist from Leyden University was called to a maternity ward to facilitate the communication between a Sudanese diplomat's wife who had come for her delivery and the maternity ward staff (Buskens 1978). This incident also led to

Nawal El Saadawi's lecture at the first Women's Studies post-graduate major in the Netherlands, organized and facilitated by the second author and her colleague, Teresa Fogelberg.

5 Toubia's perspective in this matter has not shifted since the time of this interview, as she shared with Einas Madhi Ahmed Mahdi on three occasions in the period 2009–12.

6 Reported potential consequences are infertility, cysts, menstrual problems, pain during intercourse and childbirth, maternal and child morbidity and mortality and loss of sexual pleasure. Such medical reporting has been criticized by the Public Policy Advisory Network (2012), which stated that 'Western media coverage of female genital surgeries in Africa is "hyperbolic" and "one-sided"' and that much of the subsequent health consequences are exaggerated. This stance, however, has in turn been critiqued, for example by Dr Nawal M. Nour, an obstetrician-gynaecologist and director of the African Women's Health Center at the Brigham and Women's Hospital in Boston. Nour affirms that her patients have endured both major and minor long-term complications from FGM/C. She also states her concern that the Advisory Network's presentation of data is biased. For example, she writes that the statement that 'a high percentage of women have rich sexual lives' would be more plausible if 'high' were changed to 'some'. Nour cites a large meta-analysis showing that 'women who had undergone genital cutting were more likely to report dyspareunia, no sexual desire, and less sexual satisfaction'. 'Speaking as both an African woman and an obstetrician-gynecologist', she writes, 'I hope that this practice

ends during my lifetime' (third commentary to Hastings Center Press Release 2012).

7 Kizilhan (2011) studied three groups of Kurdish girls aged between ten and sixteen who had undergone FMG/C type II in Iraq. One group of girls was circumcised and two were not. Symptoms of depression, psychosomatic conditions, sleep disturbances and post-traumatic stress disorder were found to be above normal levels among the circumcised girls and congruent with findings on traumatized and abused children. The results of the study also showed that symptoms of depression and low self-esteem constituted an index able to discriminate between the three groups with statistical significance. The circumcisions had taken place between five and eight years previously.

8 Some Muslims claim that the prophet Mohammed advocates a mild type of female circumcision, a symbolic operation where nothing at all or only a tiny part of the clitoris is removed. There is a weakness in the chain of transmission of this Hadith, however, which causes some scholars to claim that there is no Sunna to comply with in the matter of female circumcision. According to Nussbaum (1999: 125), the one reference to the operation in the Hadith classifies it as a *makrama*, or non-essential practice. The most frequently quoted Hadith in the literature is the one about how Prophet Mohammed talks to a circumciser on her way to perform the procedure. Prophet Mohammed then says, in one of many possible translations into English: 'Do not overdo it, because it [the clitoris] is good fortune for the spouse and delight for her.'

References

Abbas, R. (2013) 'Female genital mutilation campaign in Sudan slammed for "not getting message across"', *Huffington Post*, 19 August, www.huffingtonpost. com/2013/08/19/female-genital-mutilation-sudan_n_3779524. html, accessed 25 May 2014.

Abdel Magied, A. and Omran, M. (1999) 'The uncircumcised female is an ideal state of circumcision: a case study from Sudan', *Ahfad Journal*, 16: 2–15.

Abusharaf, R. M. (1995) 'Rethinking feminist discourse in female genital mutilation – the case of the Sudan', *Canadian Woman Studies / Les Cahiers de la Femme*, 15(2–3): 52–4.

— (2000) 'Revisiting feminist discourses on infibulation: responses from Sudanese feminists', in B. Shell-Duncan and Y. Hernlund (eds), *Female 'Circumcision' in Africa*, Boulder, CO: Lynne Rienner, pp. 151–66.

— (2001) 'Virtuous cuts: female genital circumcision in an African ontology', *Differences*, 12(1): 112–40.

Ahmed, S. A. H., S. Al Hebshi and B. V. Nylund (2009) 'Sudan: an in-depth analysis of the social dynamics of abandonment of FGM/C', Special Series on Social Norms and Harmful Practices, IWP-200908, UNICEF.

Behrendt, A. and S. Moritz (2005) 'Posttraumatic stress disorder and memory problems after female genital mutilation', *American Journal of Psychiatry*, 162(5): 1000–2.

Berg, R. C. and E. Denison (2013) 'A tradition in transition: factors perpetuating and hindering the continuance of female genital mutilation/cutting (FGM/C) summarized in a systematic review', *Health Care for Women International*, 34(10): 837–59.

Berggren, V., G. Abdel Salam, S. Bergström, E. Johansson and A. K. Edberg (2004) 'An explorative study of Sudanese midwives' motives, perceptions and experiences of re-infibulation after birth', *Midwifery*, 20(4): 299–311.

Berggren, V., S. Musa Ahmed, Y. Hernlund, E. Johansson, B. Habbani and A. K. Edberg (2006) 'Being victims or beneficiaries? Perspectives on female genital cutting and reinfibulation in Sudan', *African Journal of Reproductive Health*, 10(2): 24–36.

Boddy, J. (2007) 'Clash of selves: gender, personhood, and human rights discourse in colonial Sudan', *Canadian Journal of African Studies*, 41(3): 402–26.

— (2008) 'Legislating against culture: attempts to end Pharaonic circumcision in colonial Sudan, 1937–1949', *Suomen Antropologi*, 33(1): 17–32.

Buskens, I. (1978) 'Clitoridectomy with the Kikuyu', paper presented at Towards the Equality between Women and Men, Dubrovnik, 17–28 April.

El Sadaawi, N. (1980) *The Hidden Face of Eve: Women in the Arab World*, London: Zed Books.

Federal Ministry of Health, Sudan (1999) *National Safe Motherhood Survey*, Central Bureau of Statistics, United Nations Population Fund, www.popline.org/node/562940#sthash.0FiX8ydZ.dpuf, accessed 5 June 2014.

Gilligan, C. (1993) *In a Different Voice: Psychological Theory and Women's Development*, Cambridge, MA: Harvard University Press.

Gruenbaum E. (2005a) 'Socio-cultural dynamics of female genital cutting: research findings, gaps, and directions', 7(5): 429–41.

— (2005b) 'Feminist activism for the abolition of FGC in Sudan', *Journal of Middle East Women's Studies*, 1(2): 89–111.

Hastings Center Press Release (2012) 'Western media coverage of female genital surgeries in Africa is "hyperbolic" and "one-sided"', www.eurekalert.org/pub_releases/2012-11/thc-wmc111312.php, accessed 12 October 2013.

Herieka, E. and J. Dhar (2003) 'Female genital mutilation in the Sudan: survey of the attitude of Khartoum university students towards this practice', *Sexually Transmitted Infections*, 79: 220–3.

Hernlund, Y. and B. Shell-Duncan (2007) 'Transcultural positions: negotiating rights and culture', in Y. Hernlund and B. Shell-Duncan (eds), *Transcultural Bodies: Female Genital Cutting in Global Context*, New Brunswick, NJ: Rutgers University Press, pp. 1–46.

Izett, S. and N. Toubia (1998) *Female Genital Mutilation: An Overview*, Geneva: World Health Organization.

Jordan, J., A. G. Kaplan, J. Baker Miller, I. P. Stiver and J. L. Surrey (1991) *Women's Growth in Connection – Writings from the Stone Center*, New York: Guildford Press.

Kizilhan, J. I. (2011) 'Impact of psychological disorders after female genital mutilation among Kurdish girls in Northern Iraq', *European Journal of Psychiatry*, 25(2), http://scielo.isciii.es/scielo.php?pid=S0213-61632011000200004&script=sci_arttext&tlng=en, accessed 21 May 2014.

Lejeune, J. and G. Mackie (2008) 'Social dynamics of abandonment of harmful practices: a new look at the theory', Innocenti Working Paper, IWP-2008-XXX, UNICEF.

Mackie, G. (1996) 'Ending footbinding and infibulation: a convention account', *American Sociological Review*, 61(6): 999–1017.

— (2000) 'Female genital cutting: the beginning of the end', in B. Shell-Duncan and Y. Hernlund (eds), *Female 'Circumcision' in Africa: Culture, Controversy, and Change*, Boulder, CO: Lynne Rienner, pp. 253–82.

Ministry of Health (2002) *Strategy and Action Plan to Abolish Female Genital Mutilation in Sudan*, Khartoum: Ministry of Health.

Moore, H. (2007) 'The failure of pluralism?', in Y. Hernlund, and B. Shell-Duncan (eds), *Transcultural Bodies: Female Genital Cutting in Global Context*, New Brunswick, NJ: Rutgers University Press, pp. 311–30.

Mottin-Sylla, M.-H. and J. Palmieri (2011) *Confronting Female Genital Mutilation: The Role of Youth and ICTs in Changing Africa*, Dakar: Pamzuka Press.

Nussbaum, M. C. (1999) *Sex and Social Justice*, Oxford: Oxford University Press.

— (2000) *Women and Human Development: The Capabilities Approach*, Cambridge: Cambridge University Press.

— (2003) 'Capabilities as fundamental entitlements: Sen and social justice', *Feminist Economics*, 9(2–3), 33–59.

Public Policy Advisory Network (2012) 'Seven things to know about female genital surgeries in Africa', *Hastings Center Report*, 42(6): 19–27.

Sen, A. K. (1999) *Development as Freedom*, Oxford: Oxford University Press.

— (2001) 'Many faces of gender inequality', *Frontline*, 18(22), www.frontline.in/navigation/?type=static&page=flonnet&rdurl=fl1822/18220040.htm, accessed 14 October 2013.

Shweder, R. A. (2000) 'What about "female genital mutilation"? And why understanding culture matters in the first place', *Daedalus*, 129(4): 209–32.

Toubia, N. (1994) 'Female circumcision as a public health issue', *New England Journal of Medicine*, 331(11): 712–16.

— (2002) 'Changing attitudes to female circumcision', *BBC News*, 8 April, http://news.bbc.co.uk/2/hi/health/1916917.stm, accessed 21 May 2014.

Tronto, J. (1994) *Moral Boundaries: A Political Argument for an Ethic of Care*, London: Routledge.

UN Women (2012) 'United Nations bans female genital mutilation', 20 December, www.unwomen.org/en/news/stories/2012/12/united-nations-bans-female-genital-mutilation, accessed 21 May 2014.

UNICEF (2010) 'In Sudan, Saleema campaign re-frames debates about female genital cutting', www.unicef.org/infobycountry/sudan_55692.html, accessed 21 May 2014.

— (2013) *Female Genital Mutilation/Cutting: A Statistical Overview and Exploration of the Dynamics of Change*, New York: UNICEF.

UNICEF Innocenti Insight (2010) 'The dynamics of social change: towards the abandonment of female genital mutilation/cutting

in five African countries',
UNICEF.

United Nations High Commissioner
for Refugees (2013) 'Too much
pain: female genital mutilation &
asylum in the European Union –
a statistical overview', www.
refworld.org/docid/512c72ec2.
html, accessed 13 October 2013.

Wade, L. (2012) 'Learning from
"female genital mutilation":
lessons from 30 years of academic
discourse', *Ethnicities*, 12(1): 26–49.

World Health Organization (2014)
'Female genital mutilation',
Fact Sheet 241, www.who.int/
mediacentre/factsheets/
fs241/en, accessed
17 April 2014.

World Health Organization, UNICEF
and UNFPA (1997) 'Female genital
mutilation: a joint WHO/UNICEF/
UNFPA statement', www.childinfo.
org/files/fgmc_WHOUNICEF
Jointdeclaration1997.pdf,
accessed 21 May 2014.

17 | Finding new meaning, creating new connections: ICT empowers mothers of children with special needs in Egypt

NAGWA ABDEL MEGUID

Introduction

For Arab populations in general and Egyptians in particular it is important to marry someone whose parents and ancestors have a good reputation and whose family shares values, beliefs and lifestyles with one's own family. Hence, the most obvious in-laws are often blood-related kin such as cousins, and for reasons of tradition and convenience consanguineous marriages occur among approximately one-half and first-cousin marriages among more than one-third of Egyptians. Studies of parental consanguinity in the Egyptian population show frequencies ranging from 33 per cent to 42 per cent (Tadmouri et al. 2009; Yamamah et al. 2012).

Unfortunately consanguinity has been associated with adverse child health outcomes: stillbirths, spontaneous abortions, infant death, congenital abnormalities, intellectual disability, deafness, beta-thalassaemia and chronic renal failure (Mumtaz et al. 2010). Adhering to traditional marriage customs thus increases women's risk of giving birth to a disabled child, yet the mothers will be blamed and shamed for their children's birth defects by their husbands, families and communities while the fathers are not stigmatized.

While Egypt has shown considerable progress in prevention and combating of infectious diseases, genetic disorders have remained a major health problem. The National Research Centre (NRC) located in Dokki, Cairo, established the Centre for Human Genetics in 1975.[1] In 2002 I introduced a proposal for a new Clinic for Children with Special Needs in the unit for health services attached to the NRC, of which I became director in 2002.

Every three months, about a hundred mothers (referred from private clinicians and public hospitals or self-referred) visit the clinic with their children, mostly from Cairo and the surroundings and some from other governorates. Ninety per cent of these mothers are literate, at least 80 per cent do not combat the stigma and face their hardships alone, 50 per cent end up divorced and 80 per cent become unemployed as they leave their job to raise the child. Having a child with a disability can thus be traumatic, life-changing, stressful and devastating, with a catastrophic impact on a family and on finances.

As information communication technology (ICT) has unequalled potential for information dissemination, knowledge construction and human connection, I wanted to find out how ICT could be used to help such mothers. ICT can empower women, allowing them to connect with each other and access information (Grimshaw and Gudza 2005; Buskens and Webb 2009; Unwin 2009). Whatever one may think of content found online, the Internet encourages people to share freely what is meaningful to them and to find others with the same interests.

In order to ensure that our efforts would make a difference to the lives of these women, we designed a research approach comprising two phases: in the first (exploratory) phase we conducted interviews focusing on the mothers' experiences, thoughts and emotions around having a disabled child. In the second phase we involved the mothers in interventions that facilitated access to knowledge and information about the genetic nature of children's disabilities with the possibility to connect with others sharing the same fate.

Exploratory phase

Methodology

We had access to personal interviews done with all mothers (about a hundred) upon entry to the genetic counselling service for disability at the Clinic for Children with Special Needs. We conducted in-depth interviews with nine of these mothers who agreed to participate, and our research was approved by the Ethical Committee of the NRC. In our transcriptions we have tried to keep phrases and words as in the spoken language but acknowledge that some information could be lost when translated into written English. When we started interviewing we realized some respondents were embarrassed and felt inconvenienced; we tried to make them comfortable by providing drinks and food at the start and asking them to help us create a spirit of harmony and love.

Our candidates had lived with silence and loneliness for many years, so we had to undertake substantial effort to establish an interview relationship of mutual trust and respect. We wanted to get to know them on a deep and intimate level, because we needed to unveil the phenomenon of stigmatization so that we could understand how to help them beat it. We learnt that six of the nine women were computer literate and three had access to a computer at home or at work.

Sadness, guilt, shame, shunning and isolation We observed that the mothers were very sad and suffered from feelings of guilt. We found that they had isolated themselves from family and community out of fear of being stigmatized and hurt. This withdrawal had broken social bonds, even with loving friends. Fear of stigmatization had also affected the mothers' treatment-seeking behaviour for themselves and their children. When asked why there were mothers who would not go to treatment centres, participants said they either despaired about their problems or feared the discriminatory label that they would be given when seen. Because they did not want to share information about their health problem with non-affected mothers, they ended up isolated, without hope and resigned to living a life of being stigmatized.

Abandonment and impoverishment Deep-rooted cultural understandings about women and motherhood led to these women's dehumanization, belittlement and isolation. The husbands, in adherence to societal norms and views (including those of their own families), usually abandoned moral and financial support for their disabled children and their mother and started a new life. Thus the mothers automatically lost their rights as housewives and acquired the status of divorcees. All women who participated in this research, however, dreamt of being loved and married again. Respondents also lost access to resources and livelihoods as they were often required to leave their employment or were unable to attain employment due to discriminatory attitudes and because they had to spend so much time taking care of their children.

Feeling betrayed Having done everything right as girls, women and mothers, the shaming, shunning and abandonment fostered intense feelings of betrayal in these women, alienating them even more from their families, communities, culture and society and also from themselves. Even when such mothers succeeded in overcoming obstacles in attempting to live a 'normal' life, they were sometimes no longer recognized in the family as a wife and hence as a respectable woman (two of my respondents). Experiencing such ostracism, many lost self-confidence and the incentive to take care of themselves. Having been abandoned by loved ones, they abandoned themselves.

Understanding the stigma Understanding of what caused the birth of a disabled child, whether genetics or environmental or nutritional factors, varied among the mothers attending the clinic and also among the nine respondents. Genetic susceptibility was the most frequently reported cause, and belief in this played a central role in stigmatization: mothers who gave birth to disabled children were automatically perceived as having 'faulty bodies'. To stigmatize is to label people and see them as different and inferior because of an attribute they have. These differences are then attributed to bad behaviour, which results in loss of status and discrimination. However, stigmatization and subsequent discrimination can be countered by carefully targeted programmes (Warner 2005).

ICT-based intervention possible? About 70 per cent of mothers visiting the clinic were computer literate and 40 per cent had access to computers at home or at Internet shops. Six of the nine in-depth-interview respondents were computer literate and three had Internet access at home. It would thus be possible to investigate whether an Internet-based intervention could help alleviate the effect of stigmatization, encourage women to relieve themselves of their self-blame and create avenues for them to take action.

Intervention phase

We developed an educational website so that the mothers could inform themselves about the medical facts, and arranged mobile phones for them to connect with one another. The nine mothers participated in the interventions, but mothers from the bigger group also became involved to various degrees. We conducted workshops and offered the educational material that featured on the website in hard copies and on CDs; the CDs included material about genetic inheritance and explained it simply. All the tools were offered in Arabic and suited the abilities and lifestyles of Egyptian mothers. They were simple and easily accessible, and we provided training when computer skills were needed.

Web portal: a virtual open clinic

The web portal was user friendly, and, while written in Arabic, the language could be changed to English (see www.graceability.net). The web portal gives access to scientific facts about genetic defects, containing lots of easy-to-grasp information about genetics in general as well as basic information about disability and its genetic background, in scientific and layman's terms. It also contains knowledge about proper parenting, norms and milestones, and health and safety to shape parents' other cognitions and practices and influence optimum child development. It documents inspirational success stories on facing the challenges of bringing up a child with a disability. We also paid attention to the 'failures': when framed as learning experiences, failures cease to be so. The website we developed became a virtual open clinic, allowing intense sharing and knowledge exchange between mothers.

Audiovisual and printed materials

As some of the mothers might not have been acquainted with advanced ICTs, we complemented the website with print and audiovisual material about genetic diseases and modes of inheritance so that women could benefit from the information at home. Between 20 per cent (based on the interview sample) and 30 per cent (based on the total population of mothers at the centre) predominantly used the written and/or audiovisual material.

Workshops

We conducted two workshops explaining the scientific basis of the diseases of the women's children, the diseases' aetiology and progress, whether the diseases were genetic or not, who was responsible and whether the diseases were related to consanguinity or not. We tried to provide information about places where the women's children could have good training, rehabilitation and support. I worked on acquainting mothers with ICTs by providing a computer terminal connected to the Internet in the clinic so they could access knowledge. We discussed the experiences of the group of nine who participated and also opened up to other mothers by giving them mobiles and allowing or training them to use the computer and/or access the website.

Mobile phones to establish a mothers' network

We gave mobile phones to a group of fifteen mothers who visit our centre; these phones facilitated the formation of a community that helped mothers gain increased knowledge. Mobile phones have become ubiquitous and more accessible as their costs have decreased; they offered mothers the ability to move freely while staying in contact. Mobile phones now reach many parts of Egypt, enabling mothers to speak with one another in areas where it was not formerly possible.

Findings and outcomes

Power of access When we conducted the ICT training sessions (helping mothers coming in for their appointment to use the website and access the Internet), we could observe how happy they became when holding the mouse and starting to browse. Sometimes they would come into the clinic just to connect to the Internet and with each other. We witnessed their elation and saw how powerful it was for them to realize that they held the power to reach out and connect in their own hands. They visited not only the graceability web portal but also many others. This definitely improved the mothers' morale; they came out of isolation and started to connect with others through mobile phones in addition to browsing the Internet, where they gained new friends.

Empowerment through knowledge Through their use of the website, respondents started to develop a more creative relationship with knowledge. As they became able to source, create, disseminate, store, exchange, communicate and use knowledge and information about the disabilities of their children, they found other helpful general health information. One respondent reported enthusiastically on how she had transmitted her new knowledge on ovulation cycles and the thickening of the uterine walls (the mechanism of menstruation) to her daughter, who was planning for pregnancy.

Documenting success stories on the website detailing how women have faced the challenges of bringing up a child with a disability inspires other mothers to face their own challenges. Roehrer et al. (2011) witnessed a similar phenomenon whereby the use of ICTs in chronic disease management raised individual patients' self-awareness of their conditions. However, when it comes to using knowledge, knowing facts is not the whole story; accepting the knowledge and making it one's own are what matters. Internalizing new knowledge and actually believing it proved essential for the mothers to be able to use the new knowledge, especially when it was in direct contradiction to what the community had received and taught through the generations. For example, when a mother of an autistic child realized the causes of the disability were genetic and environmental, she started to explain this to other mothers of autistic children.

A new community arises: mutual understanding and support The mothers were encouraged to use skills and information gained during this project to navigate their way through the next step in their journey. Mothers obtained new perspectives through debating with each other on opinions and on new methods to deal with their children and sometimes their feelings. Sharing their fears helped them to realize they were not alone; it felt like a support group. Some participants were encouraged to describe their experiences of second-child-related decision-making after the birth of a child with autism.

Parents' understanding of normative child development, both developmental processes and abilities and the accomplishments of children as they grow, developed greatly. Parents' awareness of practices and strategies for maintaining and promoting children's health and coping with children's illness also increased. Using ICT in this way created a space where women felt encouraged to connect with each other to communicate their experiences and support one another. Their new knowledge empowered them, and the support system they developed strengthened them. For many, participation in this project became a life-changing experience. Not only did they start taking care of themselves again but they also started reaching out to their environments with new self-confidence.

Finding themselves again Limited attention has been paid to the experience of what it means to be a parent of a disabled child. The perspectives of professionals and service providers involved with these mothers have been represented to a degree (Alvarez McHatton and Correa 2005). Resources concerning mothers of children with disabilities are very few (Altschuler and Dale 1999). Women are usually the primary carers, and are often isolated with no one with whom to share their thoughts, feelings and concerns. It became obvious that the graceability website started to become more than a mere source of knowledge and information. In their discussions with each other about the new knowledge they were sharing, the mothers found the words to share with each other and admit to themselves what they were feeling and experiencing. It became apparent that their isolation was not only caused by the lack of scientific knowledge that left their stigmatization unchallenged. The fact that they did not have the words for or understanding of what they were feeling and experiencing, and could not discuss the reality of their daily lives and the challenges that they faced, are what created the social and cultural void these mothers lived in. In starting to acknowledge what they were experiencing to themselves and others they regained a deeper relationship with themselves and confidence in reaching out to others.

Creating reality: a very special initiative A very special initiative that arose out of this group was the construction of a new centre to care for children with special needs by Saida Sherbibi,[2] one of my respondents. This centre is unique in Egypt and possibly in the Arab world in being a care centre for special-needs children that employs mothers who have experience with special-needs children and in being an interdisciplinary clinic specializing in the diagnosis, evaluation and treatment of children with complex developmental disabilities; it creates a plan of care, finds support through others with similar experiences and looks up community-based resources on the Clinic for Children with Special Needs website. Realizing that public policy has to address many interests from many groups, Saida responded to her calling to stand up for the rights of children with special needs and extended her advocacy to become the main policy-maker in this field in Suez Governorate.

The role of ICT in changing mindsets, attitudes and society at large The website we developed has enhanced our visibility both as a network and as individuals with a story to share with our communities and society at large. This is important, especially as 'having a disabled child' and genetic causes of this phenomenon have been (and to a degree still are) taboo subjects in Egyptian society.

The role of human support and connection Mothers started to recognize that behind the denominator of 'mother' there is still a 'woman', and started to recognize themselves in new ways. Once they were able to talk and get out all the fears they had, the mothers no longer felt alone and could share their concerns. Some said that no one had ever asked them about their concerns or how to alleviate or face their anxieties; they were never asked about their problems, and no one tried to help them find solutions. One respondent who was infected with hepatitis C virus said: 'I had been infected with virus C, I did not ask for treatment, even though I recognized that it is a serious disease. I did not care; I felt depressed and rejected, unwanted and unloved. Until you came and you provided me the emotional support I needed.'

My personal journey as principal investigator As women in Egypt we are socialized to be modest. I remember after I started to work at the NRC the director asked me, 'Woman, you want to be a scientist, a professor?' and I said, 'Yes I want to be a professor, yes I want to be an internationally known scientist.' We would joke about it, but I believed it. But I suffered for a long time, and dreamt of being a man. The mentality that women cannot take up certain positions is still entrenched in some of my male colleagues. Yet when I started my research I would tell my respondents that all things are possible for those who believe in their capabilities and work hard, so I touched my life with theirs. However, finding a good relationship with myself seemed to be harder!

Learning to love myself started with a conscious decision to become happy and stop worrying about the fact that the world is dominated by men. I spent time thinking about what I could do to contribute to changing this situation. This was answered through my work with my respondents – so now I celebrate myself! I started to see myself as a valuable person in my society and am now able to relax and enjoy myself without feeling guilty. I accepted that I can change and may change for the better, and I love to talk about this with my respondents and find out how they see things.

The website documents success stories, and the courage and persistence of these mothers continues to inspire me and other mothers to face challenges. I learnt to practice counselling not only from the genetic point of view but also from both a social and a scientific perspective. Using knowledge and expertise gained from participating in my GRACE project provided me with the opportunity to influence policy discussions within my community. I have been writing and telling stories in newspapers; I did an interview on television sharing my knowledge and expertise; and I felt encouraged to influence policy within my institute and the greater community.

I now know that it is not what happens to us that causes our distress and stigma but how we interpret what happens to us. I started to write down inspiring quotes and exciting events in my life and those of my respondents. Now I believe that everyone draws their own path – we don't have to go a certain way to get to our destination.

Discussion

Isolation from family, community and society as well as from mainstream social, cultural and economic life led to mothers of disabled children lacking access to information and communication about their children's diseases and needs for special care. This made them even more vulnerable and prey to accusation and blame. The ICT-based interventions used by and for the research participants in my study contributed to a fundamental change in their well-being, their motivation to take care of themselves and their knowledge of how to care for their children. They found relevant information through the website and other means we offered, and acquired enough knowledge to minimize their feelings of guilt. They could talk about the truth they had discovered regarding the real causes behind their children's diseases, and this set them free.

When we look closer at what brought about the change in these mothers, we see the essential role of three components of this 'empowerment process':

- mothers engaging themselves in active knowledge construction, where they could test their new knowledge against the old;
- the emotional support they were able to receive from clinic staff and give to and receive from each other;

17 | Meguid

235

- the fact that they could express their experiences and so recognize themselves in giving substance to what they were thinking and feeling, which halted the process of self-alienation.

The way in which ICT has been used in and through my centre has made it possible to extend these possibilities and opportunities; this was our intent, and we were able to work together to accomplish it.

Conclusion

Raising the awareness of people about bearing and raising disabled children and allowing an open conversation and dialogue about it has become the first step in a larger campaign to carve a new path of positive change for Egyptian society.

After conducting the survey on sources of stigma with the mothers, we are now targeting other family members to set up an anti-stigma project to try to change attitudes. Another important development is the fact that mothers themselves have started, via the website, to address the rights of newborns with disabilities and the right of mothers to make the decision to abort upon prenatal diagnosis. Thinking about these issues is a challenge that the mothers are presenting to society at large. Changing mindsets is the first step in changing attitudes in a society; such change will come through raising awareness and affecting the way people think about issues.

Egyptian society has chosen to make women feel bad about their disabled children, and not men. One could speculate that the unconscious reason for this was to make women feel bad in order to control them better. To do this effectively, stigma around a disabled child was used as a tool. Whatever the case, inspiring women to feel good about themselves while having a disabled child is a revolutionary act in Egypt, and bound to influence society as a whole. Changing themselves, these mothers have also changed their environments.

It is quite thinkable that the change process that this group has started will have wider and more powerful ripple effects in Egypt and beyond. Their dream is not only to influence the cultural norm of blaming mothers for children's genetic birth defects but also to diminish the rate at which such defects occur. From victims of stigma these mothers have become change agents, creating a more hopeful future for themselves, their children and generations of mothers and children to come.

While ICT has been an essential ingredient in this success, the story was and is a journey of women standing up for themselves and their children in defiance of a culture that set them up for failure and feeling bad about themselves.

Acknowledgement

Special thanks for Dr Mona Anwar for her assistance during the interviews.

Notes

1 The importance of medical genetics in paediatric departments of Egyptian universities was well appreciated in the early 1960s at Cairo and Ain Shams Universities. In 1975 the specialized study of human genetics was established at the NRC. In 1967 a medical genetics unit was established at the Medical Research Institute in Alexandria, followed by initiation of medical genetics units in other universities such as in El-Mansoura Governorate.

2 Saida Sherbibi (omaya_sh@hotmail.com), director of the new centre for children with special needs: Elsafaa Society for Special Needs Kids (www.youtube.com/watch?v=8TkVENi8Ty4).

References

Altschuler, J. and B. Dale (1999) 'On being an ill parent', *Clinical Child Psychology and Psychiatry*, 4(1): 23–37.

Alvarez McHatton, P. and V. Correa (2005) 'Stigma and discrimination: perspectives from Mexican and Puerto Rican mothers of children with special needs', *Early Childhood Special Education*, 25(3): 131–42.

Buskens, I. and A. Webb (2009) *African Women and ICTs: Investigating Technology, Gender and Empowerment*, London: Zed Books/IDRC/UNISA.

Grimshaw, D. and L. Gudza (2005) *Gender Equality and Women: Empowerment through ICT*, New York: United Nations.

Mumtaz, G., A. H. Nassar, Z. Mahfoud, A. El-Khamra, N. Al-Choueiri, A. Adra, J. C. Murray, P. Zalloua and K. A. Yunis (2010) 'Consanguinity: a risk factor for preterm birth at less than 33 weeks' gestation', *American Journal of Epidemiology*, 172(12): 1424–30.

Roehrer, E., E. Cummings, L. Ellis and P. Turner (2011) 'The role of user-centred design within online community development', *Studies in Health Technology and Informatics*, 164: 256–60.

Tadmouri, G., P. Nair, T. Obeid, K. N. Al Ali and H. Hamamy (2009) 'Consanguinity and reproductive health among Arabs', *Reproductive Health*, 6: 17–22.

Unwin, T. (2009) *ICT4D: Information and Communication Technology for Development*, Cambridge: Cambridge University Press.

Warner, R. (2005) 'Local projects of the World Psychiatric Association programme to reduce stigma and discrimination', *Psychiatric Services*, 56(5): 570–5.

Yamamah, G., E. Abdel-Raouf, A. Talaat, A. Saad-Hussein, H. Hamamy and N. A. Meguid (2012) 'Prevalence of consanguineous marriages in south Sinai, Egypt', *Journal of Biosocial Science*, 45(1): 31–9.

18 | Serving self and society: female radio presenters in Uganda effect social change

SUSAN BAKESHA

The end of state control of radio broadcasting in Uganda in the early 1990s brought about exponential growth in private radio stations[1] and creation of employment opportunities for women with the required qualities and skills. Radio can have a significant impact on the listeners, given its accessibility and reach.[2]

The women radio presenters who participated in my research entered the field for various reasons: for employment, to profile their music career, to make use of their good voices, to participate in political debates or to contribute to resolving social issues. In exploring and discussing the potential of women to join the broadcasting industry, and the general constraints and challenges they face, I sought to understand my respondents' experiences with regard to their job, how they used their space on the airwaves to pursue what they believe in and what the impact on their listeners was.

In this chapter I focus on two exceptional women who made use of the airwaves to pursue their passions, forge powerful careers and have a substantial impact on the well-being of their communities of listeners.

Data collection and processing

The study engaged feminist participatory and interactive approaches that provided the researchers and respondents with an opportunity to engage with and discuss the issues related to their work. The respondents were purposively selected using contact persons in the media industry. Qualitative techniques of data collection were engaged including participant observation, in-depth interviews and focus-group discussions.

The research took place over the period October 2009 to July 2010. The researchers were able to visit the studios with the intention of understanding the work environment under which the women operated. Fourteen women radio presenters and four station managers were interviewed, and two focus-group discussions with women radio presenters were conducted.

All interviews were recorded to ensure accuracy and comprehensiveness. The interviews and observations were complemented by a questionnaire that was administered to obtain background information on the respondents. To obtain information about issues related to human-resource management and administration in relation to the women's needs, interviews were held with four station managers. The Nvivo qualitative software was used to sort the data and analyze it into thematic areas.

Meeting the criteria of a radio presenter

All respondents demonstrated that getting to the point of becoming a radio presenter, let alone designing one's own programme, involved managing a range of criteria. These include attributes such as a good voice, creativity, general knowledge and ability to attract listenership. Specialized education in broadcasting is not mandatory, and some radio stations run programmes in the local dialect, making it possible even for people with basic education to become programme hosts.

In a country such as Uganda where women's literacy rates are low, radio broadcasting is an area where women with the above-mentioned attributes have an opportunity to join formal employment. Nine of the fourteen respondents interviewed had no prior training in radio broadcasting and had not previously envisaged it as a profession; they were recruited based on having the above attributes, especially a 'good voice'.

Titie and Rebecca, who were music artists before joining radio work, said they were inspired to join radio broadcasting by their managers in the music industry because of their good voices. Jackie said she joined radio because her friends told her that her voice was good to listen to. However, the description of a 'good voice' presented some limitations, especially for women. According to station managers a good voice is deep, audible and good to listen to; sharp and high-pitched voices, generally associated with women, are considered inappropriate because they irritate the listeners. This implies that, based on this preference, most women would be excluded from recruitment as programme hosts.

In addition to voice, radio proprietors seek out individuals who are known by the community and are easily recognized by listeners while on air. This includes popular individuals from the entertainment industry: 'I think they liked my voice and the fact that I was a musician and already had followers,' said Titie when asked why she thought she was hired as a radio host. Recruiting individuals such as Titie with established status as an entertainer is mutually beneficial for both radio proprietors and presenter. Titie brought her music fans on board as additional listeners to the radio station and increased her fan base as she reached out to a larger audience through her programme: 'people got to know me more and even if you did not like my music, at least you love the radio programme and when you love the radio programme you end up listening to me, and this has slightly increased my fan base'.

Constraints and challenges for women presenters

Fitting the time schedule

Senior management reserves the right to set times for radio programmes based on market demand. In most cases, the hosts are expected to fit into the time allocated to them, including early-morning and late-night sessions. Most stations have a staff van, but this is only used to take staff home and not to bring them to work. Some respondents experience situations that compromise their personal safety and mobility while on duty:

> Sometimes we have to wake up at 4am to come; if you do not have a car it becomes a problem. One of us had to leave the job because she could not manage coming very early and she was pregnant. (Juliana)

> This place is conducive, the workmates are okay, the management is okay, our bosses are really so cool except in the night, I am alone here. They were even forced to put locks on this door, I lock myself in when everyone is out ... my show ends at midnight and the next person is supposed to come in at midnight on the dot ... so one time this person walks in, and he wanted me (because he had listened to my programme before), he was all drunk, I was scared ... he had red eyes, I don't know if he had some weed [cannabis] on him. I thought it was the end of the world for me. So it is like you work, but protection is minimum and it is risky, especially for women. (Prosy)

Some former presenters attributed their change of career to this challenge:

> My family grew, I now have four children. Then I had one; the challenges increased, so some of that hectic work of leaving at midnight, or being assigned a job at midnight became uneasy for me, and I had to find another job. (Joyce)

Sexual harassment

In preparing their programmes most presenters conduct interviews with key persons with specialized knowledge on topical issues, and attend functions and meetings that are sometimes held late. During these some were exposed to sexual harassment, as shared by one former presenter:

We did receive a lot of harassment ... from men, men who think journalists are available, and they are free. You go in to get a story and you are supposed to receive a story ... that would kind of be hard, and because you work at night people would just be thinking, well she is working at night, she must be available or something. I didn't like that about that job. (Barbara)

Sexual harassment was also reported as common at the workplace, although none of the current presenters were comfortable sharing their personal experience for fear of jeopardizing their work. Former present-ers had the courage to do so, probably because they had nothing to lose. Stalking and unwelcome sexual advances from men, even while on air, were reported as a major challenge by most presenters. Only one of the radio stations included in the study had a sexual harassment policy and encouraged staff members to make use of it to protect themselves against perpetrators.

'We shall call you back'

Maternity leave is considered a constraint on women's job security. Private radio stations operate as business entities, and absence from work for extended periods of time may not be tolerated because it inter-rupts the flow of programmes, which might affect the level of listenership and sponsorship. It was reported during one of the focus-group discus-sions that many presenters lose their job during maternity leave; authori-zation of maternity leave is often accompanied by the statement 'We shall call you back', implying indefinite leave. This was reported as common for presenters with no written contract. Due to high unemployment lev-els, most private institutions find it easy to recruit and offer employment under a non-contractual arrangement, where it is up to the employer to determine how much money is paid to the employee and when to termi-nate their services.

From radio presenters to radio personalities: two case studies

With growth and transformation of broadcasting, women recognized opportunities provided by occupying space on the airwaves to improve their personal well-being and contribute positively to resolving social issues. Operating within a complex situation where the success of a radio presenter largely depends on ability to attract listenership and spon-sorship to their programme and not necessarily to meet their personal and community needs, there have however been cases where both the presenter and radio station's priorities influence each other to produce unprecedented social and political actions. This was demonstrated in the way in which the careers of Omulongo Sarah Babirye and Betty Nambooze unfolded.

Omulongo Sarah Babirye and the Ekooti Y'amaka *(Family Court)* programme

Presenters have freedom to select the content and presentation format of their programmes, as long as they respond to the station's objectives. Like any other business enterprise, most FM radio stations are established with the sole purpose of generating profits, each programme representing a different product on the market. To meet this expectation, presenters are tasked to be innovative and to design programmes that attract and retain listenership.

One such innovation is the programme *Ekooti Y'amaka* (Family Court) hosted by Omulongo Sarah Babirye, popularly known as Mulongo.[3] The programme airs on weekdays between 10 a.m. and 1 p.m., and listeners write letters to the presenter giving a detailed account of the situation they are going through and requesting support from the public on how to overcome it. The presenter reads out the letter on air and afterwards engages listeners to offer solution(s) and support the writer by calling in or sending text messages. Discussions with Mulongo revealed that most of those who wrote in were women, who raised issues relating to family conflict, domestic violence, lack of child support, witchcraft, land disputes, property-grabbing and infidelity.

In order to extend support beyond individuals whose letters are read on air (about ten a day were received at the time of the study), Mulongo mobilized support from individuals and institutions through a number of initiatives. These included a bursary scheme providing education scholarships to underprivileged children, marriage-counselling sessions for men and women, and a trust fund where money is collected and given to people in genuine need.

The research team was able to participate in a meeting organized by Mulongo to register children in need of scholarships, at which over three hundred pupils and students were registered as beneficiaries of bursaries offered by various private schools and vocational institutions. Discussions with some head teachers revealed their appreciation of the programme because it contributed to an increase in student enrolment and improved publicity for their schools. The parents, mostly women, expressed gratitude to Mulongo for her kindness and generosity; through her programme they were able to obtain free or cheaper education for their children.

It was, however, noted that the success and sustainability of Mulongo's initiatives were largely dependent on her desire to invest extra time and money and her passion to protect the rights of the poor and marginalized. For instance, in order to verify the authenticity of letters she had to call, confirm and cross-check with local authorities. Where support is extended to the writer, she facilitates meetings with their benefactors. Related costs are not covered by the radio station, which sometimes presented a challenge:

> You can't ask the Corporation for money all the time, there are no specific funds ... I use my own money, and in case I fail to get to some place because it's far, I give up. I ask the person if they can bring themselves so we can talk from here. But if it is too much for me I just give up, because I use my airtime. (Mulongo)

Mulongo experienced constant threats, including death threats, from individuals whose negative acts were exposed through the programme:

> sometimes I am threatened; I have messages on my phone. Other people have been tortured and threatened to be killed by those that owe them money. When I get involved they start the threats, they ask me who do I think I am, they tell me about the dead bodies in the papers and who do I think kills those people.

Despite the challenges, she continues to do her work because of her love for her job and the personal satisfaction she derives from helping those in need: 'I do my job with satisfaction and love it. When I solve an issue to completion I am proud of myself, I feel satisfied, it keeps me going.'

Promoting civil and political freedom: Madam Teacher

'I feel like a human rights activist, that's what I feel mostly. I feel I want to fight for people's rights. That is how I ended up in politics' – this is how the Hon. Betty Nambooze described herself when asked why she became a politician. At the time of the interview she was a member of parliament representing Mukono district, located about twenty-five kilometres away from Kampala, the capital. In her early forties and married with children, she is one of few women who competed for and won a mainstream parliamentary seat. She is a member of the Democratic Party, one of the opposition parties in Uganda.

Betty's involvement with the media dates back to the late 1990s, when she worked as a reporter for a local daily newspaper as a side job to her formal post as head of the Metropolitan Police for Mukono district. She was later invited by two radio stations to become a panellist on a weekly programme discussing topical issues. In 2001 she joined active politics and declared her intention to contest a parliamentary seat.

Betty's views and intention to stand for a political position attracted reaction from government, since she intended to unseat a member of the ruling party. In 2002 she was arrested, charged with corruption, jailed for eleven months and released after the charges were dropped for lack of evidence. She lost her job as a public servant but continued with her political activism, participating in political debates hosted on various radio stations.

In 2003 she was recruited as a radio presenter by the Central Broadcasting Station (CBS). CBS is owned by the Buganda Kingdom, one of the biggest cultural institutions in the country. Since independence the Buganda Kingdom has had a volatile relationship with the central government due to unresolved issues dating back to before independence. The Buganda Kingdom was the first part of Uganda to be colonized, and from it the colonialists spread to other parts of the country. Its inhabitants are called Baganda and speak Luganda. Most Baganda are loyal to their Kingdom and have great respect and reverence for the Kabaka, its head. Uganda derives its name from this region, and the capital city of Kampala is located there.

Betty was tasked to design and present a programme to raise the listener's civic consciousness and advance the Kingdom's interests, such as recognition of its special status within the country and return of the Kingdom's properties seized by the colonial government.

As an individual Betty wanted to put right some historical facts about the Kingdom. According to her, historians did not provide a true record of the events that shaped its political history in relation to the whole of Uganda. Her mission was to correct this distortion through her programme:

> I first did research and I realized that history was very unfair, because so many have written the history of this country and place Buganda at the helm of the country's problems. So my concern was to correct that thinking and make the people realize that Buganda was not the problem, it was some leaders that who didn't want to follow the law … So for me, one way or another I wanted to rewrite the history and I think I achieved it. I rewrote it, and I even published my book.

Betty's programme aired every Sunday evening from 10 p.m. to midnight, presented in a story-telling style using a local dialect, Luganda. Some minutes were allocated for an interactive call-in question-and-answer session. The programme presented political views considered divergent and anti-development by the ruling government. Consequently

244

the presenter was subjected to a series of arrests and charged with various crimes, including treason. Ironically the arrests exposed her to the limelight of the media, thereby increasing her popularity among listeners, who considered her brave.

As a result her programme became very popular and listeners gave her the name 'Madam Teacher' in appreciation of her efforts to educate them about their history. Their loyalty to the Kingdom was strengthened and they began to question some government actions towards Kingdom activities. This was partly demonstrated by the September 2009 riots that spread across the Buganda region, protesting the government's decision to stop their king, Ronald Muwenda Mutebi II, from carrying out one of his periodic visits to his subjects in Kayunga district, citing security concerns.

The event was highly publicized on air, forcing the government through the national broadcasting regulator the Broadcasting Council to close down a number of radio stations, including CBS, accused of promoting sectarianism and inciting violence. Betty lost her job as a presenter – but her political career flourished. In 2011 she competed with men and won a heavily contested political campaign to become MP for Mukono municipality.

Betty's success was to a great degree made possible through the support she received from her husband; he facilitated her mobility and provided her with security while on duty:

> Sometimes we used to sleep in a hotel, sometimes we would drive back. But I want to tell you that all the time I was with my husband. He would bring me, wait for me, in fact sit in the studio with me and keep quiet, and after the programme, if we had planned to drive back to Mukono, we would set off. If not we would stay in a hotel and then return in the morning.

Betty's husband narrated how he took on the role of a mother to their children while his wife was in detention. He prepared meals, took them to school and visited those in boarding schools. His actions attracted public ridicule and isolation from his peers, who perceived him as weak for not divorcing such a 'loud-mouthed woman'.

To ensure a continued presence on air while away on other duties or during maternity leave, Betty pre-recorded her programmes, which were broadcast during her absence. She would then respond to listeners' questions by connecting and calling the studio. Due to the sensitivity of her programme, Betty invested a lot of time reading and researching to get the facts rights before presenting them on air:

I used to do a lot of reading. Every Friday I would be reading for that programme specifically. And I would move into the studio with all these books ... I had decided on one thing, which is never to say anything without a reference for quotation.

The role of radio in promoting Madam Teacher's political career Betty attributed her success as a politician to the radio: 'Oh my friend, the radio has made me the politician that I am,' she asserted. Through her work on radio, both as a panellist and as a radio presenter, she gained the confidence and eloquence required to participate in a vigorous political campaign with men. Although women in Uganda have the right to compete for political positions, they still find it difficult to succeed due to various challenges, including limited access to and use of the public space during campaigns. This is largely informed by cultural stereotypes and gender roles constraining their mobility, and lack of adequate financial resources to pay for publicity. The airwaves provided Betty with a free platform to advance and publicize her political agenda, giving her an edge over her competitors:

> First of all I had a forum where I shared my opinions, people got to know me ... People would appreciate my views, and I got to be known and popularity came in, because in politics you need to publicize yourself. This was free publicity for me. In Uganda working on radio makes you a star instantly.

Analysis and conclusions

Radio presents a unique space for women to exercise their freedom and exploit their potential to grow and have an impact on their community of listeners. As broadcasters they regularly communicate with and relate to individuals and communities, which enables them to create social networks facilitating their personal growth and career advancement. Although work norms and expectations constrain women's performance given their biological functions and social responsibilities, it is possible for women to function within the confines of the structural challenges and achieve personal success as well as have a positive impact on their communities, as reflected in the cases of Mulongo and Betty. The success of their programmes can largely be attributed to their creative and innovative approaches to radio broadcasting, their hard work, their personal investment and, as demonstrated in Betty's case, spousal support.

Both women chose a specific presentation styles that appealed to and sustained the interest of listeners. Mulongo reached out to and established a personal relationship with her listeners by reading out their letters on air and providing them with a platform to seek and obtain solutions to their problems. This raised her profile to become a celebrated radio presenter. Similarly Betty's presentation style allowed her listeners to relate to her through the call-in sessions, which earned her the status of an educator and the nickname Madam Teacher.

Through their programmes these presenters affected their communities in various ways. Mulongo's programme created a community of listeners who addressed local problems through initiatives such as the school bursary scheme. These initiatives focused more on charity than on enhancing people's ability to identify and address structural injustices within the social system. By offering school bursaries to children without addressing the root causes of their lack of school fees, the programme did not facilitate listeners taking strategic actions to change their social environment.

For Betty, her programme enabled her to share her views and influence listeners to support her cause to increase people's loyalty to the Buganda Kingdom as well as build a political career. Betty created a community of listeners who believed in her message and accepted her as a leader in a male-dominated field. Through the air waves she was able to challenge patriarchal and cultural perceptions that usually constrain women's participation in leadership. By the time she presented herself to the public her supporters were mainly interested in her 'brain and not her brawn' (Wajcman 2010: 147). Her decision to compete with men for a political position redefined the roles and responsibilities of women in Uganda, thereby contesting patriarchal norms.

Hafkin (2000: 17) envisioned a situation where African women could use and transform information and communication technologies to create an information society to accommodate their needs, aspirations and visions. Women such as Betty and Mulongo provide a learning experience regarding how women can use radio as a platform to enhance their capabilities and contribute to the well-being of others. They illustrate personal determination to shape their own destiny by becoming agents of their own change and in changing their communities.

It can be argued that these women helped maintain a working environment that was in fact unworkable and that perpetuated gender injustice and social inequality; and that the causes they laboured for were more about charity than progressive social change. However, through their initiatives on causes that were personally meaningful to them and the way they responded to the interests and needs of their audiences, meaningful development and community renewal did indeed take place.

Notes

1 By February 2009 over two hundred private commercial FM radio stations were registered and operational in various parts of the country, forty-two based in the central region, where they compete for listenership and business.

2 In a survey carried out by InterMedia (2005) it was estimated that 100 per cent of the population had listened to the radio in the past year, 93 per cent in the past seven days and 74 per cent as recently as the day before. The 2002 population and housing survey revealed that 50 per cent of households owned a radio. It also showed that about half of the households (49.2 per cent) in the country reported that word of mouth was their main source of information, followed by radio (47.8 per cent) (Uganda National Bureau of Statistics 2002).

3 Among the Baganda, the word *balongo* means "twins," and *Omulongo* or *mulongo* is a title given to a single twin.

References

Hafkin, N. (2000) 'Convergence of concepts: gender and ICTs in Africa', in E. M. Rathgeber and E. O. Adera (eds), *Gender and the Information Revolution in Africa*, Ottawa: IDRC, pp. 11–21.

InterMedia (2005) *Uganda: Media and Opinion Survey Data for Developing Countries*, Washington, DC: InterMedia.

Uganda National Bureau of Statistics (2002) *The Uganda Population and Housing Census: Census Atlas: Mapping Socio-economic Indicators for National Development, Uganda*, Kampala: National Bureau of Statistics.

Wajcman, J. (2010) 'Feminist theories of technology', *Cambridge Journal of Economics*, 34: 143–52.

19 | Challenging the silence, secrecy and shame: transforming ICT's role in increasing pre-marital sex in Sudan

IKHLAS AHMED NOUR IBRAHIM

Introduction

Sudan is a conservative society with multiple rules of ethics and morality that are defined by men and dominated by male interests. Men have the prerogative to decide the nature of the punishments for contravening the rules and can implement their decisions with total liberty. Women remain completely at the mercy of the males in the family. To kill an unmarried girl or woman accused of illicit sexual relations or of being pregnant is considered within a male relative's rights and a righteous punishment.

For a long time Sudanese society tried to control the sexual behaviour of its youth by citing the traditional negative consequences of sexual experiences, such as loss of virginity and family honour and unwanted pregnancies. Because discussing sex is a big taboo in Sudan, people cannot easily communicate about it, and find it particularly difficult to express their thoughts about it in relation to their children. Now and then articles about this issue have appeared in the local press acknowledging how this silence affects Sudanese society and especially women. They are the ones severely affected by the silence and shame around sex, as the burden of sexual responsibility is carried by women and not by men (Hekayat 2009; Alahram Alyoum 2010).

Mobile phones have been used in Sudan from the moment Internet services were introduced there in 1997. Especially among Sudanese adolescents and youth, mobile phones quickly became popular for the transfer of money, songs, pictures, short videos and SMS (text) messages. However, access to mobile phones and the Internet has also prompted young people to use this technology to seek contact with one another to talk about dating, romance and sex.

The use of mobile technology by the youth has thus created a social revolution for which the country and its people are ill-prepared. When young women fall pregnant outside marriage they are severely punished by their families and communities. Many young women will thus attempt to avoid the shame and fear by abandoning their babies (throwing them away), opting for a back-street abortion or committing suicide.

Correlations have been made between the use of mobile phones and the number of unwanted pregnancies and 'thrown-away babies'. There is no formal adoption agency in Sudan where unwanted babies can be adopted. The number of abandoned babies in Khartoum has increased considerably since use of mobile phones has become popular: the Mygoma Orphanage used to offer shelter to about four hundred babies per year, but in 2008 this number rose to a thousand. Nearly 10 per cent of 'thrown-away' babies die yearly (Mohamed 2009).

Some people thus hold that mobile phones are contributing to immorality and the increasing divorce rate among young people, because they have given women the opportunity to be masters of their own networking and to establish contacts without parental oversight (De Bruijin et al. 2009). It is true that unrestricted and unsupervised contact between the sexes is traditionally not allowed in Sudan. The recent rush among youth to have mobile phones and Internet access has provoked considerable interest because of the way it facilitates talk about love, sex and dating at any time and in any place. Such unrestricted sexual contact was not possible before and is still not allowed (Dafalla 2010).

Sudan's capital, Khartoum, was selected for this study as it represents a cross-section of all of the cultures of Sudan, due to the migration of people because of drought and ongoing war. A key figure for this study has been the president of Ana Sudan, a non-governmental organization (NGO) that maintains a shelter for unwanted children in Khartoum. Dr Mohamed Elgemiabby is famous for his pioneering work in this field; he was the first and for a long time the only public figure to openly discuss issues relating to adolescent sexuality; the relationship between pre-marital sex and cultural changes brought about by information and communication technology (ICT), especially mobile phones and commercial television; and the fate of the unwanted children who result.

The explosive use of mobile phones in combination with fundamental gender injustices regarding sexual matters prompted us to study the current reality of young women using mobile phones for the purpose of and within romantic relationships. Because ICT has become so important in young people's lives, we also wanted to investigate whether ICT could be used in a drive to support them in making responsible decisions on these matters, and hence prevent harm to young women and their unwanted babies.

The second part of our study was an action research project that focused on the design and implementation of ICT-based interventions to stimulate responsible sexual behaviour. We learnt a lot in this inter-vention phase, and although we did not do an official evaluation of our interventions we comment on our learnings in the latter part of this chapter and include them in our recommendations.

Research methodology

First phase: exploring the issue

The first part of the study explored the relationship between adoles-cent mobile dating and the real-life consequences of the sexual relations that resulted from this. The respondents we selected had all had sexual relations before and outside marriage. As this was a study of a particu-larly sensitive nature and with a particularly vulnerable group, the high-est form of secrecy and confidence had to be maintained. Because the researchers needed to get facts and perspectives (opinions, experiences and emotions), an iterative, exploratory, qualitative research design was developed. This design allowed for the integration of narrative data derived from in-depth interviews with informal observations, conversa-tions and a survey.

The data were organized into a set of categories grounded in the follow-ing research questions: What are the context of the family and community culture and the social and economic situation of the family? What is the impact of family and community? With whom are young people able to dis-cuss sex and sexuality? What are the types of communication they use; what are the costs? Does mobile phone use indeed facilitate pre-marital sexual activities? What is the educational level of young people involved and what is their knowledge about sex, sexually transmitted diseases (STDs) and the use of contraceptives? With whom do they partner and where and when? What are the reasons for getting engaged in premarital sex?

These categories were then used to give meaning to the various research findings. The use of colloquial language proved helpful. The main challenge of the study was getting access to respondents; there-fore direct, secret interviews and direct observations were initially used to facilitate understanding of the question. A communications plan including a survey was developed and executed to support the involve-ment of NGOs and all other related bodies such as the Governor's Office. Collection of accurate data, especially in face-to-face interviews, on sen-sitive activities such as sex posed a number of challenges: where to find and meet the respondents, how to earn their trust and how to get the cor-rect information.

Fortunately we found that the president of Ana Sudan NGO, Dr Mohamed Elgemiabby, was prepared to collaborate with us. We had to seek his permission and help to be able to meet the girls and young women who trusted him, as he had helped them in highly precarious situations. The second step was a series of mobile phone calls with the respondents to encourage them to participate in in-depth interviews in his office, and to convince them of the importance of their contribution in this research to explore causes and problems related to premarital sex. Fortunately, after preliminary discussions we were able to secure sufficient involvement in the study.

The in-depth interviews with the young women followed a free-flowing format in which we avoided interrupting their narratives. We spoke with our respondents several times until we had an understanding of their lives and the circumstances in which their sexual life history had unfolded. Apart from multiple in-depth interviews, these case studies were grounded in participant observation and informal observations and conversations during visits to Ana Sudan. On the basis of the knowledge acquired from these case studies, a survey was designed to assess the impact of social and cultural factors such as premarital sexual experience, socioeconomic status and types of ICT used. These structured interviews were done face to face. The questionnaire was filled in by forty young people, half of them male, with the main language being Arabic.

Second phase

Students, graduates, university staff and households collaborated in the survey; radio was recommended by them as an intervention tool for the second part of the study because it has the widest reach. Radio is also accessible to the majority of adults and older people, who are often not familiar with using computers or the Internet. Furthermore, most of the young women and men use their mobiles to listen to the morning radio programmes broadcast by the radio station that is popular within the community and among teachers, researchers and formal and informal community leaders. These programmes give them access to information from regional, national and international sources. Three radio series were broadcast on the FM100 morning programmes of the Albeit Alsudany (Sudanese house) programme Sabah al Beiut. People listen to this programme because it discusses social problems. They listen in on local transportation on the way to work and women listen at their homes. As a second tool, Internet platforms, mainly Facebook and a blog, were recommended by the students and the university staff as these give participants time for reflection and they can participate when it suits them.

First-phase findings

Impact of premarital sex in Sudan

All the respondents we worked with had had premarital sex that had resulted in an unwanted pregnancy; this selection was done intentionally to understand the causes and impact of premarital sex on their lives. The respondents' ages varied from fifteen to thirty-five years; 15 per cent were between fifteen and nineteen years of age, 15 per cent between thirty and thirty-five years and 70 per cent between twenty and twenty-nine years old. We observed that none of the NGOs in Sudan had done research to investigate the causes and impact of premarital sexual relations and the harm inflicted on young women, while a lot of effort had been made to care for the abandoned children. Dr Elgemiabby had so far been the only one who had taken the young women's case to heart. Using the mobile phone he could reach out to and connect with the girls in ways that helped protect their privacy. Young women who have experienced premarital sex need to be handled carefully as the bad treatment they have received at the hands of their families and society at large have profoundly damaged their physical, emotional, mental, psychological and social well-being. They need careful and compassionate rehabilitation. Ignorance and harsh punishment will only turn them into abusers of other women (Adil and Elgemiabby 2009). Vocational training through special programmes offered by some governmental organizations and NGOs give these women the opportunity to stand up for themselves and learn how to make more life-affirming choices.

Among the respondents early sexual experimentation took place at between fifteen and nineteen years of age. Most women were sexually active (60 per cent) after the age of twenty and 30 per cent of them before twenty years of age; 95 per cent of the boys and young men were sexually active before the age of twenty. It appeared that the majority of women had had a single partner: either a lover who promised marriage or a relative from the extended family. Men had had multiple partners. About 70 per cent of both sexes were knowledgeable about STDs, more particularly about HIV through the media; however, they were not using contraceptives. Girls and young women especially believed that contraceptives would cause infertility.

The respondents had acquired their sexual knowledge from television, the Internet, Facebook and friends; very few had read books about sex. It was not possible for them to discuss sex with their parents because of the commonly held belief that information about sexuality and safe sex encourages sexual activity. Mothers therefore withheld information from their daughters that is imperative to understanding sex, sexual relations and reproductive health. While a great proportion of young men reported curiosity or the desire to gain experience as motivations for their sexual debut, the women held more negative attitudes towards premarital sex as they were often discouraged from thinking about it by their parents.

A twenty-two-year-old girl shared as follows:

> I used to talk by mobile with my lover for three hours at night where the price for calls was reduced, discussing sex and love because we cannot talk about it face to face, and this excited us to try sexual intercourse once, but unfortunately I get pregnant. The boy arranged for an abortion through the mobile, but I was afraid to do it because sometimes abortion is carried out by an inexperienced person and results in death.

A twenty-three-year-old wealthy young man said:

> I and other friends use the mobile to buy condoms from a friend; to buy condoms from the pharmacy is a risk because we may be seen by a person who tells my parents. Rich men and women are wise and have enough money to protect them and their poor partners and friends.

An eighteen-year-old girl expressed her wish for a different relationship with her mother: 'I wish that my mother would talk with me about everything that concern sex and sexuality.'

Another girl, aged nineteen, said: 'I cannot say no to him because I love him.'

A twenty-four-year-old man confessed as follows: 'I will not marry a woman that had sex with me before marriage because she may practice sex with other men after marriage, I will not trust her.'

A twenty-eight-year-old woman said: 'If a man uses the condoms it means he was practicing with many women – I will not accept that. Also I believed that using contraceptives causes infertility when I would get married.'

Factors leading to premarital sexual relationships

Boys start having sex at an early age (fifteen years or younger) to gain experience and fulfil their sexual desire. They also seek multiple partners in order to impress friends, while young women look for true love and marriage. Because of the precarious economic situation, desertification, drought and war, many people migrate to the capital, Khartoum, with little money, if any. So some young women consented to sex because of poverty.

Rural students migrating to the city without money need accommodation, food, transportation and education. Unemployment and idleness leave the youth frustrated and they cannot marry because of the high costs of marriage. When families break up, children are left with the extended family, leaving girls vulnerable to seduction by male relatives. Peer pressure combined with class differences and the need to accommodate more powerful friends and show off lead young men to approach girls for sex. Left alone at home the young people watch media such as television, films, Internet and videos, which often feature sex programmes. Sometimes girls were bullied into consenting to sex; sometimes they fell for the promise of marriage. A combination of sexual desire and lack of sexual awareness and education would lead young people to go too far. There is no behaviour without reason. Adewale (2009) found that many young people engaged in premarital sex as a result of curiosity; they wanted to experience it themselves and emulate what they had seen in the media. Sometimes girls would be greedy for money or presents. A general theme was the lack of good sex education. Since parents and government have refused to educate the youth on sexual matters, the youth have resorted to getting information from wherever they can.

Boys and men often do not care about their partners because they are brought up in a state of ignorance and irresponsibility; the community believes that men cannot do wrong regarding sex issues. Men can take advantage of the fact that their lack of virginity cannot be proven (Adil and Elgemiabby 2009; Mohamed 2009). They keep persuading the girls that sex is natural, and after sexual intercourse if the girl falls pregnant they either deny that they were responsible or insist on an illegal abortion. Men cannot marry the girls they have premarital sex with because they will not trust them and their families will not accept such a marriage. This tragic double standard is a consequence of contradictions inherent in the traditional cultural norms people adhere to.

Today both young men and young women spend longer in school and marry later. During this extended period of adolescence and young adulthood they may have sexual relations, putting themselves at risk of unintended pregnancies and STDs, which damage their mental, physical and social well-being.

Is mobile phone use facilitating premarital sexual activities?

Mobile phones were found to be the most important ICT tool used by both sexes as a platform to exchange messages of love, sex and romance. Mobile phone companies offered free or subsidized calls during nighttime. This is a convenient time for dating, and young people would find a private place (his, her or a friend's home) when their families were away. Boys and men would buy mobiles for the girls and young women, pay their calling costs and also use the mobiles to send the girls money for other expenses. The young people would exchange phone numbers when they met at schools, at universities, on local transportation, at social events and via friends. Sometimes they would get just get a call from an unknown person; they would start chatting and then keep the number for further communication. Girls and young women would get to know men in shops as they were attending to them as customers. It also became apparent that use of mobiles gave boys and men a great deal of freedom to escape a relationship, especially when the women fell pregnant; they would simply change their telephone number. Furthermore, mobiles also facilitated easy communication between the young people and midwives for the purpose of arranging an abortion or re-circumcision.

Is mobile phone use contributing to an increase in female genital mutilation?

Abdel Magied et al. (2000, 2009) state that, from a legal perspective, any unmarried woman who keeps quiet about her lost virginity has experienced premarital sex and has thus committed adultery. However, it seems that about 40 per cent of girls and young women can marry if what happened is kept top secret, while 60 per cent can marry because they can be circumcised and stitched. This means that female genital mutilation enhances premarital sex, as the mobile phone facilitates communication with midwives or women who practise circumcision. It also means that these illicit sexual encounters increase the incidence of circumcision and re-circumcision.

Re-circumcision is practised by 10–15 per cent of girls between the ages of sixteen and twenty-five, as a camouflage to restore their virginity. It retightens the vagina so that they can avoid future social complications just before marriage. Our study has confirmed this as a regular practice. One of the respondents shared: 'My partner arranged for delivery by the mobile with a mediator who arranges the place and fate of the baby and the circumcision process.' Female genital mutilation reflects deep-rooted inequality between the sexes and constitutes an extreme form of discrimination against women. Although attempts have been made to eradicate female genital mutilation/circumcision over the past fifty years, through an intensive campaign involving religious groups, the media and women's organizations (see Chapter 16), the increase in adolescent sex has definitely also increased this practice.

Second-phase interventions: use of workshops, radio and Facebook to disseminate results and attempt to effect change

In this second phase of our study we were led by the following question: how can social change and transformation take place through the use of ICTs to empower girls and women?

We followed a three-pronged approach: we organized a national workshop in which we presented our research results and invited other experts in the field; we started a series of radio programmes about the issue, which were the first of their kind in Sudan; we started a Facebook page inviting wide participation; and we created a personal blog.

The workshop

Three famous speakers were invited to participate in a workshop arranged to present, reflect on and discuss the findings with NGOs, policy-makers, religious men, university staff, students and guests. Abdelbagi Dafalla, an activist, researcher and doctor, gave some examples from his research on university students and SMSs; the results showed that romance and sex were the topics mostly covered in these. Professor A. Alzaki spoke freely about the influence of Western culture through ICTs. He said Islamic *sharia* laws should not be implemented before community awareness of the Islamic laws and responsibilities, because knowledge is the basic platform for a proper Islamic community. The Qur'an poses the question: 'Are they equal those who know and those who do not know?' (39: 9).

Dr Elgemiabby said that the problem is the need for family, community and religious and government bodies to break the silence. The relationship between the sexes will not change unless there is real community change and awareness about the importance of ICTs as an effective tool for sex awareness and education, with different programmes being designed to suit different ages.

The radio programmes

Three radio series were broadcast through FM100's Albeit Alsudany programme from 8 a.m. to 10 a.m. The programme was presented by famous radio presenter Shadia Khalifa and Abdelbagi Dafalla (mentioned above). For the radio presenter it was the first time such a taboo subject had been openly and directly discussed live on air on a national broadcasting channel. The programme sparked many telephone calls and direct inquiries from the audience, asking for more information and discussion.

One young woman caller said:

Thank you for sharing this problem. Women are suffering from
mobile abuse either with lover or other persons who sometimes get in
contact through wrong number and keep calling, especially during the
night, asking for dating where communication companies offer free
hours. Women, especially girls, need awareness about the important
issues like premarital sex and its causes, because this taboo will not be
discussed with the families due to shame.

A middle-aged man said:

Parents and extended family must take the responsibility to inform
the children about sex, including diseases, birth control and limits
that they see necessary. Behaviour change in society is needed because
discussions about sex are not allowed.

Another young woman said:

There are double standards set by the Sudanese Islamic societies that
turn a blind eye towards men for being promiscuous before or after
marriage and only blame women, don't respect them and punish
them if they lose their virginity. It is very important to discuss sexual
issues openly in our society to protect the current generations and the
generations to follow.

The Facebook page: Ikhlas Nour اخلاص نور
Facebook has been very instrumental in opening doors to discussions
about sex and sexuality that were previously taboo. This is because young
people feel free to write about their thoughts and feelings without supervision, using nicknames to keep their true identities unknown because
they want to avoid being shamed. Young people who have experienced
premarital sex cannot talk to their parents or family members about their
abuse and the emotional effects, because of the shame and harsh punishment they fear. This fear traps and silences them; thus they cannot find
help to recover, as they cannot find a trusted adult to help them because
of the taboo. Two girls wrote:

Parents ignore the consequences of sexual unawareness. Lack of
scientific understanding about sex makes all people vulnerable to
mass media with their portrayal of sexual behaviour. Adolescents are
ashamed and embarrassed to seek knowledge or advice from parents.
Girls/women have no say in decision-making and control over their
own sexual behaviour. [There is a] belief that awareness about sex and

sexual education encourages sexual activities that are not part of our culture and not approved by our religion.

Newly introduced types of marriage are a threat to morality; some young couples resort to unconventional forms of marriage like common-law marriage [*urfi*] where a paper is written between the man and the women to acknowledge that she is his wife, without informing her family and based on confidentiality and non-announcement, in order to sanction their sexual relationships.

The blog

A blog was created to open doors for people to write about and discuss sex and sexuality, with special emphasis on premarital sex. Unfortunately no one has written anything to open the floor for discussion. This may be because most people seem to prefer to use Facebook.

Conclusion

Sexual behaviour has been inadequately researched in Sudan; it is important that the taboo around discussing sexual matters be broken in order to enlighten and educate people. It has become clear through this study that ICT can play an important role in this field. Facebook offers users privacy and confidentiality when they want to inform themselves or share experiences. This is a crucial prerequisite in a culture where sexual matters are shrouded in controversy and where shame and secrecy are weapons of moral control.

The detrimental role that ICT, especially mobile phones, plays in the increase in premarital relationships and the harm this has brought to young women is fuelled by and fed on the secrecy, silence and shame that are so tightly woven around sex and sexuality in Sudan. This study has shown that ICT can also be used to break open this web of secrecy and silence. ICT-based interventions have created opportunities for young women to question that they, the most vulnerable group of all, carry the burden of the silence and shame and suffer the consequences of premarital adolescent sex on behalf of Sudanese society.

The way forward for Sudan as a society in the light of this research thus seems to be to enlighten and educate, especially the youth, on sex and sexuality. However, sex education without a concerted effort to change the gender relations will not change the double standards in which the shame and blame are put on the girl while the boy escapes unscathed, which is neither fair nor realistic. Being properly educated about sex may prevent many young women from falling pregnant and many unwanted children from being born. However, it will not necessarily contribute to better relationships between the genders and more respect for women.

The perception that women can bring shame on their families and community members and the concept that men have the right to kill them form the context in which the lack of sex education can bring such harm to young women and their unwanted children. It is this core set of patriarchal beliefs and customs that has to change for ICT to be used optimally for women's empowerment in North Sudan, whether in sex education and awareness or other areas of life.

Recommendations

It is imperative that sex is taken seriously at all levels of Sudanese society, so that there is no longer any need for silence, secrecy and shame around sex and sexuality. Sexual education in the broadest sense, including its physical, psychological, social and religious aspects, needs to be designed and facilitated in a way that is coherent with the Sudanese culture of mutual respect and modesty and the importance of the family and the community. Such education needs to be grounded in the understanding that sexual responsibility should be equitably shared between the genders and hence special programmes should be designed for boys and young men. Given the popularity of the various ICTs, from radio and television to mobile phone and the Internet, sexual- and gender-awareness programmes can be presented through these channels. To this end it is important to forge a collaboration between government authorities, universities, NGOs and religious leaders. When the silence and the secrecy around sex can be transformed into communication and collaboration, women abandoning their babies or committing suicide out of shame and fear will become a thing of the past.

References

Abdel Magied, A., A. S. El Balah and M. K. Dawood (2000) 'Re-circumcision: the hidden devil of female genital mutilation case study on the perception, attitudes and practices of Sudanese women', *Ahfad Journal*, 17(1): 3–14 (Reprinted in *Violence against Women & Children*, 11(1–2): 66–79).

Abdel Magied, A., I. E. Tayeb and M. E. Hassan (2009) 'Practice and attitudes of Sudanese midwives towards: re-infibulations', *Ahfad Journal*, 26(1).

Adewale, B. (2009) 'Causes of premarital sex', http://ezinearticles.com/?Causes-of-Premarital-Sex&id=2908790, accessed 21 May 2014.

Adil, A. and M. M. Elgemiabby (2009) 'Causes of increased number of abandoned children' [television programme], Harmony, 12 September, presented by F. Sadiq.

Alahram Alyoum (2010) 'Screaming of a newborn baby thrown by his mother in a well' [in Arabic], *Alahram Alyoum*, 28 September, www alahram.com.

Dafalla, A. (2010) 'Youth and mobiles: SMS University of Khartoum, Sudan', unpublished data.

De Bruijin, M., F. B. Nyamnjoh and I. Brinkman (2009) *Mobile Phone: The New 'Talking Drums of Everyday Africa'*, Cameroon: Langaa RPCI, Bamenda.

Hekayat (2009), 'Do not throw your baby to the dogs' [in Arabic], *Hekayat*, 1 October.

Mohamed, H. (2009) 'Foundlings in Sudan ... sad realities and uncertain future!' *World Pulse*, 3 September, http://worldpulse.com/node/13022, accessed 24 May 2014.

20 | Reviving the power of community: how Radio Rurale Femme de Mbalmayo in Cameroon became a catalyst for equality and democracy

GISELE MANKAMTE YITAMBEN

In Cameroon generally and in Mbalmayo and its environs in particular, women are trapped within a matrix of discriminatory systems of thought and practice. These reduce women's capacity to take care of themselves and their families and offer limited protection in cases of domestic abuse. To address this a group of women from this area established Radio Rurale Femme de Mbalmayo (RRF) with a UNESCO grant in 2000. RRF has contributed to improving life for women in the region by directly influencing prevalent gender discourses and relationships, setting in motion a process of successful social change.

What happened and what needs to be fully understood so that learning can be transferred to other contexts? This chapter discusses the history and context of RRF and the prevalent matrix of women-discriminatory systems of thought and practice. I apply Charles Duhigg's (2012) theory of social change to my observations.

Community radio in context

The introduction of community radio in Cameroon is relatively recent. In 1995 the French Agency for Cultural and Technical Cooperation set up and installed five rural community radio stations in the country. Since then this project has been taken forward under the auspices of several international organizations, such as the Food and Agricultural Organization (FAO), the United Nations Development Program, the Canadian and Japanese cooperation agencies Canadian Cooperation and Japan Cooperation. Since 2000 the major donor, UNESCO, has contributed to a further sixteen community radio stations,[1] with twenty-one formally recognized stations now in existence.

Rural radio in sub-Saharan Africa has evolved as development evolved: from agricultural radio in the 1960s to radio clubs in the late 1960s through to the mid-1970s, conventional rural radio or educational radio in the late 1970s and local rural community radio in the 1980s (Ilboudo 2001). Previously considered a top-down methodology for communication using theories of diffusion, 'communication for development has evolved to become a bottom up and participative methodology' (Tedesco 2008).

Mbalmayo

Mbalmayo[2] is a lowland forest region forty kilometres south of Yaounde with five tribes living in the area: Ewondo, Mvog Manze, Nvog Ekobena, Nvog Ndiand Otolooa.[3] The total population, including eleven villages nearby, is estimated at 800,000 to 1.5 million people, and is covered by RRF.[4] Apart from Radio France Internationale and Radio Cameroun, RRF is the only station available and it relays national news. Programmes are in the native languages to encourage the youth to speak their local languages, since they learn English and French at school. The local languages of the Ewondo are dominant (about 70 per cent), with French, English and other languages making up the rest. Said Ms Mbazoa, director of the RRF:

> Programming takes into consideration the time that the local farming
> population is available to listen ... Each age group has its programme.
> The themes cover the whole spectrum of issues that are pertinent
> to the interests of the rural community: from agriculture to health,
> nutrition, animal husbandry, hygiene, fishing, pharmacopoeia [use
> of African medicinal plants and herbs for curing disease] and general
> information on what is happening in the community.

Radio Rurale Femme de Mbalmayo

We chose to study RRF as a model of how a community radio station could contribute to social change, because of what we observed:

- Ekombitie now has a female traditional ruler: Her Majesty Sophie Okala (aged fifty-eight, single mother of five). According to her it was because of the radio programmes that she was elected traditional ruler after her father passed away. She says the station sensitized the villagers on gender discrimination and had a positive impact on the lives of villagers in other ways: the men became very collaborative and did not offer any resistance to her taking office.
- Many international volunteers have written glowing reports on the impact of this radio station. Katharina Atze, a German volunteer with UNESCO, wrote: 'The radio is a catalyst in the lives of women. Women have been able to come up and share their experiences with other women over the radio and this has led to a lot of awareness among the women folk.'

- A visit by UN Secretary-General M. Ban Ki-moon to RRF during his working trip to Cameroon from 9–10 June 2010 (UNESCO 2010b) confirmed that the community radio achieved concrete results.
- Collaboration of civil-society organizations and national-government institutions such as the Delegation of Women's Empowerment and the Family (UNESCO n.d.) and the Delegation of Social Affairs with RRF is impressive and ongoing, contributing educative programmes for women on health, home management, agriculture, the law and other relevant topics.

Matrix of women – discriminatory thought systems in the south of Cameroon

This matrix comprises three clusters of thought and practice that together and in interplay have a near-complete stranglehold on women's capacity to care for themselves and their families, and offer limited protection in cases of domestic abuse. Capitalism and Christianity together hold women confined to domestic labour, subsistence farming and petty trade, and prevent them from seeking political influence and participating in public decision-making. Cultural traditions do not acknowledge women's independent access or rights to land, and lack of gender justice in modern and traditional legal frameworks complicate women's capacity to seek recourse.

Capitalism, Christianity and gendered division of labour

Mbalmayo women are farmers carrying out subsistence agriculture on small farms, growing food crops to feed their families. They are also the main labour force on cash-crop farms controlled by men. The men sell their coffee, cacao and palm oil to the urban market or multi-nationals, contributing virtually nothing to the women's subsistence farming. As is understood in Marxist feminist theory, men and women are not exploited equally under capitalism. Women do not receive wages for their unpaid caring work and subsistence farming. The control over and exploitation of women's labour means men benefit materially from patriarchy; they benefit economically from the subordination of women (Abeda 2011).

Financing and extension services first put in place by colonial administration and today reinforced by development assistance programmes essentially aim at promoting cash-crop farming, excluding women from training and financial means for developing their agricultural activities. Christians consider women to be submissive to men and their main roles to be mothers, wives and housekeepers (1 Peter 3: 1). Neo-colonial extractive global capitalism perpetuates the economy that is holding Cameroon (and much of the developing world) ransom, and thrives on and exploits social inequalities, especially gender inequality.

This division of labour and family responsibilities is the visible face (Post 2013) of a social order grounded in a concept of gendered task-sharing, where women give natural priority to domestic and private work while men devote themselves to productive and public activities. Because the work that women do both in the house and on the fields is unpaid, they directly subsidize the economy while becoming dependent on men, who have become sole breadwinners.

Women's limited presence in decision-making can, according to the Fatou (1995), to a certain degree be attributed to colonial prejudices that oriented training of women more towards reproductive work (bringing up children, care-taking, hygiene) than economic productivity. Only belatedly did extension and technical programme services take into account the fact that women are 60–80 per cent of the labour force in agriculture.

Women are rarely approached as farmers, even when in charge of farming operations. Women's needs and experiences are perceived as deriving more from the domestic than the agricultural economy, and hence women's labour has drawn less attention from national economic policies. The capitalist economic system, Christian mindset and national policies collude to maximize the profits of large enterprises and maintain women's exploitation.

Traditional cultural thought and practice

Men have the right to have more than one wife, without the reverse being possible. Laws regarding adultery favour men: male adultery is only established in the case of a sustained relationship with the same extra-marital partner.[5] For women the law is very strict, and female adultery is established on the basis of a single event.[6] Widows' property rights vary according to traditional cultural laws; most women in this area cannot inherit land, nor do they have the right to use the land. Their husbands allocate them land to work on and their status is that of a labourer on the family farm. This generally does not enable them to build up independent financial security. When their husbands pass away they are at the mercy of the family council, which decides their fate. Whether they are allowed to continue farming depends on various factors outside their control: their status within the family, whether they have children (especially sons), how in demand the land is and whether they are taken in levirate marriage by one of their husband's family members (Fatou 1995).

Regarding dowry, the predominant place of money in the local economy as a consequence of the influence of and integration within the capitalist system has rendered all traditional institutions precarious. Dowry, whose value was traditionally more social than economic, has to an extent made women tradable goods. Some parents request gifts and expensive presents from boys who ask for their daughter's hand in marriage (thus reinforcing the future husband's hegemony over their daughter). Reimbursement of dowry constitutes a substantial impediment when women seek a divorce, because the woman's family often does not want to reimburse the money or goods. Traditional institutions by which women could seek recourse have been corrupted.

No gender justice under the law

The feminist movement in Cameroon has pushed the government to adopt policies aimed at advancing the situation of women by, among other measures, inclusion of gender parity in the constitution. In addition to adding binding measures in modern law, the state has created a ministerial department to facilitate political socialization of women and sensitization of men to value women's worth.

However, coexistence of two legal systems – written law and customary law – has generated confusion among women, who are often not aware of their rights within the constitution or feel too downtrodden to pursue their rights. On issues concerning inheritance, marriage or sorcery, one can choose to take one's case either to a customary court or a modern tribunal. In modern law women have equal access to family heritage. They can create and manage an income-generating activity without prior consent of their partners, but cannot inherit their husband's property: legally they are considered to be merely usufructuaries.

Conflicts arise from the coexistence of these two different legal systems. Women pursuing a certain action may find protection against discrimination under one law while putting themselves at risk under the other. The dowry is an example of this. In Cameroonian modern law, the total or partial payment of the dowry, or execution or non-execution of any total or partial marriage agreement, does not affect the validity of the marriage. Any action concerning the validity of a marriage based on total or partial non-compliance to an agreement or marriage dowry is inadmissible.[7] Without payment of a dowry, however, the marriage is not acknowledged in customary law. When the dowry is not paid in full,[8] a man's authority over his children will be refuted, he cannot bury his wife and cannot claim a dowry for his daughters (instead maternal uncles will claim such dowries). The dowry seals the bond between two families for several generations. These social ties form a sort of protection for women, because they open up their household to the social control of a wider community. However, customary marriage has no 'positive' legal value in Cameroon; to be considered valid it must be recorded in the civil registry of the place of birth or residence of one of the partners.

When a woman wants to leave her husband, her family has to reimburse the dowry. If they refuse, the woman is often stuck. If she insists and leaves, the husband may have her arrested and jailed for abandoning the matrimonial home. Yet under modern law the woman could get a divorce without going through all of this. Women's ignorance and the resistance of many men to change mean many women continue to suffer in silence. Even when informed, many cannot find the energy to confront and resist these practices. With two legal frameworks coexisting without being fully harmonized into one law binding upon all, much space is left for arbitrary, highly subjective interpretations. These are often not in the interests of women, because the judicial system remains a reflection of the patriarchal system and most judges are male.

In a rentier economy in which men are those who accede to wealth and where money has rotted the dowry system, taking women's traditional protection away; in an environment that encourages women to stay at home and take care of man and children while polygamy is allowed; and where women have lost traditional means of seeking recourse while being unable to access a modern legal system (which is still far from fair and gender just), it is clear why women's situation has become so dire.

This and general under-investment in policies for women's rural development have had a disastrous negative cascading effect, leading to insufficient agricultural production. This in turn has led to food insecurity, causing maternal and infant mortality.

How did RRF succeed in bringing about significant social change?

RRF supported women in their capacity to take care of themselves and their families with a wide variety of programmes. Describing these programmes is not the focus of this chapter, and it has been done elsewhere (Marsaud 2001). Here we focus on the way RRF has been able to accomplish its mandate of social change to empower women in the area. According to Charles Duhigg (2012) in his book *The Power of Habit*, social change takes place when:

- an individual strongly desires a situation to be different and starts doing things differently or challenges the status quo even if breaking existing laws;

- this individual is supported by strong ties of friendship, even when socially and legally vulnerable due to breaking laws;
- 'weak ties' of the community exert social pressure on others to change their behaviour;
- a leader gives people a new identity, which acknowledges the new values and supports the new behaviour, so that eventually enough people in the community take up the new values, identity and behaviour.

While all of the above-mentioned items are necessary components of a social-change process, they do not follow in a logical sequence. The story of the establishment of RRF and unfolding of its meaning and significance in the Mbalmayo community follows, keeping these social-change components in mind.

The story of RRF

In 1998 a small group of people originally from Mbalmayo thought of initiating development projects to be controlled by local women to contribute to the elimination of discrimination against women. Mrs Owona Constance, wife of one of the most influential politicians of the country and leader of one of the region's women's associations, had been dreaming of a rural educational radio station to help reduce discriminatory practices against women. When informed that UNESCO had launched a programme for implementation of community radio in Cameroon (UNESCO 2010a), a small group of people requested and received finance to equip the radio station. According to Mme Sophie Beyala Bekolo, Coordinator of Radio Programmes and the Community Multimedia Center in the sub-regional bureau of UNESCO for Cameroon, Tchad and Centrafrique (whom I met in 2011), UNESCO consented because Mbalmayo was an area with many strong women's community groups, and the idea to set up the radio station came after the merger of two hundred women's associations there. These organizations had constituted themselves into one large umbrella organization called Concertation des Associations Feminines de Mbalmayo (CAFEM). In 2001 networks were formed in all administrative units in the Mbalmayo area.[9] In the process of starting the radio station, dialogue was initiated between UNESCO, CAFEM and other stakeholders.

RRF was created in 2000 with the following objectives:

- informing women about their rights and handling questions of interest to them;
- serving as a space where women could express themselves and share problems, and where women and men could work together towards a harmonious evolution of the community;

- providing a platform for women and sympathizers with women's emancipation to eliminate discriminatory practices against women.

For love of a woman ... the men came

Upon the launch of the radio station, however, women did not come forward to air their preoccupations; men came to discuss problems their sisters, mothers or neighbours faced. The women did not feel confident to come forward, as their voice had been silenced, ignored, despised and rejected for so long; but after a while the women came. Traditionally a woman with a marital problem would go to the 'wise men council'. Said Martine:

> It does not serve anything to go and see the 'Wise men council', for all that is of interest to them is the fine that they will make your husband pay, that is to say crates of beer that they will drink together. After that the man will still continue to harass you. I prefer going to the radio and putting across my problem where others will provide solutions spontaneously.

The power of weak community ties to exert social pressure

Slowly but surely, the radio became a 'public square' where women would bring issues into the open in the hope that public pressure would bring solutions. Harassment issues brought forward by women often aroused the solidarity of the audience: the fear of public opinion enables the finding of solutions – for instance, the story of twenty-nine-year-old Susanna, who got married at the age of eighteen as the fourth wife to an octogenarian. For eleven years of a marriage that yielded six children, Susanna felt ill-treated, so she decided to end the marriage. However, according to tradition the dowry had to be refunded by her family. Susanna knew that her family would be reluctant to do this, so patiently and secretly she started to set aside part of her earnings from her farm work.

When her family indeed refused to return the dowry, Susanna's husband thought this would force Susanna back. However, Susanna managed to come up with 90 per cent of the dowry.[10] Taken unawares, the husband was forced to accept the money, but did not leave her in peace. He wanted her back home and kept harassing her. Susanna then went to the radio station and explained her predicament, declaring that she had refunded her former husband's dowry. It was only after that radio appearance that he stopped worrying her because many people rang in to condemn the attitude of the said husband. Susanna finally got her freedom and her peace.

RRF's director

When RRF started, its director, Ms Mbazoa, was a young, unmarried woman. This represented a challenge in her wish to work for social change. Traditionally she would have had no say in this very patriarchal region. Ms Mbazoa found things very difficult from the start: 'Men even threatened me with death. They say that I am making their wives "grow fat heads".' When she got married she retained her maiden name without attaching her husband's name, and the community found that a bad example. (Little did they know that adopting one's husband's name is not a traditional custom in the area but a practice imposed during colonial times.) Thanks to the unwavering support of their promoters, RRF kept Ms Mbazoa in her position. She had a clear vision about the change she wanted to see, and was not going to be deterred.[11]

Broadcasting a new female identity

The female programming staff also experienced friction: 'Certain men go as far as warning their wives against getting into contact with women working at the radio,' one employee told us. People went as far as trying to set the female employees' husbands against them. Even when their husbands were proud of them because they worked at the radio, they did not always share their viewpoints, which created dissonance at home. The male workers, all bachelors, were ridiculed for working under female authority. The female radio staff realized that change cannot be rushed, and that they had to respect the community's sensitivities: 'The population has you in the eye, your behaviour is being monitored with lenses,' the programming director shared.

The radio as a community forum

The radio extended local authorities' capacities for outreach: the commissioner of police, magistrate and even the clergy proposed taking care of certain problems after having heard about them over the radio. The president of Mbalmayo Court regularly intervened on radio to ask women with problems to come and see her. Thanks to her, many women sued successfully and obtained the inheritance or divorce that family councils had been blocking.

The radio became more than a replacement for social institutions and provided a safety-net for women. The silent majority that previously did not have the possibility of expression can today express itself under cover of anonymity. Since these expressions of opinion are not tied to a person's status, they are considered on the basis of their inherent value and judged by the community on their pertinence, usefulness and rationality. In this way not only the women and their families benefitted but also the community as a whole.

Discussion and conclusion

Applying Duhigg's thinking offers a useful explanation as to why and how RRF could successfully influence some of the gendered thinking and behaviour in Mbalmayo and its environs.

There was an obvious need for change as perceived from within the community, as many women and their families were suffering and existing social institutions were failing. The radio, having become partly a public forum, offered the community a platform where the power of social pressure could be wielded to solve social problems, replacing to a degree traditional options for protecting women through exerting social control. Because challenges to dysfunctional gender thinking, behaviour and relationships were shared publicly, both the process and successful outcomes strengthened the sense of community.

The strong ties of friendship (and love) brought the first cases to the radio and kept the female director and staff in their positions. The role of a leader offering the people a new identity, with new values and new behaviour, was clearly filled by the radio director and strengthened by the personalities and behaviour of the programming staff.

The radio station was first adopted through traditional pathways: the men would come forward to speak on behalf of women. As the women themselves started to come forward and the function of RRF expanded to become a true community forum, its original vision of contributing to harmonious evolution towards more inclusion and social and gender equality became a reality.

Studying the unfolding story of RRF provides insights into mechanisms of a successful process of social change, but it also brought up some questions:

- Is this process of solving problems encountered by the community going to really challenge traditional gender power relations?
- Will we see, for instance, an end to polygamy accomplished through community radio programming?
- Will we see a fundamental departure from the deeply entrenched patriarchal system in Mbalmayo and its environs?

I guess that another way of phrasing these questions would be: What is needed for a real shift in gender power relations to happen in rural Cameroon?

Recommendations

1. A network of community radios should be formed in order to enable the sharing of success strategies, promote emulation and encourage the establishment of more radio stations. This transformatory approach can help to shake the gender-power relations in Cameroon.

2. The communities' radios network thus constituted will become an instrument that enables the people and their communities to discover and identify the enormous potentialities that they possess in order to become the builders of their own well-being and further push the boundaries of policy. This measure is within the capabilities approach as defined by Sen (1999) and deepened by Nussbaum (2000), who applied the capabilities approach to feminism. Nussbaum thinks that it is not necessary for individuals to be contented with rights but that they should be made to deploy their potentiality to build a good social well-being given that they are the only ones capable of identifying their needs and knowing what to them is useful. In this perspective every member is a resource to him/herself and for others.

3. Community radio can be an appropriate medium for promoting participation of women in national dialogues. For example, it could facilitate women's contribution to the formulation of the pending family code.

Notes

1 According to Sophie Beyala, program coordinator for radios and community multimedia centers in the sub-regional office of UNESCO in Cameroon, Chad and the Central African Republic, personal communication, June 2011.

2 Mbalmayo stands for 'Mbala me yo', which was the name of the first chief of the area before the Germans took over as colonizers. Mbala me yo was consulted by the Germans as they sought to become acquainted with the region, and since then this name has become established in the area.

3 Mbalmayo also harbours inhabitants from other parts of the country, such as the Bakossi, Bakweri, Bamilekes, Bamoums and Bayangi, to mention but a few. There are also foreigners from countries such as Equatorial Guinea, Gabon, Niger, Nigeria and Senegal.

4 These villages are Akoèman, Dzeng, Ekombitie, Mengueme, Metet, Ngomedzap, Nkolgock, Nkolmetet, Nseng-long, Olama and Zamakoe. The population from other villages expressed some dissatisfaction with UNESCO because they were initially told that the whole Division of Nyong and So'o would be able to get radio reception, and this did not happen.

5 Men are encouraged to spend family revenue on issues that they determine alone, while the wife bears alone the family burden of feeding the household and bringing up the children. Women are furthermore at risk of sexually transmitted diseases from their husbands, who are allowed to have multiple sexual partners.

6 Article 361 of the Penal Code, the customary law, is particularly unfavourable to women. In several customs the woman is part of the property of her husband in the same way as goods. She cannot expect to inherit, and the belongings of her husband come under the control of his family when he passes away.

7 Section 357 of the Penal Code punishes the excessive requirement of dowry with imprisonment of from three months to five years and/or a fine of XAF 5,000–500,000 (Journal Officiel de la République du Cameroun 1967).

8 When the dowry is deemed insufficient or not paid at all, the woman may be exposed in that her own family may believe they have not benefitted enough from their investment in their daughter. In this regard, occult practices might be used (sanctioned by the family of the woman) by dissatisfied persons or because of non-payment of dowry to direct infertility or marital instability at the woman.

9 These networks, established with letter No. 01/07/L/Mincof/SG/Depv/CECO of 5 November 2000, included: REASFECOM (Réseau des Associations Féminines de la Commune de Mbalmayo / Network of Women's Associations of Mbalmayo Council Area); L'UNADA (Union des Association pour le Développement d'Akoèman / Union of Development Associations of Akoeman); Le REFACOM (Réseau des Femmes Actives de la Commune de Mengueme / Network of Active Women of Mengueme Council Area); Le REFAN (Réseau des Femmes Actives de Nkolmetet / Network of Active Women of Nkolmtet); and RAFEZ (Rassemblement d'Association Féminine a Zamakoe / Group of Zamakoe Women's Associations).

10 Susanna cultivates food crops (cassava, cocoyam, groundnuts, maize and potatoes) on a piece of land that she rents and that belongs to a family in the village. She is a member of two women's Contribution Meetings in the village. She regularly saves in those Contributions a part of her earnings from sales of excess produce from her farm, after consumption. At the end of years of effort, she succeeded in raising the amount to pay to her former husband.

11 I am reminded here of Tim DeChristopher, renowned environmental activist, when he speaks about conscience and adhering to values 'rather than working from, you know, what corporations tell us they'll accept, we're going to work for what we actually want, something that's actually in line with our vision for society' (Moyers 2013).

References

Abeda, S. (2011) 'Patriarchy and women's subordination: a theoretical analysis', *Arts Faculty Journal*, July 2010–June 2011, www.bdresearch.org/home/attachments/article/nArt/A5_12929-47213-1-PB.pdf, accessed 25 March 2013.

Duhigg, C. (2012) *The Power of Habit: Why We Do What We Do in Life and Business*, New York: Random House.

Fatou S. (1995) 'Femmes rurales chefs de famille en Afrique subsaharienne' [Rural women family heads in Subsaharan Africa], Food and Agriculture Organization, www.fao.org/docrep/x0237f/x0237f00.htm, accessed 21 May 2014.

Ilboudo, J.-P. (2001) 'Histoire et évolution de la radio rurale en Afrique noire: rôles et usages' [History and evolution of rural radio in sub-Saharan Africa: rules and practices], Food and Agriculture Organization, www.fao.org/docrep/003/x6721f/x6721f02.htm, accessed 2 November 2011.

Journal Officiel de la République du Cameroun (1967) www.vertic.org/media/National%20Legislation/Cameroon/CM_Code_Penal_Cameroun.pdf, accessed 16 June 2013.

Marsaud, O. (2001) 'Radio des femmes de Mbalmayo au Cameroun: pari réussi' [Mbalmayo women's radio: a succss story],www.afrik.com/article2211.html, accessed 15 June 2013.

Moyers, B. (2013) 'Why Tim DeChristopher went to prison for his protest', *Truthout*, 25 May, www.truth-out.org/news/item/16586-why-tim-dechristopher-went-to-prison-for-his-protest, 26 May 2013.

Nussbaum, M. (2000) *Women and Human Development: The Capabilities Approach*, Cambridge: Cambridge University Press.

Post, E. (2013) 'The gendered division of labour, the wages for housework movement, and the law', *Academia*, www.academia.edu/827795/THE_GENDERED_DIVISION_OF_LABOR_THE_WAGES_FOR_HOUSEWORK_MOVEMENT_AND_THE_LAW, accessed 15 June 2013.

Sen, A. (1999) *Development as Freedom*, Oxford: Oxford University Press.

Tedesco, M. (2008) 'Communication pour le developpement et radios communautaires: le cas du Népal' [Communication for development and community radios: the case of Nepal], Master 2 Professionnel, University of Paris,www.univ-paris1.fr/fileadmin/Centre_doc_ufr11/M2P_CIAHPD-tedesco.pdf, accessed 20 May 2013.

UNESCO (n.d.) 'Mbalmayo and Meiganga women's community radios', www.unesco-ci.org/ipdcprojects/content/mbalmayo-and-meiganga-womens-community-radios, accessed 20 May 2013.

— (2010a) 'Premier forum national des radios communautaires du Cameroun' [First national forum of community radio of Cameroon', *Lettre d'Information Bureau Multipays Yaoundé* [Newsletter Cluster Office Yaoundé], November, http://unesdoc.unesco.org/images/0019/001903/190385f.pdf, accessed 13 Novembre 2011.

— 2010b) 'Visite du secretaire general des nations-unies a la radio femmes-FM de Mbalmayo' [Visit of the UN Secretary General to RFB], *Lettre d'Information Bureau Multipays Yaoundé* [Newsletter Cluster Office Yaoundé], June, http://unesdoc.unesco.org/images/0018/001886/188631f.pdf, accessed 6 June 2014.

21 | Transforming relationships and co-creating new realities: landownership, gender and ICT in Egypt

SANEYA EL-NESHAWY

Introduction

Egypt's female landowners – 97 per cent of whom do not manage their own land (United Nations Development Programme 2005a) – feel frustrated and limited due to their male relatives' authority over their land, and because they find that these male relatives are controlling and restricting their agricultural success. Women are accustomed to their subordination to male family members and the customary practice of these relatives having responsibility for managing their land. Women are unable to control the use of or take decisions regarding their land as a result of inherited cultural norms and beliefs that give rise to and sustain gender inequality in the control and management of women-owned landholdings.

When women inherit land in Egypt their inheritance comes as part of a collective property-rights package called *shuyu*, in which they share the inherited land with other relatives. While women inherit half of a man's share, they also feel compelled to allow the part they do inherit to be 'managed' by a male relative, even when capable of doing this themselves (El-Neshawy and El-Sayed 2005), so that the whole area of inherited land can be managed as one piece. The few exceptions are women-headed households, or when the male in charge of their land is away. It is assumed that the men have greater capacity than their female relatives to be productive farmers, and thus they 'take care' of the land for the women – as is expected of them (United Nations Development Programme 2005b).

The unquestioned and seemingly 'unquestionable' succumbing to male authority over their land affects all aspects of women's lives. Women farmers miss out on the self-empowerment that comes with effective management of one's land, and the gendered structure limits and constrains their productivity, income, livelihood security, independence and public status. Their performance as farmers is constrained in a number of ways. They have less access to agricultural information because they are not encouraged or even invited by Agriculture Department staff to participate in extension services. They glean some information from radio and television programmes, and from their land neighbours. Rural women's lack of knowledge about their landowner rights further aggravates the situation. Landowners' socioeconomic rights are controlled by laws that preserve agricultural land from non-agricultural usage and guarantee land as collateral for a credit card for obtaining agricultural resources (Republic Decree No. 96, 1992).

Women's roles have traditionally been confined to carrying out household functions, including raising children and caring for elderly family members, and undertaking home-based productive activities including feeding and milking animals and selling poultry products. Without control over land management, women become vulnerable, deprived of their rights and dependent on key males in their families. This leads to men holding increased power in the family and community and women's lowered sense of self-worth. Furthermore, due to the gendered social and cultural norms, women have limited engagement in community politics and restricted decision-making power, and thus limited influence on policies that subsequently do not support their legal rights or priorities. Such limitations on women are justified by a general acceptance of normalized male roles and leadership.

How would this situation change if women landowners acquired the knowledge to productively manage their land, as well as knowledge of their legal rights as landholders, in an environment that supported unlearning subordination and pursuing their ambitions? Would a shift in the gendered control of production and decision-making occur if women gained knowledge that helped in improving production? For women to change their land status would mean changing long-standing norms.

While exploring and acting upon this question through my research with women farmers I also turned to my own situation of not managing my own land even though I have extensive expertise as an agricultural scientist. I examined why I did not manage my land and had not even claimed ownership during the thirty years since I became the hereditary owner. My journey to claim control of my inherited land as an educated woman living in town involved different challenges from those faced by the women farmers who live in their village and already work with their land, although not as decision-makers.

I inherited quite a large piece of agricultural land after my father's death. In accordance with long-standing norms my land was left in the hands of a male relative – with whom I have good relations and who I love – to farm and take care of in our village. This arrangement required my trust and submissiveness to inequitable gender norms, which was expected and acceptable in the rural society. All the women in my family followed these existing norms in the rural society in which we were brought up. I was given minimal rent for the use of my land, such that for many years my landownership did not feel like a reality. In addition I was totally engaged in my research, working hard to achieve my ambition and building my professional career.

When I designed and undertook my GRACE research I was initially not conscious of an intent to change and empower myself to reclaim my land. However, agriculture has been my passion and focus since childhood. Working closely with women farmers throughout the research process raised my interest in and desire to become a productive farmer on my own land. Seeing the changes and successes experienced by the women landowners as they recognized and came to value their own abilities and rights and became increasingly confident in their knowledge inspired me to reflect on my own relationship with my land, and increased my desire to become a rightful woman landowner. I therefore decided to face the challenges involved in reclaiming my land.

The intent of the study

My research team set out to investigate whether and how the use of ICTs, in the form of a web-based agricultural extension programme, could support women who intend to take on the management of their own land (Sharma 2001; Bakesha et al. 2009). Together with the women farmers we set out to discover whether mastering this web-based agricultural extension programme would enhance their agricultural knowledge and marketing opportunities. We recognized that deference to men and male authority is deeply ingrained in women's consciousness in Egypt (Forkhonda 2002) and that having the capacity to manage one's land would not be sufficient for women to break away from the traditional norms of their culture. We wanted to find out how the women could enhance their self-confidence and self-determination as female farmers to the point of questioning traditional male authority over their land and taking the lead themselves as effective and empowered decision-making farmers of their land.

With women's behaviours changing, agricultural productivity increasing and family well-being improving, I expected that gendered power relations would change over time. I believed that, by identifying crucial knowledge gaps and using a web-based programme designed accordingly, women were likely to change their perspective on their capacities and know-how, increasing their sense of self-determination. As women become confident in their opinions and exercise their choices in land management, they gain a sense of entitlement to management of their land and subsequently of their lives and their contribution to their community. Land management would furthermore bring women into the decision-making structure in their rural community (Republic Decree No. 434, 1999).

Engagement in the steps of the research project – which involved direct ongoing contact with women farmers seeking to expand their capacities, developing together a specific learning programme and learning to apply what they learnt to their practice of farming, and supporting them as they improved their practice and as their thinking shifted – contributed to increasing my own interest in and capacity to reclaim the management and ownership of my land from my male relative. An important part of why I designed my research with women farmers in both my village of El-Sharkia and in Ismaelia was to work closely with women farmers in the same community as where my land is located. I had started to own my personal desire to become an active farmer and manager of my own land, showing gratitude to my home town that I had grown up in and to my male relative, and to put into practice the passion of my life journey in the field of agriculture. My intent and dream was to become recognized in my community and reconnected with it as a productive, successful farmer. In this chapter I set out to describe and understand both journeys – my own and those of the women farmers – and how they influenced and were crucial to each other.

Research methodology

Twenty women landholders, their relatives and neighbours initially participated in the project. Nine of them were involved in the full process, starting from designing the extension programme and computer-skills training. Female landowners' needs were assessed through in-depth interviews carried out with the twenty women by the research team. The women indicated that a lack of information was a primary missing element relating to their ability to take on the management of their land. They reflected on their dreams to manage their own land through the process of dream drawings in conjunction with free attitude interviews (Buskens 2005).

Based on the in-depth interviews, the research team designed an extension programme named 'Empowerment of female farmers in the field of landholding and marketing through access and use of ICTs' (www.gracemena-elneshawy.com/index.php?page=subject). The focus was on crop production, marketing, funding availability, land rights, landowner credit cards, registration of land credit and the agricultural cooperative association. The interviews were complemented by the use of posters, videos or computer presentations, workshops and group discussions to identify, review and prepare the needed information. Female landowners were mentored on computer skills and how to approach and use the web-based programme's content as well as other online agricultural information resources. The programme evolved through cycles of learning, implementation, sharing and reflecting.

The methods I used to gain my own land back were different as agricultural knowledge was not the missing element for me. While my passion for agriculture shaped the focus and design of my research, it also became a process that enabled me to fully recognize and pursue my dream, a dream that I hoped to share with other women (family, friends, other women in my communities), to show them that this desire can become a reality. My process involved a great deal of personal writing, using dream drawings (see Chapter 22) myself to explore what I would love to see, communicating with various authorities, debating with my family and sisters (who are in the same situation) and discussing with agricultural colleagues who are in a similar situation. At the same time I was attentive to my need to retain close bonds with my male relative, to recognize the criticism he would bear for turning my land over to me and to be respected by the community I was raised in, which saw me as an educated urban woman with no need for – and perhaps not deserving – my land and its produce.

Outcomes of the research process for the women farmers

Gaining expertise, confidence and change strategies

The research process created opportunities for women farmers to connect with each other, reflect on their dreams and identify what information and knowledge they needed, and these interactions affected many dimensions of their journey to becoming successful farmers. Their connection with each other allowed them to recognize shared problems, obstacles and solutions concerning their land production and to share the ways they went about convincing their male relatives to recognize their capacity to manage their own land. Reflecting on their dreams highlighted the large gap between their present status as farm workers and the manager relationship with the land they own that they wished to achieve.

The lack of information relating directly and indirectly to farming strategic crops and becoming farm managers was responded to through offering use of the web-based programme, which was also made available on CD and as a paper document, and through my provision of training, including regular visits to the women's fields. The web-based programme was found to be useful in many ways. For example, through the knowledge gained, female landowners could protect their crops by checking daily weather predictions on the Internet. This helped them plan for sudden increases or decreases in temperature, high winds, heavy rain, floods or drought. Some found a new approach to developing high-nutrition feed for animals instead of relying on grazing. Women who previously let their animals eat Nile-flowering plants growing on the surface of uncovered canals, which are classified as toxic, learnt that residues of the toxin are found in animal meat and milk and so they alerted farmers to change where they grazed their animals.

On the basis of the information accessed, sharing my knowledge in agriculture with the women farmers and organizing the research processes to include team and group work to share and increase their expertise, increases in the women's self-confidence and success stories became tangible in terms of land management, including production increases and thereby income increases. They could show their male relatives, who held the decision-making power over their land, that women could become equally capable, just like the few women who head their own households and hold their own land credit cards and provide for their families. Thereby they showed that they deserved to possess their land credit cards themselves. Sixteen of the women farmers' revenue from their crops increased by 40 per cent over two successive planting seasons. Their effective use of computers and the Internet increased from being a characteristic of 30 per cent of the participants (six out of twenty participants) at the start to 75 per cent upon completion of the intervention. The number of women who became the managers of their own land also increased: fourteen women out of the twenty became managers of their own land subsequent to the research intervention.

Access to a computer and the Internet also resulted in economic benefits related to gaining national and international information on intermediary companies that deal with marketing agricultural products. Some women began to sell their produce through these companies. In other cases, as a result of women's increased confidence and knowledge, their male relatives who owned agro-business stores asked them to market their own produce through the male relative's company, indicating the male relative's recognition that the women were becoming increasingly informed and prepared for these tasks.

Shifting gendered norms

Women landowners' increasing productivity, revenue and subsequently self-determination started to change the customary social norms that had previously restricted their communications with the public (it had been considered morally shameful for a woman to be in public or in the company of another man without her husband). With their growing self-confidence they started to communicate freely and speak with those they wished to, even if they were men, as needed for farming support and to make their own land profitable. Having gained the know-how and self-assurance to deal with their land, they began personally signing contracts with the merchants who would market their harvested crops and with companies that executed certain agricultural operations on their land, and would reserve farm labourers prior to the planting season with no restrictions or fear. The women could also use their farming profits to look after some household expenses, which was considered by their male relatives and other family members to be a concrete example of increased self-sufficiency. They have more say in family financial decisions, responsibilities and household-related matters. One woman shared the payments of purchasing a taxi with her husband, using her extra income to strengthen the family's financial well-being.

Shifting these social norms also began to change the restrictions on women's movements in rural society, which increasingly were waived and no longer adopted by men as they realized that many aspects of their life and well-being were being affected by women's effective contribution to their land. By showing their husbands that they are good and reliable farmers and experiencing a sense of freedom because they knew what to do and could rely on themselves in managing their land, women had a sense of breaking free of constraints imposed on them and overcoming their fear of male authorities:

> We now have the liberty to move around freely and that helps to give us space to use our personal signatures or stamps while visiting the agriculture authorities for purchases, to reserve our share of seeds, pesticides, fertilizers, or mineral nutrients, which were not allowed before.

How the journey of the women farmers was essential to my own journey to claiming my land rights

Seeing the sense of connection and love farmers have with their land revived my own deep-seated bond and desire to stay close to the farm and enjoy the environment I was raised in. Having the opportunity to work land directly, unmediated by hired farm workers, and visiting farm lands regularly as the women farmers applied various agricultural practices under my supervision, I acquired a close connection and sense of cohesion with the land.

Self-trust and confidence

Working closely with the women farmers gave me the sense of 'deserving' control over my land, and increased my confidence to ask my male relative for my land back to farm under my own direction. Whenever the women farmers whom I taught and trained succeeded in regaining their land and became able to improve their productivity and enhance their status as farmers, I would ask myself, 'Why not me?'

My ability to change from the position I had kept for thirty years, of leaving my inherited land in the hands and care of my male relative, was contributed to by the regular meetings and the leadership I experienced with the women through training and mentoring them; by experiencing their nature and customs, which I could draw upon later when hiring other women farmers to work on my land; by understanding their way of thinking as practitioners on their land; and by the satisfaction I gained from doing what I see as my duty towards farmers with regard to my professional career. My intent for my research process of increasing women farmers' self-empowerment became my own.

ICTs were also part of my journey. Coming from a different position (a professor in agriculture) from the women, by creating a project website that explained our project and introduced the women farmers online, I could use this avenue to promote how the knowledge and information that created and resulted from the project originated in my career experience in agriculture, particularly my focus on farmers' performance and disseminating knowledge in rural areas. The project website promotes my name and reputation as a scientist in agriculture among a limitless virtual community. I also asserted my expertise in the villages by using an institutional vehicle when making weekly visits to the women farmers in Ismaelia and El-Sharkia. I used and applied seeds, fertilizers, nutrients and organic matter with the official stamps and approval of my institute.

Challenging the manifestations of male authority

For all the expertise, experience and professional profile I had, and the ability to acquire and apply knowledge, my male relative's management of my land was a very sensitive issue to be dealt with. I realized what worried me most and what I had to overcome was the fear of confronting male authority. It was the first barrier I had to break; it meant going against my own learnt and practised submission to existing cultural norms in my community. My relative's traditional male role far outweighed the value of my knowledge, profile and inherited right to the land.

At the beginning my male relative rejected my demand. I persisted in raising the issue in a friendly way with no involvement of any other person or authority. He showed no interest in what I was asking. I was able to speak the truth to my male relative and the rest of my family members, saying that I wanted to reclaim my land, but I was very careful not to break family bonds or create distance between us. I started with personal and calm communication. I would allude to and exhibit my passion to work personally on my land; I visited my land accompanied by the women whom I intended to hire to work on my land with me. Conducting my GRACE research, which was seen as part of my employment and career and which was respected by my male relative, seemed to him to be a logical reason for my taking over the management of my land.

I carefully moved forward to the formal procedures involved, but he would procrastinate when I needed him to request the official land documents. When we got to the point of separating my piece of land with fencing, he refused to let me go with him in case people saw me and said that his sister was taking the land from him. Such experiences left me feeling sad and regretful; it was not pleasant convincing my male relative or the farmers who had been working the land for a long time that they could no longer consider it theirs. Once I was managing my own land, I had to take a certain approach to gain their acceptance and change their beliefs regarding their acceptance of my landownership and management. For example, I grew and gave my male relative gifts of the most desirable vegetable crops.

My experience affected one of my sisters, who started to behave as I did, asking to reclaim her land and for it not to be sold to the male relative managing it for her. The personal transformations among family members went further: my nieces similarly asked for their land. Women agricultural scientists in my research team also claimed their inherited rights to land and built houses for themselves in their villages. Some female farmers who are workers next to my land have been motivated to 'not only have their inherited land documents and even practice the agricultural tasks, but also contribute to the agricultural plan for the following seasons', benefitting from my experience, they explained.

How our two journeys each made the other possible

The fact that I have extensive technical expertise in farming but did not work my own land or have a deep connection with my place of birth and landownership, whereas the women farmers wanted to acquire such expertise and were already grounded in their community and worked on their land, meant that our interests were complementary. We both sought to manage our rightful land.

My journey with women farmers benefitted me as their diligence, satis-faction, tacit knowledge, activities, patience and early rising were inspir-ing. I learnt from the way they convinced their male relatives through proving their abilities to manage their land, while I also used diplomacy in my approach to my male relative. Seeing them manage their own land gave me the inspiration and confidence to take the steps needed to gain control of my land, so that I was able to become a farmer applying my agricultural knowledge on my own land. From this I also gained more confidence to become an example and teacher for other female farmers, and thereby expanded the circle of the women farmers who adopted and benefitted from the same stance of wanting to regain their land to man-age and farm.

Getting my own land back increased my credibility among women farmers. When they asked me as an agricultural scientist to bring them crop nutrients that I had developed during my laboratory work, I could determine the nutrients' benefits through trials and experiments on my own land. My position as an agriculture professor with knowledge and extensive experience and with the power and experience to be a decision-maker needed to be grounded and put into practice through my actual management of my own land. Seeing this – in combination with their acquisition of additional knowledge, their growing self-confidence and their approaches to regaining their land from their male relatives, along with having suitable ground to work on to maximize their productiv-ity – the women became better farmers, made more money and gained increased status as female farmers.

Gaining management of our own land: changing ourselves and transgressing social norms and gender roles

Our starting points were very different, and our dreams and needs too, except for the shared purpose of becoming the managers of our own land. We each desired and needed to expand who we were, in a number of ways, and learn how each of us could best act upon our common purpose.

The women farmers wanted to increase their revenue as extra income from increased crop production was an important issue from a household-economy perspective. They were determined to learn how to use comput-ers and the Internet to benefit from the specific and relevant information these media could make available to them. This learning was designed as a social and responsive process – it drew on what they knew they needed, from the perspective of knowing their land, their community, their needs and their sociocultural environment. The learning was situated in shared spaces and was collaborative, both indoors and in the fields. The women dedicated themselves to learning how to best practise – in their fields – what they learnt under my guidance and training, while also learning from each other as they worked on applying their increasing capacities in the most effective ways to shift traditional norms. They were strategizing together, reinforcing each other and their own confidence regarding how best to gain decision-making power in the management of their land and crops, without losing respect in their families and community.

As the women farmers increased their expertise, produced successful and varied crops and expanded their market options and revenue, social norms that restricted their success had to fall away. Their husbands recognized the value of their contributions and the women themselves became more confident in their know-how and more comfortable transgressing cultural norms that inhibited their progress. They had managed to change themselves and the social norms and practices of their community while increasing their status, self-confidence and self-determination.

I too had to find the best way to gain the right to manage my own land, counter to established practices. My agricultural know-how was not the issue, but also was not what it took. I had to overcome my resistance to challenging values and practices built on acceptance of male authority and upheld by my community of origin, from which I had become distanced by my education, years living away, status and absence from the land. Thus I too had to change and expand who I was in relation to all these aspects in order to reach my dream of managing my land while preserving an increasingly strong sense of connection with my community, family and self.

What enabled me to change and expand involved first increasing my trust and confidence in myself. I turned to my accomplishments – academic and in the rural fields – as a teacher and a producer of crops. I also needed to become accepted and grounded in my own community. My research project and working closely with the women farmers provided me with avenues to once again become familiar to and with my community and to develop my understanding of local ways of thinking and being as a woman farmer.

For both the women farmers and myself, our experiences of gaining management control of our land and all this entailed transgressed social norms and existing gender relations, yet we maintained (or in my case regained) the respect and interdependencies essential to rural social well-being. This involved the use of ICTs to improve our own condition and contest existing power relations, rather than allowing existing social forces to prevail (Hafkin 2000; Gurumurthy 2004) while at the same time changing and expanding ourselves. We had to build within ourselves the capacity for and legitimacy of our pursuits, given how these were counter to how we were raised and to the communities that connect us to who we are. We had to expand our visions of ourselves and then have social constraints on our capacities and identities let go of to make room for our expanded selves. Our personal changes, as women with increased self-determination, agency and capacity to contribute to family and community well-being, were recognized and over time understood and embraced by our families and rural societies.

Conclusion

Regaining my land has grounded me as an agricultural scientist. I now practise what I teach and speak from my own experience. I relate physically to the land: smelling its mud, seeing its green produce, feeling the texture of the soil. Having a physical relationship with my land connects me with my father and through him to past generations of my family who owned that land. It has absolved the feelings of being cheated out of my birthright and subsequently out of the family bonds of interdependency, my land rights and my sense of connection to my origins. Thus the actual management and ownership of the land also create a spiritual bond for me of belonging to the land, to the earth and, through the rural community, to my own origin and Egypt. From this expanded sense of myself I have gained more confidence – and have the first-hand experience in what it takes – to become a teacher of female farmers whose dream and purpose is to regain their landownership while retaining their respect and connection in their community.

References

Bakesha, S., A. Nakafeero and D. Okello (2009) 'ICTs as agents of change: a case of grassroots women entrepreneurs in Uganda', in I. Buskens and A. Webb (eds), *African Women and ICTs: Investigating Technology, Gender and Empowerment*, London: Zed Books, pp. 143–53.

Buskens, I. (2005) *Free Attitude Interview Manual*, http://issuu. com/gracenetwork/docs/fai__final, accessed 20 May 2014.

Council of Minister for Regulation of the Rules of Land Ownership (1992) *Republic Decree No. 96 (1992)*, Cairo: The Cabinet.

Council of Minister for Regulation of Women's Leadership of Small Enterprises (1999) *Republic Decree No. 434 (1999)*, Cairo: The Cabinet.

El-Neshawy, M. S. and A. A. El-Sayed (2005) 'Women's participation in production, marketing, and storage of fresh horticulture crops for local consumption and export', paper presented at the International Conference on Women's Impact on Science and Technology in the New

Millennium, Bangalore, 21–25 November.

Forkhonda, H. (2002) 'Horizon of sustainable agricultural development: increasing production and export', paper presented at the Women and Rural Development Conference, National Council for Women presentation, Cairo, 19 May.

Gurumurthy, A. (2004) 'Gender and ICTs overview report', www.unesco.org/new/fileadmin/MULTIMEDIA/HQ/SHS/pdf/Gender-ICTs.pdf, accessed 21 May 2014.

Hafkin, N. (2000) 'Convergence of concepts: gender and ICTs in Africa', in E. M. Rathgeber and E. O. Andera (eds), *Gender and the Information Revolution in Africa*, Ottawa: IDRC, pp. 1–16.

Sharma, C. (2001) 'Using ICTs to create opportunities for marginalized women and men: the private sector and community working together', paper presented at the World Bank, Washington, DC, 18 December.

United Nations Development Programme (2005a) 'Gender equality and empowerment of women through ICT', www.un.org/womenwatch/daw/public/w2000-09.05-ict-e.pdf, accessed 21 May 2014.

— (2005b) 'Human development report for Egyptian provinces', Cairo: Ministry of Planning and Local Development.

FOUR | **Methodology**

22 | Research methodology for personal and social transformation: purpose-aligned action research, intentional agency and dialogue

INEKE BUSKENS

Introduction

This chapter sets out to explain the main ingredients of the GRACE approach to research, capacity-building and networking. The vision that binds the GRACE researchers together is a world where all people are free, and where women and men are equals and treat each other with respect as partners. Such a normative, future-oriented perspective inevitably influences individual choices in terms of research process and design, over and above the various directives that originate in disciplinary background and/or methodological and theoretical preference. The knowledge that was sought by the GRACE researchers was meant to contribute to social change and this often implied that the theories that were applied were not so much 'about the action as it took place' but more 'for the action that was deemed desirable', either within the framework of the individual projects themselves or for another research or intervention at a later stage. In a concrete sense this meant that the researchers aligned their projects with a three-fold purpose of social change: a purpose that was specific to their particular project, a purpose that was specific to their region and the purpose that was behind the overall GRACE Network process (see Introduction).

In order to design and conduct normative, future-oriented research, whether actual action research or research for action at a later stage, certain capacities are needed. The capacity to think in alignment with purpose and integrate a research question with a specific purpose of social change, while adhering to the traditional criteria for research quality, requires being able to think 'trans-disciplinarily' and develop the conceptual meta-capacity that allows one to define, search or create a theory that meets the needs of a specific iterative research process at a specific moment in time.

Imagining being part of a different future and being able to design and conduct research that is aligned with that future will inevitably confront researchers with questions about the self: what do I want and need to become in order to be part of this new future? What do I need to learn in order to do the research I want and need to do? Since coherence between the envisaged future and one's future self is key to the validity, credibility and effectiveness of the research project, researchers have to be able and willing to engage processes of conscious and willed personal transformation. This requires a stance of taking responsibility for the self, a commitment to grow in self-awareness and the development of intentional agency. The personal becomes methodology, not only because the research methodology is an expression of the personal (which it is in any kind of research) but also because the person of the researcher is an intrinsic ingredient of the research design and a crucial dimension of the research process and any other action that may follow from it at a later stage. Apart from the technical quality standards pertaining to all types of research, there is no external standard to test a future-oriented normative research process in terms of its process and impact other than the future vision and the ideals that support it and hence the importance of the person of the researcher living such ideals.

In conjunction with these two capacities, the capacity for dialogue is crucial: as a method for self-exploration (conducted either intrapersonally or interpersonally), as a research method (in conversation with team members, respondents and other stakeholders) and as a networking method (to ground the research process and results in the various relevant research contexts and knowledge communities).

These three capacities speak to each other, support and complement each other and also balance each other. The degree to which conversation partners can align themselves with a shared purpose and bring their intentional agency to bear upon it will define the quality of the dialogue. In dialogue, conversation partners may obtain greater clarity about their intentionality and about the nature of the purpose they have aligned themselves with and what this alignment takes in terms of self-awareness and personal transformation. And it will be in dialogue that stakeholders will decide what would be a desirable purpose for social change in a given context, and the degree to which they are aware of their own intentions and capacities will define their deliberations and choices. These three capacities were consciously developed within GRACE, during workshops and ongoing dialogues online and offline.

To assist the researchers with navigating the complex fields of sometimes conflicting and disappointing emotions, thoughts, aspirations, experiences and perspectives that their projects would inevitably generate and to facilitate the various levels of dialogue about these, while staying aligned with the researchers' three-dimensional project purpose, various sets of visual aids were developed. These visual aids functioned as maps that the researchers could use to reflect on and communicate about their relationships with their projects and the social change that would ensue, as well as their relationships with themselves and the processes of personal change, which they themselves had set in motion.

This chapter comprises three parts. The first part, 'Purpose-aligned action research as meta-theory', focuses on the purpose-aligned process logic that informed all the projects. The type of knowledge that the GRACE approach would yield had to be knowledge that would be 'able to do things', to 'make things happen' and change people's behaviour and environments. Regardless of the specific research methods that were eventually chosen, such as surveys, qualitative interviews, participant observation or discussions, the main research question guiding the research design was aligned with a purpose of social change and this influenced both design and execution on many levels. The meta-theory informing the GRACE project is illustrated with two graphics: Figures 22.1 and 22.2.

The second part, 'Self-awareness and intentional agency', explores the capacities of self-awareness and intentional agency and explains the two personal trajectory maps (Figures 22.3 and 22.4) that the researchers used to navigate their (relationship with themselves in relation to their own) processes of personal change. Women and men who align themselves with purposes of social change in and through their research will invariably meet the gendered parts of themselves that do not resonate with the future they want to see but with the gender inequality and sexism they have grown up with and in. For researchers who want to act as ethical agents in the knowledge quest for social change, enhancing their capacities for gender (self-) awareness and for intentional agency is thus pertinent. However, while the development of cognitive and affective capacity are extensively examined, the study and development of intentional capacity are neglected in Western psychology and in reflections on research capacity-building. The second part will therefore attempt to fill some of this gap and explore some of the conceptualisations and reflections from various academic fields that are pertinent to this capacity and its development.

In the third part, 'Partnership and dialogue', the dialogical aspect of the GRACE research, capacity-building and networking approach is explored. Because the success of social change efforts depends so much on the quality of researchers' abilities to communicate their findings and perspectives, regardless of the variation in research questions and methods in the various projects, the spirit of every research design was dialogical.

Researchers are used to communicating in and about their work, in many fora and for many purposes. These research conversations each require their own specific spaces and the use of their own specific techniques, to suit their respective purposes. Presenting a scientific paper at an international conference is a different form of communication from facilitating a neighbourhood meeting in a community action research project. In the same vein, conducting a critical collaborative dialogue for the purpose of enhancing personal (gender) awareness and intentional agency, to obtain clarity about a shared purpose and the journey as it unfolds, will of course also need to have its own space and be conducted according to its own rules. This is the form of dialogue that was used in GRACE between researchers and their team members and respondents, between the GRACE members and between the researchers and their mentors. The fifth visual graphic, Figure 22.5, represents the space in which the various dialogical relationships could develop.

Part I: purpose-aligned action research as meta-theory

Because of its alignment with a positive purpose instead of a problem to be solved, our approach builds on the work in appreciative inquiry (Ludema et al. 2001). Because the researchers had the option to act as change agents themselves and often did so, our approach built on the tradition of pragmatic action research (Coenen 1987); and, because researchers infused their designs and processes with their own future-oriented values and aspirations, our approach built on the tradition of normative action research (Babüroğul and Ravn 1992). The approach also resonates with emancipatory action research (Buskens and Earl 2008) and the planning, monitoring and evaluation method 'outcome mapping' (Earl et al. 2001).

Furthermore, the project logic must be able to accommodate various stakeholders joining at various moments, with these stakeholders bringing various knowledges and various knowledge interests. Such a process should be facilitated in such a way that the various participants are able to (learn to) share and communicate with each other, without letting the power differentials decide on the process and outcomes of their conversations. It is thus important to develop a shared project language; Brown (2010: 128) refers to a 'pattern language with a strong focus and fluid boundaries'. Figures 22.1 and 22.2 represent the space in which such a language can develop.

Keeping the project language open and transparent will also resonate with the purpose of cognitive justice and hence with the type of knowledge democracy that has become ever so important in the Information Age (Visvanathan 2009). An inclusive, open system of knowledge construction

Zed Books, 7 Cynthia Street, London N1 9JF

Sales 020 7837 4014 Editorial 020 7837 0384 Production 020 7837 8467 Marketing & Publicity 020 7837 8466
Finance 020 7833 1985 Fax 020 7833 3960 Email zed@zedbooks.net Website www.zedbooks.co.uk

Syemania,

Please find enclosed a copy of 'Women and ICT in Africa and the Middle East' as requested.

With Compliments

Nikki

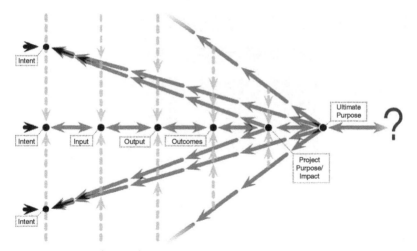

FIGURE 22.1 Project trajectory map 1.

that strives for cognitive justice will in itself also be a driver of project success, because it will generate the widespread support needed to 'make things happen'. It was this thinking that led to the development of the Purpose-Aligned Action Research Process, originally named the Quality and Impact Framework (Buskens 2001).[1]

Figures 22.1 and 22.2 show how the research purpose and the values behind the purpose (the more transcendental vision of a world where everyone is free) give temporal and spatial parameters to the research process and encourage researchers to use a procedural rationality to explain their process of discovery (Smaling 2013). In other words, the research process itself will indicate what is needed step by step through the unfolding changes it effects and the influences on the process the researchers become aware of during the journey. With the researchers explaining the rationality of this unfolding procedure, the processes of discovery and justification (which normally are kept separate in social science research) are brought closer. This methodological transparency allows for more inclusion and participation of various stakeholders at various times throughout the project and also by others at a later stage. Social reality is complex and it will be difficult for any research or intervention project to claim to have effected certain outcomes and impacts in isolation from other efforts for social change that are happening in the same research environment. Furthermore, while these future-directed orientations influence the research choices being made in line with this future vision, emergent phenomena can also be linked retroductively to the project's purpose by reasoning backwards. Hence, the arrows point both ways:

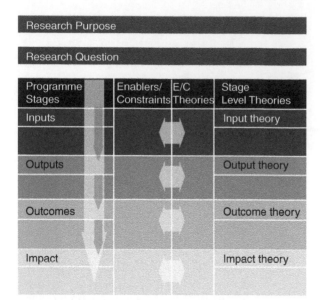

FIGURE 22.2 Project trajectory map 2.

from researchers' initial intentions to their purposes and vision beyond, and from the vision and the purpose back to the researchers starting their journey with certain intentions. The unfolding research processes have the following characteristics:

1. The researchers use their inside knowledge pertaining to the norms, beliefs and ideologies that form and inform the cultural environment as well as all relevant factors affecting the situation and the living conditions. While the logic that aims to guide the knowledge quest can be designed beforehand, the researchers will remain open to the unfolding of this research journey in the environment and adapt and change and add whatever is needed in terms of knowledge, research methods and techniques. The research process is thus iterative and open-ended, with everybody involved willing and able to participate in ongoing reflection and learning.

2. In terms of theory and conceptualizations, the research is trans-disciplinary; the search for disciplinary knowledge, concepts and theories is prompted by the needs of the knowledge quest and is not defined by or limited to the disciplinary knowledge brought into the process by the scholars involved at the initiation of the research.

3. The main research question is not a hypothesis to be tested nor a hermeneutic-interpretive question focusing on respondents' perceptions, emotions or rationalizations. The main research question is a

'how to' question that is grounded in the social change the researchers, research respondents and participants want to see. The knowledge constructed will hence be pragmatic knowledge and may prompt the introduction of theoretical knowledge or construction of new theory at various moments of the journey.

4. The quality criteria pertaining to the research process and research results are not only informed by questions of reliability, validity and methodological objectivity but also by the degree to which they (research processes and results) facilitate the project's purpose of accomplishing and understanding social change, the degree to which the underlying theory of change is explicated by the research design and the degree to which every research decision is coherent with this theory of change and the ultimate project purpose.

5. At all moments of the research process a 'reality check' can be made as to how the project has progressed in relation to the ultimate purpose. This will facilitate communication about the research process and such dialogical intersubjectivity is an important strategy in striving for research quality (Smaling 1995, 1998). An approach that has 'alignment with a purpose of social change' integrated into its project logic is of necessity complex (Byrne 1998; Walby 2003; Smaling 2013).

Figure 22.2 shows an overview of the various moments where decisions about adoption, adaptation or development of theory have to be made: for instance, what thinking guides the knowledge creation that will inform the intervention design at input or output level? The map is meant to facilitate coherence between all of the various theories used. This map makes clear that it is the process that will indicate at every step what the appropriate theory use or adaptation is. This requires a certain mixture of theoretical mastery and lack of attachment to a particular theory.

Part II: self-awareness and intentional agency

Key to the GRACE approach towards research, research capacity-building and networking is the emphasis on and nurturing of self- and gender awareness and intentional agency in both respondents and researchers. McNay explores the work of Ricoer, Bourdieu and Castoriadis to restore a positive dimension to the concept of agency in feminist theory, a concept that acknowledges the creative aspect in action and the importance of radical imaginaries over and above agency as resistance and subversion (McNay 2000).

Intentional agency is described as conation (Huitt and Cain 2005; Gerdes and Stromwall 2008), purposeful action and will-power (Campbell

1999), intent (Moddel 2009; Buskens 2010, 2011, 2013, 2014), the capacity to aspire (Appadurai 2004) and (volitional) agency (Sen 1999, 2004). Conation and the human capacities for cognition and affect are often portrayed as the innate tripartite 'hardware' of human mental capacity (Militello et al. 2006: 240).

The conative aspect has been neglected in research and in education in Western Europe and North America since the 1920s. To make things happen intentionally by one's actions is, as Bandura states in his work 'Social cognitive theory: an agentic perspective', the quintessence of humanness. For the most part, however, psychological theories have granted humans little, if any, agentic capabilities (Bandura 2001).

The various concepts and the capacities these concepts allude to are related, and the differences in conceptual perspective resonate with the disciplines of the respective proponents. Moddel (2009), a phenomenologist, frames intent as 'the impetus to form meaning or to perform a specific act'. He asserts (2009) that:

> ignored in classical science and without a place in cybernetic emitter/receptor descriptions of communication, the ubiquity of intent has been left unacknowledged and yet without it no unit of meaning would enter our minds and we would be zombies in a world totally out of reach.

Appadurai (2004: 63), an anthropologist, brings the 'capacity to aspire' into dialogue with Sen's (1999) concept of capability and Hirschman's (1970) concept of voice. While his treatise focuses on the poor, his reflections can be extended to women: 'The posture of "voice," the capacity to debate, contest, inquire, and participate critically' (2004: 70) is the capacity to engage social, political and economic issues in terms of the ideologies, doctrines and norms that are widely shared and credible and hence this capacity is reflexively related to the capacity to aspire: 'It is through the exercise of voice that the sinews of aspiration as a cultural capacity are built and strengthened, and conversely, it is through exercising the capacity to aspire that the exercise of voice by the poor will be extended' (2004: 83). Inspired by Taylor's (1995) politics of recognition, Appadurai speaks of the 'conditions and constraints under which' disempowered groups 'negotiate with the very norms that frame their social lives' (2004: 66).

Appadurai treats the capacity to aspire as a cultural meta-capacity and, although the human capacity to aspire is indeed to a degree a function of our cultural learning and hence our environment (Appadurai 2004), an essential dimension of that capacity is formed and informed by our will –

that is, the force of our intentionality, the conative drive for action and the individual determination to get things done.

Campbell (1999: 59) suggested that the most fundamental and significant power is that represented by agency and that human beings should be viewed primarily as agents who possess the power to transform themselves and/or their environments, in conflict with behavioural resistance from their own conditioning or environmental resistance. As conation is linked to intrinsic motivation and the capacity to exercise will for its own sake, it is thus also connected to values, beliefs and our desire to accomplish meaningful and purposeful action.

While Malabou (2008) asserts in *What Should We Do with Our Brain?* that our brains are plastic but that we do not do enough with this plasticity of our brains, Leys claims that Malabou evades the 'very problem which is at the center of the mind/brain debate, namely, the nature of intentionality' and despairs about the fact that, according to her understanding, Malabou offers as a solution that 'the claim *is* that intentional agency just is the biological process that can produce the desired-for "gaps" or differences that characterize freedom' (Leys 2011).

Whether consciousness and hence intentionality is an emergent property of the human brain or the primary cause of mental human capacity and/or human existence, the nature of intentional agency or conation is a transformational capacity that can be trained (Huitt and Cain 2005; Huitt 2007; Gerdes and Stromwall 2008). In GRACE this capacity was trained very explicitly and purposefully in many different ways, during the annual workshops and during the ongoing mentoring both online and offline. In a way, working with purpose alignment in research processes will inevitably train conative capacity.

Figure 22.3 represents a model that can be used to focus thought intentionally, not in the sense of an action plan but in creating a representation of something to which one aspires, through which the mental force of conation is activated. In focusing on one's dreams, these 'dream drawings', as they are called, map one's journey in terms of the emotions, thoughts and experiences within one's personal doing, being and relating, and bring the resources and challenges within one's environment to awareness. The alignment with one's intended state of being or experiencing makes the journey visible and can explain why certain internal and external hindrances arise. Because of the transformations that often happened as a result of this focus on and intention to bring about personal or social change, this exercise came to be called the 'transformational attitude interview or process' (TAI for short). Its representation is now known as the 'personal trajectory map'.

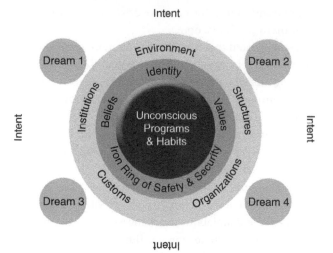

FIGURE 22.3 Personal trajectory map 1.

In the centre are situated unconscious programmes and habits. The ring immediately around the centre is the 'iron ring of safety and security', where one holds one's sense of identity: beliefs and value systems. In the ring around that, the environment is pictured with its institutions, rules, regulations, structures and so on. Intent functions as a vectored energy and can thus be placed in any of the other aspects of 'self': one's dreams, one's identity, one's environment or one's unconscious programmes and habits. Taking intent as one of the elements of self, this map portrays five elements of our mental capacity, of 'how we know and relate to ourselves'.

When we understand intent as a vectored will that can embody itself in any of the other four elements of self, we can speak of intent as 'positioning itself' (speaking in terms of the personal trajectory map) in one's dreams or one's identity or one's environment. When one is not consciously placing one's intent in any of these three known aspects of self and is not consciously aware of it, the will and thus one's intent can be assumed to inhabit one's reservoir of unconscious fears and desires. When the self is drawn to a new experience, a new horizon, a journey is set in motion where the self will be aligned with a possible future self that is not yet familiar but is very attractive (Markus and Nurius 1986). At a certain point the vectored energy of the self will feel more at home in the dream and as part of that dream, and the future self will at that point have become the present self.

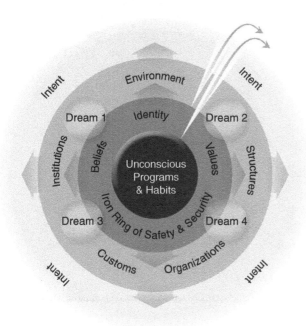

FIGURE 22.4 Personal trajectory map 2.

During this period, where various selves can be habituated simultaneously, there may be unease or even anxiety. The self now has
broken out of its 'comfort zone'. The part of the identity self that needs
to know itself as familiar may feel 'broken into' or even 'falling apart'. In
the process of expanding to new experiences and a new 'self', one may
also become aware of some unconscious habits and programmes. The
moment one starts to change and occupies a new self, one has a better
perspective on what the old self 'was'. When the self makes what was the
dream now part of daily reality and adds a new dimension to the identity ring, the self will feel expanded and may also simultaneously feel
the excitement of this expanded state, and start adding new experiences
and habits to its actions, thoughts and emotions. And so a newer, more
expanded self emerges, with a new daily reality, a new sense of identity
and a new environment. Perhaps new positions and new friends will now
come into one's ambit.

It needs to be emphasized that this map intends to be a way of working with the self without claiming this to be all there is to what we are as
human beings. This map is much too simple and simplistic for that. It
does not pretend to be anything more than a heuristic device that can be of
assistance when one needs to 'manage' one's journey of personal change

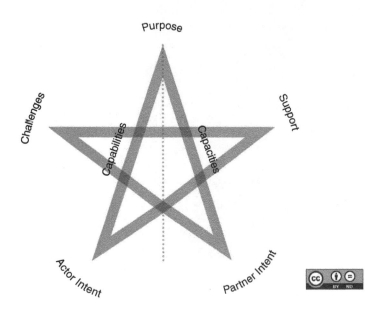

FIGURE 22.5 Relational map.

and transformation. Its value is that it has been created in response to researchers in need of the self-understanding to allow them to continue their work. But in itself a simple tool like this cannot function outside a community of people who have a shared language and can relate to the meaning of the journey of self-expansion.

Part III: partnership and dialogue

Because of the imperative for social change that has been the mandate of this Network from the beginning, alignment with a purpose of social change became key to the research and intervention approach in the Network's second phase. The relationships between researchers and other stakeholders (respondents, mentors, policy-makers, peers) were thus grounded in the purpose, in the dream that was shared and the intentional agency the partners would bring to bear towards their shared dream.

Partnership is sought because the person of the partner or the resources such partnerships bring can contribute to the realisation of the actor's purpose, which in and through the relationship has become a shared purpose. The capabilities (Sen 1999) that the partner enjoys and that are grounded in the partner's capacities, intentional agency and environmental support structure reflect the actors aspirations and will thus stimulate the actor's capacity development. In this sense,

Appadurai's concept of the capacity to aspire can be seen to anchor Sen's concept of capabilities in an empowerment approach: 'empowerment has an obvious translation: increase the capacity to aspire' (Appadurai 2004: 70).

Characteristics of a critical dialogue

The form of dialogue that seems most suitable towards the purpose of supporting researchers in their journey of integrating gender awareness in their research is what research methodologist Adri Smaling has described as the 'critical dialogue' (Smaling 2008; Buskens 2014). Smaling first describes the characteristics that a critical dialogue should have in order to optimize its fruitfulness and then compares the critical dialogue with the critical discussion and the debate.

In the first place, the relationship between the conversation partners is rooted in the shared topic and hence the alignment with this topic is primary and will lead the process and content of the conversation. Without this shared topic, there would be no conversation and possibly not even a relationship. Characterizing the nature of this relationship, Smaling speaks of the relationship a researcher has with her/his object of study as a subject–object (S–O) relationship, the relationship with a co-researcher as a subject–subject (S–S) relationship and a critical dialogue between researchers focusing on a shared topic (which could be themselves) as a subject–subject–object (SSO) relationship (Smaling 2008). Smaling's (2008: 22–5) characteristics of a critical dialogue can be summarised as follows:

1. The partners are equal in terms of power, which implies equal chances for participants to initiate, continue or stop acting and reacting, talking and listening, discursive speaking and empathic feeling.
2. It should involve mutual trust.
3. It should involve mutual respect.
4. It should involve mutual openness, implying open-mindedness (being open to the partner and her sharing) and open-heartedness (not holding back issues, feelings, insecurities or embodied experiences when they are relevant to the conversation). While open-mindedness is more a general state of mind, open-heartedness is explicitly expressed vis-à-vis the other. It knows its expression in relationships. Smaling (1995: 29) acknowledges the risk that exclusive focus on either open-mindedness or open-heartedness might degenerate into a perverted form. Open-mindedness might degenerate into a distant awareness and even an impressionistic narcissism. Open-heartedness might

degenerate into an expressionistic narcissism and even exhibition-
ism. When this happens, true dialogical openness is not possible.
However, a dialectical relation between open-mindedness, open-
heartedness and dialogical openness will potentially lift all three
strategies to a higher level (Smaling 1995).

5. It should involve mutual understanding. In order to accomplish this,
the partners should use their empathic capacity, relying on emotion,
knowledge and interpretations so that the most suitable interpretation takes the lead, as such making mutual understanding a truly
hermeneutical act.

6. It should be argumentative.

7. It should exhibit good will – that is, positive, constructive intentionality towards one another, which leads to optimal interpretation.

8. It should be reflective in character.

9. It should be evaluative.

10. It should be collaborative.

Critical dialogue in juxtaposition with critical discussion and debate

Juxtaposing the critical dialogue with the two other main forms scientific researchers use to communicate with one another, the critical
discussion and the debate, Smaling (2008: 26) distinguishes certain characteristics between these three forms and emphasises that the critical
dialogue, although critical, is about mutual support and trust and the willingness to understand each other and collaborate as conversation partners
instead of compete and endeavour to beat an opponent (see Table 22.1).

The GRACE dialogue

The type of dialogue that suited our purposes of building partnerships, stimulating self-exploration and developing intentional agency
is, however, a very specific form of a critical dialogue between two (or
more) scientific researchers and their partners on a shared topic that
may include themselves. Talking about dreams that are not reality yet
can make aspects of self conscious to the self that from that point on
need to be integrated. While for some becoming aware of hidden aspects
of self can be a light and joyful journey, a natural continuance of personal growth and expansion, for others it can be filled with conflict and
resistance.

In the following section I will describe the five conditions that should
be added to Smaling's critical dialogue in order to describe the form of
dialogue that developed in the GRACE Network (Buskens 2014).

TABLE 22.1 Critical dialogue in juxtaposition with critical discussion and debate. Translated and abbreviated from Smaling (2008: 26).

Dimensions of Difference	Critical Dialogue	Critical Discussion	Debate
Metaphorical typification	Agora (public square for community meetings, conversations and trade)	Palaestra (wrestling or boxing school close to gymnasium), later sports terrain; strict rules for behaviour	Arena (sand-covered middle section of a Roman amphitheatre, space for fights to the death); less strict rules
Means of persuasion	Logos, argumentatively sound	Logos, argumentatively sound	Logos and ethos and pathos, not necessarily argumentatively sound, sophistries
Type of interpretation	Optimal interpretation, benign	Optimal interpretation, benign	Not optimal or even minimal interpretation, not benign or worse
Mutual relationship	Cooperation, much mutual trust and respect; mutual understanding, mutual learning processes, sharing experiences, participatory; not aimed at consensus	Regulated competition, solving of a difference of opinion, sufficient mutual trust and respect, but it is about winning and losing, and reaching consensus is important	Possibly violent competition, struggle, fighting; winning or losing can be very personal and *ad hominem*

Five GRACE dialogue conditions

First, the dialogue must be grounded in post-sexist futures (Buskens 2014: 12, 13). Exploring visionary post-sexist concepts and perspectives is essential for researchers because it is impossible to create what cannot be imagined. The fact that humanity has to create a future that is different from the current socio-economic-politio-religious state of affairs cannot be refuted any longer. But these visionary concepts and perspectives are also important methodological tools. They create mental spaces that can counteract the sexist discourses and mindsets that all research stakeholders inevitably will bring to the research process. Especially women, and in this case female researchers and research respondents, have often adapted their visions of the future and thus of development outcomes to the conditions of the sexist environments they have grown up in. Offering them a counter-balancing mind-field and discourse can enable them to collaborate with development research processes in a useful, valid, relevant, ethical and visionary fashion. Imagining and thinking from a 'mental space' where all human beings genuinely respect themselves and each other and appreciate gender as an expression of being human and thus deserving of respect will enable the conversation partners to hold a reference point for all the thoughts, emotions, aspirations and intentions that unfold during the conversation. Making use of their capacities for experimentation and imagination, conversation partners will inevitably come to reflect on themselves, their lives, their relationships and the world and as such draw from and also enhance their capacity for reflexivity in a wider sense.

Second, conversation partners must realize that their dialogue will be a meeting in imperfection. Nobody can claim to live, think, act, know, be and relate in a manner that is consistently free of sexism (yet) (Eichler 1991). No country can claim that it has resolved its gender issues. Nobody can be considered to be gender aware in the sense of being able to approach a person or a situation without sexual prejudice of any sort and apply the awareness pertaining to the gender issues that are relevant to any particular situation, in an appropriate way. It is important that this 'imperfection' is acknowledged openly and frankly (Buskens 2014).

Third, since no conversation partner is free from sexism, the giving and receiving that will take place is therefore not about freedom from sexism. One cannot give what one does not have. The exchange in and through the conversation will be about the courage to discover and acknowledge one's own sexism and the commitment to overcome it. Supporting others in becoming gender aware has to be grounded in the capacity of supporting oneself in becoming gender aware. Self-disclosure as an expression of open-heartedness is an effective dimension of a critical dialogue, but it is important to keep its use as a technique in balance with the purpose of the conversation, which is about the shared dream and the development of intentional agency and self- and gender awareness.

Fourth, research projects often give researchers the opportunity – and at times even urge them – to reassess their gender perspectives and intentionalities. However, in the face of research data that speak clearly about a gendered reality that is not coherent with researchers' own gender perspectives, researchers have been known to resist even blatant evidence when such does not fit in with their sexual prejudice. Even a feminist consciousness can be biased towards women's gendered reality and dismiss the rationality of their choices. Such resistance makes eminent sense, however. So much of human identity is formed and informed by gender relationships that gender beliefs, about one's own and the other gender(s),

relationships that gender beliefs, about one's own and the other gender(s), have been continuously affirmed in the effort of confirming and firming the self. Therefore, rather than seeing 'things as they are', human beings often use their rational reasoning to confirm erroneous prejudices and deny the reality of conflicting experiences because the dissonance between beliefs and reality would be too psychologically daunting to accept.

Finally, safety is paramount, psychologically and thus also in a spatial sense. What is shared during the conversation must be held confidential by the conversation partners. There should be no obligation, no pressure to share. On the other hand, if sharing would be valued, this could be agreed upon as an additional resource for increased self-understanding.

Standing together looking in the same direction

The approach to research, capacity-building and networking in GRACE, which was grounded in purpose-aligned action research, intent and dialogue, created a very specific community culture. While participation in this community was both demanding and rewarding, it was probably this shared culture that made this book possible. As a result of the freedom given to all research teams to choose their own research topics, respondent groups, research methodologies and purposes of personal and/or social change, the twenty-one research teams could very possibly have delivered a completely incoherent and chaotic collection of work. Yet, with all its rich diversity, common threads and issues emerged and allowed us to speak to pertinent concerns in the field of information and communication technology for development and gender and of development studies in general. We thus think that our approach warrants further exploration. Standing together in shared space and looking in the same direction allowed us to acknowledge and explore our individual differences. The convergence that emerged became so rich because the various perspectives, intentionalities and experiences that each of us brought to our dialogues became ever so many mirrors in which all of us could recognize, renew and reclaim ourselves. The space we created together was thus not only the container that kept us aligned to the purposes we all stood for, it also became a most powerful catalyst for personal and social change.

Note

1 Ineke Buskens and Matthew Smith designed the original Quality and Impact Framework, which was used to train the GRACE researchers in the second phase and to facilitate the integration of an overall research question with a purpose for change. Figure 22.2 was inspired by Terry

Smutylo's Graphic representing 'relative influence along the results chain' (Earl, Carden and Smutylo 2001: 9) and was designed by Kiss Brian Abraham. The forerunner of the Purpose-Aligned Action Research Process was a research project aiming to contribute to a decrease in cervical cancer death in Khayelitsha, South Africa, conducted by Ineke Buskens in 2001. The majority of clients and health-care workers considered the act of women exposing their private parts to an examiner as shameful and the vagina itself as shameful and ugly, a part that had to be hidden. Since the biggest impediment for women to come for regular screening was this sense of shame, which furthermore even hindered their capacity to discuss their experiences, anxieties and needs, a praise-singer was asked to create a song to praise women's vaginas and their reproductive sexual organs. The poems intended to directly challenge this state of mind and create a mental space around the constellation of fixed thoughts and emotions women held around their private parts. While the ICT technology was 'old' in the sense that the praise-singer's performance was recorded on video to be played in the waiting rooms of the clinic, the content was innovative, revolutionary to an extent and definitely transformatory. Seeing the video and discussing the poems together with other women visiting the clinics allowed the respondents to open up and explore their feelings, thoughts and experiences. This research design was a typical example of normative action research where the researcher's intent was transformatory in a context where respondents were conflicted between their desire for health and their cultural shame and thus were not able to freely participate in the research discussion before the intervention (Buskens 2002). It was this research project that was used as an examplar during the GRACE 2 project conceptualisation training workshops to explain the Purpose-Aligned Action Research Process in the context of gender research into ICT for women's empowerment.

References

Appadurai, A. (2004) 'The capacity to aspire: culture and the terms of recognition', in V. Rao and M. Walton (eds), *Culture and Public Action*, Palo Alto, CA: Stanford University Press, pp. 59–85.

Babüroğul, O. N. and I. Ravn (1992) 'Normative action research', *Organization Studies*, 13(1): 19–34.

Bandura, A. (2001) 'Social cognitive theory: an agentic perspective', *Annual Review of Psychology*, 52: 1–26.

Brown, V. (2010) 'Multiple knowledge, multiple languages: are the limits of my language the limits of my world?', *Knowledge Management for Development Journal*, 6(2): 120–32.

Buskens, I. (2002) 'Constructing knowledge for health: women's perspectives on cervical cancer prevention procedures, research report, New York: Engender Health.

— (2010) 'Agency and reflexivity in ICT4D research: questioning women's options, poverty and human development', *Information Technologies & International Development*, 6: 19–24.

— (2011) 'The importance of intent: reflecting on open development for women's empowerment', *Information Technologies &*

International Development,
7(1): 71–6.

— (2013) 'Open development is a
freedom song: revealing intent
and freeing power', in M. L.
Smith and K. M. A. Reilly (eds),
*Open Development: Networked
Innovations in International
Development*, Cambridge, MA: MIT
Press, pp. 327–52.

— (2014) *Developing the Capacity for
Gender Awareness in Development
Research: Some Thoughts and
Suggestions – A Think Piece for the
IDRC's Information and Networks
Team*, Ottawa: International
Development Research Centre.

Buskens, I. and S. Earl (2008)
'Research for change: outcome
mapping's contribution to
emancipatory action research
in Africa', *Action Research*, 6(2):
171–92.

Byrne, D. (1998) *Complexity Theory
and the Social Sciences: An
Introduction*, New York: Routledge.

Campbell, C. (1999) 'Action as will-
power', *Sociological Review*, 47(1):
48–62.

Coenen, H. (1987)
*Handelingsonderzoek als
Exemplarisch Leren* [Action
Research as a Form of Learning
through Exemplars], Groningen:
Konstapel.

Earl, S., F. Carden and T. Smutylo
(2001) *Outcome Mapping: Building
Learning and Reflection into
Development Programs*, Ottawa:
International Development
Research Centre.

Eichler, M. (1991) *Non-sexist Research
Methods: A Practical Guide*, New
York: Routledge.

Gerdes, K. E. and L. K. Stromwall
(2008) 'Conation: a missing link in
the strengths perspective', *Social
Work*, 53(3): 233–42.

Hirschman, A. O. (1970) *Exit, Voice
and Loyalty: Responses to Decline
in Firms, Organizations, and
States*, Cambridge, MA: Harvard
University Press.

Huitt, W. (2007) 'Success in the
conceptual age: another paradigm
shift', paper presented at the 32nd
annual meeting of the Georgia
Educational Research Association,
Savannah, GA, 26 October.

Huitt, W. and S. Cain (2005) 'An
overview of the conative domain',
Educational Psychology Interactive,
www.edpsycinteractive.org/
brilstar/chapters/conative.pdf,
accessed 14 October 2013.

Leys, R. (2011) 'On Catherine
Malabou's *What Should We Do
with Our Brain?*', *nonsite.org*,
http://nonsite.org/issues/issue-2/
on-catherine-malabous-what-
should-we-do-with-our-brain,
accessed 21 May 2014.

Ludema, J., D. L. Cooperrider and
F. J. Barrett (2001) 'Appreciative
inquiry: the power of the
unconditional positive question',
in P. Reason and H. Bradbury
(eds), *Handbook of Action Research:
Participative Inquiry and Practice*,
London: Sage, pp. 187–99.

Malabou, C. (2008) *What Should We
Do with Our Brain?* New York:
Fordham University Press.

Markus, H. and P. Nurius (1986)
'Possible selves', *American
Psychologist*, 41(9): 954–69.

McNay, L. (2000) *Gender and
Agency: Reconfiguring the Subject
in Feminist and Social Theory*,
Cambridge: Polity.

Militello, L. G., F. C. Gentner, S.
D. Swindler and G. Beisner II
(2006) 'Conation: its historical
roots and implications for future
research', paper presented at
the International Symposium on

Collaborative Technologies and Systems (CTS'06), Dayton, OH, 14–17 May.

Moddel, P. (2009) 'Intent and the process of becoming conscious: a phenomenological view' [video], *Society for Scientific Exploration*, www.scientificexploration.org/talks/27th_annual/27th_annual_moddel_p_phenomenology_intent.html, accessed 14 October 2013.

Sen, A. K. (1999) *Development as Freedom*, Oxford: Oxford University Press.

— (2004) 'How does culture matter?', in V. Rao and M. Walton (eds), *Culture and Public Action*, Palo Alto, CA: Stanford University Press, pp. 50–85.

Smaling, A. (1995) 'Open-mindedness, open-heartedness and dialogical openness: the dialectics of openings and closures', in I. Maso, P. A. Atkinson, S. Delamont and J. C. Verhoeven (eds), *Openness in Research: The Tension between Self and Other*, Assen: Van Gorcum, pp. 21–32.

— (1998) 'Dialogical partnership: the relationship between the researcher and the researched in action research', in B. Boog, H. Coenen and R. Lammerts (eds), *The Complexity of Relationships in Action Research*, Tilburg: Tilburg University Press, pp. 1–15.

— (2008) *Dialoog en Empathie in the Methodologie* [Dialogue and Empathy in Research Methodology], Amsterdam: SWP Publishers.

— (2013) 'Complexiteitsdenken en kwalitatief onderzoek' [Complexity Thinking and Qualitative Research], KWALON 52, Vol. 18, No. 2, 89–98.

Taylor, C. (1995) 'The politics of recognition', in C. Taylor (ed.), *Philosophical Arguments*, Cambridge, MA: Harvard University Press, pp. 25–73.

Visvanathan, S. (2009) 'The search for cognitive justice', www.india-seminar.com/2009/597/597_shiv_visvanathan.htm, accessed 14 October 2013.

Walby, S. (2003) 'Complexity theory, globalisation and diversity', paper presented at the Conference of the British Sociological Association, York, 11–13 April, www.leeds.ac.uk/sociology/people/swdocs/Complexity%20Theory%20realism%20and%20path%20dependency.pdf, accessed 14 October 2013.

Notes on contributors

Kiss Brian Abraham is a Zambian civil-society activist, pro-feminist gender activist and researcher, an IT expert and a journalist. Known for his political cartoons and graphic art, Kiss is a member of the Media Institute of Southern Africa and a founding member of the Zambia Social Forum and the African Regional Social Forum. Kiss established Knowledge and Information Service for Society Innovations in 2003 and is co-creator of the New Zambian platform for information- and crowd-mapping. He is passionate about creating space for the use of art and cartooning to instigate dialogue about issues in Zambian society that matter for development.

Nada Al-syed Hassan Ahmed is Associate Professor in Biology and Environmental Science and Head of Environmental Awareness at the Centre of Environmental Science, Aden University, Yemen. Nada obtained her MSc and PhD from the University of Baghdad, Iraq, is the Vice Head of the Yemeni Environmental Association for sustainable development and a member of several national associations concerned with the environment, life, health, gender and human rights. In 2010 Nada received the Yemeni President's Award for Scientific Research and, in 2014, she received the University of Aden's President's Award for distinguished work with students at the Faculty of Education.

Einas Mahdi Ahmed Mahdi is a lecturer in economics and development in the Department of Economics, Faculty of Commercial Studies, University of Kordofan and a part-timer lecturer at Elobeid Technical College and Sudan Open University. She is currently completing her PhD thesis in development studies at the University of Khartoum, Sudan. Einas has worked as a field supervisor for Care International Sudan and is executive board member of the Elobeid Voluntary Organization for Rehabilitation and Development and coordinator of Elobeid Trauma Treatment Centre, working with traumatized victims, especially women and children, who are gravely affected by the conflicts in Sudan.

Zahra Al-Saqqaf teaches English literature at the Faculty of Education, University of Aden, Yemen. Her MA dissertation and PhD thesis discuss issues of female self-fulfillment and self-empowerment, migration and the construction of female gender identity, and of mother–son and mother–daughter relationships. Zahra has published research papers and supervised MA dissertations in literature, gender studies, translation, Arabic–English comparative and contrastive studies and teaching English as a foreign language. She is a member of the Association of Professors of English and Translation at Arab Universities and of the editorial board of the journal *Gender and Development* published by the University of Aden.

Radia Shamsher Wajed Ali was the first female journalist in the Arabian Peninsula to hold a BA in journalism and information science. Active in the southern Yemeni women's movement since 1965, Radia became assistant general secretary of the executive board of the Unified Yemeni Women's Union in 2003. A founding member of several non-governmental organizations related to human rights and women's empowerment, she has received numerous awards. She has been advisor to the Women's Training and Research Centre at Aden University and has stood in two parliamentary elections. Currently Radia is a member of the Istanbul Forum's Crisis Management Initiative.

Edna R. Aluoch is an administrator by profession and a part-time freelance writer. She holds a BA degree in economics and sociology. She is passionate about helping establish organizations involved in community development work, especially the empowerment of women and the education of children. She lives and works in Nairobi, Kenya.

Huda Ba Saleem holds a PhD in Community Medicine and Public Health (Malaysia University) and a diploma in International Child and Youth Care for Development (Victoria University, Canada). Huda is head of the Community Medicine department and director of the Aden Cancer Registry and Research Center (Aden University, Yemen), a member of several international professional organizations, serves on the editorial board of international medical journals and functions as consultant and principal investigator for international organizations. In 2013 Huda received the Elsevier Foundation Award in life sciences for early career women scientists in the developing world for the Arab region.

Vera Baboun is a Palestinian politician and since October 2012 the first female mayor of Bethlehem City, Palestine. Holding the positions of secretary-general of the Association of Palestinian Local Authorities and vice president of Global Coordination of Local Authorities in the Mediterranean, Vera received the Monsignor Pompeo Award for Peace in July 2014. Prior to her election, she lectured in English literature and gender and development at Bethlehem University and was Assistant Dean of Students (2000–2006). Vera takes pride in her essay titled 'Edward Said: a mentor who sponsored speaking truth to power' (2012) and her work through GRACE.

Susan Bakesha is a gender activist, researcher and trainer, holding an MA degree in women and gender studies from Makerere University, Uganda. She has actively participated as a facilitator for a number of development projects, amongst others the National Women Candidates Training for Women Politicians in Uganda, the Gender Budget Training Programme for local government leaders in Uganda, the Women's Rights, Gender and Governance Training Programme for Development Workers in Africa and the Participatory Gender Audit for government ministries and agencies in Uganda. Susan has served as head of the GRACE Africa Secretariat and currently is the executive director of Development Alternatives (DELTA). She has served as head of the GRACE Africa Secretariat and currently is the executive director of Development Alternatives (DELTA).

Oum Kalthoum Ben Hassine is professor and supervisor of post-graduate research in marine biology at Tunis El Manar University. She is founder of the Tunisian Association of Women and Sciences and a corresponding member of the European Academy of Sciences, Arts and Letters. She has published more than two hundred articles and supervised more than a hundred theses. A long-time women's rights activist and a staunch defender of academic values, Oum Kalthoum was awarded the Emeritus Honor Diploma of the European Academy of Sciences, Arts and Letters in 2013 and a certificate of appreciation for exceptional voluntary service by the United Nations.

Kazanka Comfort is director of operations of Fantsuam Foundation and plays a strategic role in its policy direction and project implementation. She began her professional life as a teacher and later went on to study law, followed by a diploma in development studies. She is the winner of the first Hafkin Africa Prize, has worked briefly at WomensNet, is a member of GRACE and the APC Africa Women, and in 2013 she served on a global panel of women leaders in Toronto to talk about why you cannot tackle poverty without putting women at the centre of development.

John Dada is a founding member of the Fantsuam Foundation and under his watch Fantsuam was awarded the first Hafkin Africa Prize, in 2001. The foundation has been featured by the BBC and CNN, and in

2008 Fantsuam's rural wireless service was accorded recognition by the Nigerian Communications Commission. In 2008, John was awarded the Meritorious Award by the University of Queensland, Australia and served as chair of the African Technical Advisory Committee of the United Nations Economic Commission for Africa. In 2010 he chaired the team that developed a framework for Nigeria's broadband policy.

Saneya El-Neshawy is professor of plant pathology at the Agricultural Research Center, Egypt. She was awarded her PhD from Ain Shams University with partial fulfillment at North Dakota State and California Davis universities. She has been a visiting scientist and an invited speaker at various international conferences. Saneya has been principal investigator of numerous research projects and is a member of the Organization for Women in Science for the Developing World, the Bangladesh Bioethics Society and the GRACE Network. In 2013 Saneya won the Award of Innovation Contest in Knowledge Sharing in Agricultural and Rural Development for the MENA region.

Mervat Foda is professor at the National Research Center (NRC), Cairo, Egypt. She has a PhD in Dairy Science and a Licentiate in Food Engineering. Mervat has registered a patent at the Egyptian Patent Office, been awarded a bronze medal in the International Invention Fair of the Middle East, Kuwait, and been recognized as a Distinguished Scientist several times by the Egyptian Ministry of Higher Education and the NRC. A member of several women's organizations, Mervat was selected as president of The Egypt Chapter of the Organization for Women in Science for the Developing World in 2014.

Ahlam Hibatulla Ali, a professor in orthodontics at the Faculty of Dentistry, University of Aden, Yemen, was the first dentist to receive a PhD in orthodontics (Rostock, Germany) and the first woman professor in orthodontics in Yemen. After working for several years as the vice dean at the Faculty of Dentistry, Aden University, Ahlam was appointed as the dean. In 2004 Ahlam established the first Center for Cleft Lip and Palate Reconstruction in Yemen and has served as its director since. She is a member of the Yemeni Women's Association for Science and Technology, the Organization for Women in Science for the Developing World and GRACE.

Rokhsana Ismail was founder and first director of the Women's Research and Training Center at Aden University, Yemen. She established a refereed journal on gender and development, was vice president of the Organization for Women in Science for the Developing World (2005–10) and serves currently as member of the executive board (2010–14). A professor in chemistry, she founded the Yemeni Chemical Society as well as the Yemeni Women's Association for Science and Technology for Development. Since 2010 Rokhsana has been the director of the Centre for Science and Technology at Aden University. She has received numerous national and international awards.

Buhle Mbambo-Thata is Executive Director of Library Services at the University of South Africa (UNISA). She is a member of the Strategic Advisory Network of the Global Libraries Programme of the Bill and Melinda Gates Foundation. She has served as governing board member of the International Federation of Library Associations (IFLA), chairperson of the E-Knowledge Society for Women in Southern Africa, and member of the advisory committees of EIFL Found.net and the Gender in Africa Information Network. Her research interests are in women and ICT, ICT applications in libraries and library services on mobile devices.

Nagwa Abdel Meguid holds a PhD in human genetics and is a fellow of Uppsala University, Sweden and of Yale University, USA. As one of the pioneers to accurately diagnose recessive disorders in Egyptians, Nagwa is the founder of the autism clinic of the NRC. She has received numerous national and international awards for scientific and research excellence, is a member of the NRC's Ethical Committee and of the international juries for the L'Oréal UNESCO awards. She has more than 140 scientific publications to her name.

Sibonile Moyo holds an MSc degree in Computer Science from the National University of Science and Technology (NUST) in Zimbabwe. She was chairperson of that department from 2009 to 2012 and is currently a lecturer and researcher there. Before joining NUST Sibonile was a lecturer in the Department of Computer Studies at the Bulawayo Polytechnic (1996–2005) and was in charge of that department from 2004 to 2005. Sibonile feels passionate about women empowerment in technical fields and is a member of the NUST gender research cluster. She works nationally as an independent consultant in ICT-based information-systems development.

Amel Mustafa Mubarak is an agricultural economist working as assistant professor at the Department of Agricultural Economics, at the University of Khartoum, Sudan. In addition to her work as coordinator of graduate studies, Amel is actively engaged in teaching and supervising MSc students. Her research focuses on socio-economic development, agricultural and rural development and society-development services. Amel is a member of many local, regional and international organizations in her field, in addition to women's organizations such as the Organization for Women in Science for the Developing World. Amel has particular interest in women's issues, policy analysis, food security and poverty-alleviation research.

Jocelyn Muller is a strategic, multi-disciplinary researcher with an eye for innovative methods that inspire change; seeking to reveal the linkages between personal and social change. She has worked with a number of organizations, including the Energy Research Centre, Medical Research Council and the World Wildlife Fund, undertaking research in ICT4D, climate adaptation and energy sectors. Her work has encompassed environmental sustainability, gender equality and socio-economic prosperity. She has a vast skill set, but her passion lies in designing and implementing participatory methodologies. Jocelyn wishes to combine her knowledge with empowering methods by imagining, appreciating and being the change you want to see.

Nagat Ali Muqbil is associate professor of Parasitology and head of the biology department at Aden University, Yemen. She obtained her PhD in 1999 from Rajasthan University, India. Nagat is a member of several national and international councils and associations: the Yemeni Biological Society, the Yemeni Women's Association of Sciences and Technology for Development, the Organization for Women in Science for the Developing World, the National Higher Studies Academic Council, the Women's Research and Training Center, the Biodiversity Team and the Environment Protection Association. She supervises post-graduate students, has participated in several national and international conferences and has published widely on parasitology and gender issues.

Ikhlas Ahmed Nour Ibrahim is associate professor of meat science and technology, University of Khartoum. A member of the Senate and of many scientific committees, Ikhlas has more than twenty years of experience in the leadership of integrated research projects and supervision of postgraduate students. Feeling deeply about gender equality and women's empowerment, she has been involved in the design and implementation of community-based training programmes for women in sustainable milk-processing technology and dry-land husbandry projects. In the context of her GRACE research, Ikhlas hosted the first national radio programme on sexuality in Sudan, discussing the factors influencing pre-marital sex.

Salome Omamo is a gender and social-development specialist with extensive experience in gender analysis and gender mainstreaming, qualitative and quantitative research, policy analysis, monitoring and evaluation, project management, capacity-building, lobbying and advocacy, HIV/Aids, education, agriculture, food security and livelihoods, conflict analysis and peace-building and rural and community development. In collaboration with donors such as the Department for International Development – UK, the International Development Research Centre, the International Labour Organization, the Lottery Fund, USAID and various African governments, Salome has worked in countries such as the Democratic Republic of Congo, Egypt, India, Kenya, Morocco, Nigeria, South Africa, Tanzania, Uganda, the USA and Zambia.

Arwa Oweis is Professor of Nursing and Dean of Maternal and Child Health at Jordan University of Science and Technology, Jordan. She is the author of numerous articles on women's health and violence against women, serves as editorial board member and reviewer for international journals and has been a keynote speaker, presenter and organiser for numerous local, regional and international workshops and conferences. Arwa has conducted several locally, and internationally funded research projects and acts as a consultant for various national and international organizations, such as the World Health Organisation, the Jordanian Nursing Council and the National Centre for Women's Health Care.

Rula Quawas is a professor of American literature and feminist theory at the University of Jordan. She was the founding director of the Women's Studies Center at the university, and she was also the dean of the Faculty of Foreign Languages. Rula's research focuses on feminist readings of American and Arabic texts written by women writers. Rula has been honoured as a distinguished international scholar and also received the Meritorious Honor Award for Leadership and Dedication to the Empowerment of Jordanian Women. She was recently nominated for the International Women of Courage Award. Rula strongly believes in dreams coming true.

Abeer Shaef Abdo Saeed obtained her master's degree in internal medicine from Aden University, Yemen where she is an instructor at the Department of Public Health and Community Medicine. Abeer holds a certificate in emerging infectious disease research from the University of Florida, USA. She participates in research programs relating to community and public health, works as a faculty correspondent for several infectious diseases and health programs and is also a national trainer for Dengue. As a social activist Abeer is a member of several national associations concerned with health, women, youth, human rights and social justice.

Ibou Sané lectures at the University of Gaston Berger in Saint Louis, the University of Cheikh Anta Diop in Dakar and the University Assane Seck de Ziguinchor in Senegal. Ibou obtained his doctorate in sociology from the Université Lumière (Lyon 2), France. He lectures in urban sociology, political sociology, sociology of development, sociology of the informal sector and handicrafts, sociology of associative movements, project evaluation methods, research methodology of the social sciences and social theory. In his research he focuses on development, sociology of population and migration, the informal trading sector and the links between gender, ICT and development.

Gisele Mankamte Yitamben is an economist and an expert in entrepreneurship development, information and communication technology and gender equality. Yitamben endeavours to improve the lives of underprivileged people through productive resources and technical services. She is a member of the reference group advising the Director-General of UNESCO on sustainable development and a long-time Schwab Foundation fellow, having received many distinctions, amongst them being ranked among the world's 40 most outstanding social entrepreneurs for 2002. A member of GRACE since its founding in 2004, Yitamben has contributed chapters to its two books and strategic support to its leadership.

Index